Progressive Traditions

American Indian Literature and Critical Studies Series

PROGRESSIVE TRADITIONS

Identity in Cherokee Literature and Culture

JOSHUA B. NELSON

UNIVERSITY OF OKLAHOMA PRESS
Norman

Library of Congress Cataloging-in-Publication Data

Nelson, Joshua B., 1974–

Progressive traditions : identity in Cherokee literature and culture / Joshua B. Nelson.

pages cm. — (American Indian literature and critical studies series ; v. 61)

Includes bibliographical references and index.

ISBN 978-0-8061-4491-7 (hardcover : alk. paper) 1. Cherokee literature—History and criticism. 2. American literature—Indian authors—History and criticism. 3. Identity (Philosophical concept) in literature. I. Title.

PM783.5.N48 2014

897'.557—dc23

2013049103

Progressive Traditions: Identity in Cherokee Literature and Culture is Volume 61 in the American Indian Literature and Critical Studies Series.

The paper in this book meets the guidelines for permanence and durability of the Committee on Production Guidelines for Book Longevity of the Council on Library Resources, Inc. ∞

An earlier version of chapter 2 was published as "Integrated Circuitry: Catherine Brown across Gender, Race, and Religion." *American Indian Culture and Research Journal* 30.2 (2006): 17–31. Reprinted with permission.

1 2 3 4 5 6 7 8 9 10

To Tiffany, Mom, and Ronnie

Contents

Preface

ᎤᏬᏁᎵᏍᏗ ᎣᏁᎬ ᎦᏛᎩᎠ ᏥᏌ
ᎤᏂᏁᏓᎾ ᏄᏁᎲᎾ ᎤᎾᏓᏂᏨᏛ
ᏣᎬᏫᏳᎯ ᎾᏉ ᏔᏘᏄᎦ ᏗᏙᎤᎡ
ᏧᏃᏰᏂᏉ ᏕᎯᏂᏴᏎᏍᏗ ᏂᎪᎯᎸ
ᏗᏂᏲᎵ ᎦᎸᎳᏗ ᏔᏘᏄᎦ
ᏧᏃᏕ ᎢᏳ ᏣᏁᏢᏍᏗ ᎦᎸᎳᏗ

I hear someone speak sorrowfully, Jesus,
No father have they; they have been orphaned,
You are the highest; now take them to your home,
Their hands, hold on to forever.
The children, to the heavens take them,
They'll be beautiful when they live over there up high.
"Orphan Child," Cherokee hymn

No one knew what to do about the several hundred orphans strewn about the country, but they knew it was a problem sure to get worse before it got better. Families had taken in about all they could, and although the government ran an orphanage that might be able to help, the government claimed that its orphanage couldn't afford to take on any more than it already had. Besides, these other children didn't really belong to the government—they weren't citizens. That they had lost their families and had essentially no means to provide for themselves was lamentable, but politicians found it hard to justify what amounted to foreign aid when the nation faced plenty of its own internal challenges, even though the children lived inside the boundaries of the country. Thankfully, a benefactor appeared. W. T. Whitaker made his living running a couple of furniture stores. He also helped build the local school and church, which he pastored. Worried about what would become of the orphaned children and the kind of trouble they'd get into without someone to look after them, he opened his own home to as many as he could afford to care for, motley crew that they were. According to reputable sources, Whitaker sank basically all of his money and resources into housing those children.

The orphans came largely from parents without means, and many people wondered if the children had the capacity to amount to anything. Undeterred, Whitaker put them up and educated them in both the traditional classroom, in the school he helped build, and in vocational training around his farm. Boys learned about agriculture, girls about domestic arts, and everyone about the Christian gospel. Knowing how many more children there were in the country who needed aid but were denied it by his own government, Whitaker finally appealed to the government of the people from whom the children had come to kick in something for their care. The foreign government agreed and made a sizable contribution, which helped Whitaker expand his operation from the thirty-some-odd kids in his care to somewhere around a hundred at a time. They lived and worked together on what became a nearly self-sufficient farming operation, maybe like what an extended family might have done in generations past. Years later Whitaker's government, which had earlier refused to help the alien kids, turned to him for help when its own orphanage burned down and it needed a place to house its children. Though it made things cramped, he took them in.

Whitaker was Cherokee, and the orphanage he operated in Pryor Creek, Indian Territory, from the late nineteenth century until statehood in 1907 was exclusively for white children, at least until he took in the Cherokee kids from the burned-down Cherokee orphanage. In his plea for help from Congress, he wrote of the white orphans: "You know that most of the white people of the Territory are poor and not able to help me. . . . Now they are crying to us from every corner of the Indian Territory for food, clothing, and shelter. It makes me feel sad that I can not help them and to know that I am a Cherokee Indian using my own allotment and money for the support of this home, begging the people of the United States to help me care for their own people when they will not. I pray God to lead the minds of the white people and the Congress of this great United States to come to my rescue and help save the homeless children of the Indian Territory."[1] Though he owed no allegiance to the white orphans living in the Cherokee Nation, Whitaker felt compelled to do something for the children, marginalized by the nation in which they lived and the nation to which their parents had belonged.[2] His story is rare when it comes to Indian and white relations. We are far more accustomed to hearing of missionaries who came to Indian country bent on proselytizing and complicit with colonization. We are told of how they made over the Indian in their own image, according to state-sponsored civilization programs that aimed for the eradication of Indian cultural differences so that they might be assimilated into the American mainstream.

We come across narratives such as Whitaker's far less often, narratives that feature intriguing reversals in which it is the Indians who brought education and Christianity to poor, ignorant heathens, stories in which Indians civilized white folks. What are we to make of these oddities? We could write them off as peculiar exceptions to the rule, or we could dig a little deeper and see how many others like them we find. If we find enough, we might question the accuracy of the rule we've inherited. This book tries the latter approach. It challenges the conventional wisdom that tells the history of Indian tribes according to a contest between traditionally minded Indians and those inclined toward progressive changes. I contend that the distinction between the traditional and the progressive is both limiting and difficult to make. Simply put, I try to show how tribal traditions can adapt and change without losing their character. Whitaker's reaching out to a threatened and excluded people, his emphasis on education and religion, his interventions in problems at the local level, and above all, his insistence on his identity as a Cherokee exemplify how wonderfully complicated a simple act of compassion can be.

This book does not seek to revolutionize the histories of U.S. attempts to eradicate Native cultures and assimilate Native peoples into the mainstream or some Native people's complicity in assimilation. These things happened, and we need to understand how. But *Progressive Traditions* does ask if these trends make up the whole story. If the Cherokee seminaries, for instance, didn't teach Cherokee history or language in their official curricula, did that prevent students from learning these from each other and forging strong Cherokee communities there? Such countercurrents and unofficial histories, even if they fall outside the norm, are both fascinating and important. It may well be that for many past and present Cherokee people, outliers themselves in one way or another, unofficial and peculiar stories matter as much as the standard versions do. (I, for one, learned all sorts of things from my college communities that never got mentioned in the course catalog.) In reading Cherokee and other American Indian literature and thinking about how American Indian literary criticism equips us to understand how culture relates to it, I find that there's too much we haven't considered and too much that doesn't make sense. That's not because of a problem with the literature.

Since the 1990s, debates between nationalists (who advocate a critical position that strengthens the sovereignty of Native nations) and cosmopolitans (who are more interested in keeping political and identity boundaries fluid than in shoring them up) have dominated American Indian literary theory, displacing any theoretical and political arguments not immediately concerned with either camp's political programs. Looking to literature for creative articulations of communities' shapes among Cherokee people, Cherokee critics such as Jace Weaver, Daniel Heath Justice, and others, including myself, have taken Creek scholar Craig Womack's cue in approaching literature from theoretical perspectives grounded in some aspect of relevant tribal culture.[3] Major emphases in the field have included incorporation of traditional orature, ties to and relationships with the land, representation of tribal history or political problems, and connections with communities of various shapes. On the occasions that literary critics confront the problematic work of Cherokee authors such as Catharine Brown, Elias Boudinot, John Oskison, or Will Rogers and don't find what they expect, they seem compelled to explain away the writers' assimilationist appearances. In so doing, these critics adopt a historical pattern of dismissal that reduces Indian identity to a dichotomy in which Indians are either "traditional" or "assimilated," the latter being code for "not really Indian." These terms also owe something to colonialist identity measures, which insinuate inauthenticity or corruption with the terms "progressive" or "assimilated," and fixate "true" Native people in an irrecoverable past with the term "traditionalist"; either prong goads Native people out of the concerns of the present.[4] Disassembling this heteronomous binary, which has been far too long with us, requires a reassessment of what exactly is meant by "assimilation" and "traditionalism."

I'm attempting to move past these terms by first putting them together, showing how though apparent opposites, they are often part and parcel of larger shared goals, especially securing communities' vitality. We'll see the Cherokee authors discussed in the following chapters also combining old and new ways of doing things as they employ traditional adaptive strategies to resolve cultural and historical problems. At the edges of the already liminal, smaller groups of Cherokee people have long coalesced around common causes and shared interests, such as fostering traditional values, opposing colonialism, or advocating technological education, and they've done it using a surprising range of strategies. I propose that if we look carefully at the enormous variety of principles and practices available to a culture, the collection of which sociologist Pierre Bourdieu calls the *habitus*, we could begin to appreciate the importance of pluralism in Cherokee culture.[5] With the many resources already at its disposal, the Cherokee habitus, like that of many tribal groups, can respond adeptly and with restraint to the challenges that confront traditions.

I remember at a conference in Tahlequah a few years back hearing a couple of traditional folks (by most people's standards, I think) talking about different ways of using medicinal plants. They explained that each plant is thought to have seven different uses, and rarely is one person expected to know them all, certainly not for every plant. Instead, practitioners are taught to respect others' knowledge and to seek others out for consultation. I continue to admire this moment and the sentiments it embodies, so respectful of the proliferant things to know and ways of knowing and so mindful of our personal limitations. Should we critics of American Indian literature, Native and non-Native alike, open ourselves to such cooperative and pluralist ways of thinking, where we formerly found only loss of tradition, we might come to see volitional and diverse innovations of principles and practices that we might not have even understood as traditions. Even so mammoth a volume as James Mooney's five-hundred-page report to the Bureau of American Ethnology could not catalog every facet of Cherokee tradition, a word that after all is another way of naming the way(s) of life of a heterogeneous people. Neither could any one critical perspective accurately code all Cherokee literature according to one measure of tradition.

While some Cherokee theorists have formulated culturally grounded strategies for interpreting Cherokee literature, the archive's diversity escapes capture under any single paradigm. Daniel Heath Justice, for instance, explores recurrent cultural themes of belovedness and what he dubs a "Chickamauga consciousness" corresponding to patterns of accommodative conciliation and nationalist resistance, respectively. Mary Churchill elaborates the former by drawing on the religiously inflected "White Path" tradition of achieving harmony through a mediating balance of opposition. Jace Weaver emphasizes the importance of community attachments to authors and their work, a position much like that articulated by sociologist Eva Garroutte in her work on the importance of reciprocity to Indian identity.[6] I admire all of these for their insightful, energized, and energizing readings of texts, and I would be remiss if I didn't acknowledge their profound influence on how I make sense of Cherokee writing. I fear that too often, however, they tend toward a single, monistic interpretation, as if the particular tension or value each identifies is *the* differentiating or overriding principle of Cherokee literature and culture, offering the across-the-board *best* interpretations of the entire Cherokee canon. Just in terms of alphabetic writing, this body of work is now nearly two hundred years old and includes scores, maybe hundreds, of authors, in addition to infinite other nonalphabetic "texts" that we could read as cultural productions.

Existing paradigms merely gesture at the complexity and depth of the works discussed in the succeeding chapters, even when critics do not dismiss the works' authors as Cherokee in name only. In fact, this common critique, which has kept many of these authors out of print and out of our literary history, led me to the larger general critique of the traditional/assimilated binary that can be found over and over again in Native scholarship. When I was casting about in graduate school for a dissertation topic, I knew I wanted to work on Cherokee literature and was enticed by the prospect of unearthing some undiscovered masterpiece. I didn't find one, but I did over and again find brief references to authors such as Narcissa Owen, Will Rogers, and John Oskison, among others, who later critics knew were Cherokee but declined to examine as Cherokee writers because they and their material were "assimilated." Neglecting the advice not to bother with such non-Indian Indian writing, I found that these works in fact often had very much to say about and to Cherokee people, though their Cherokee contours are not always readily apparent. Of the several fascinating authors who have been so labeled and so ignored, I focus heavily on Catharine Brown and Elias Boudinot in this book, not least because I find their mostly neglected works fascinating for their illustrations of adaptive strategies to help communities cohere but also because they so often catch the brunt of the paradigmatic binaristic criticism ricocheting them away from our discussions and continuing to shape the boundaries of the Cherokee and American Indian canons. I might well have included many of these other authors who have been similarly excluded—Owen around the turn of the twentieth century, Oskison, Rogers, on up to Thomas King, Betty Louise Bell, and Diane Glancy more recently, to name just a few—but I believe that showing how to read such texts for their Cherokee elements requires a thorough and detailed (that's also to say, space-consuming) look into social circumstances as a matter of methodology.

This approach yields a work that is by no means solely concerned with nor comprehensive on the subjects of Cherokee literature or culture; neither, as it treats a relatively small number of strictly literary texts, is it a literary history. Daniel Heath Justice does a fantastic job of this with *Our Fire Survives the Storm*. *Progressive Traditions* is more like a literary sociology—I'll say more about this approach to literature read through cultural principles and practices in the last section of the introduction. In examining several types of texts, including memoirs, speeches, editorials, constitutions, novels, hymns, court cases, and laws, in addition to religious and political dispositions, the following chapters nevertheless offer up a variety of materials that I approach with similarly varied interpretive strategies borrowed from American Indian studies and cultural studies. The failure to understand how authors like Brown and Boudinot fit into the field of American Indian literature points up the need not for a newer and better totalizing framework coming from any one discipline but for strategies more varied, dynamic, and pluralist. For these reasons, I happily admit that the practice-oriented theory I advance here can be only one of many approaches. Insofar as it stands in at the outset for a range of practices, it would also have to defer to positions that describe practices with greater specificity.

In this introductory attempt, I'm not suggesting any prescribed method so much as trying to work out a broad theoretical way of finding greater cultural and identity-related significance in the many principles and practices that we have not yet thoroughly considered. I'd like to consider how our frames of reference have been constrained by the central theoretical and political concerns of nationalism and cosmopolitanism, the leading camps in Indian critical theory, which, besides some lapses into the quick-and-easy assimilated/traditional binary, also share a tendency to endorse tribal nation-states without the robust skepticism they've earned.

Acknowledgments

I owe thanks to many people, more than I can remember, for helping bring this project to life. I hope those I've forgotten will forgive me. Thanks foremost to Alessandra Jacobi Tamulevich and Thomas Krause at the University of Oklahoma Press for their support and for making the process go so smoothly. The comments and suggestions by the anonymous reviewers for the press helped strengthen the manuscript in many ways, and I'm grateful for their attention and efforts. The efforts of my editor, Abby Hayes, and copyeditor, Bonnie Lovell, are sincerely appreciated.

I owe much to Laura Donaldson, Shirley Samuels, Angela Gonzales, and Jim Adams at Cornell University for their support of my project in its early stages. At the University of Oklahoma, special thanks are due Alan Velie and Geary Hobson for their mentorship and unflagging support. Vince Leitch, Dan Cottom, and especially Ronald Schleifer went beyond the call of duty in providing feedback and helping me prepare materials. My undergraduate students have been inspirational, as have the graduate students in my Native theory and fiction seminars, especially Waleila Carey, Rain Gomez, Brian Hudson, Rachel Jackson, Liz Smith, Shannon Toll, and Lizz Toombs, who also provided venues that allowed me to try out new material. Colleagues across campus—such as Catharine John, David Mair,

Kim Roppolo, Jonathan Stalling, David Anderson, Melissa Hearn, Joanna Rapf, and the other faculty in the English department; Barbara Hobson, Lindsay Robertson, Joe Watkins, Todd Fuller, and many more in Native American Studies; R. C. Davis, Daniel Simon, and the staff at *World Literature Today*; and Vicki Sturtevant, Kristin Dowell, Dan Swan, Andy Horton, and Karl Schmidt, in connection with Native film studies—have all helped make OU a wonderful place to do this work. This research was supported in part by grants from the College of Arts and Sciences, and the Research Council of the University of Oklahoma Norman Campus. The American Indian Graduate Center in Albuquerque also provided me with financial support at a crucial time.

Susan Hall and the wonderful people at Cameron University in Lawton extended a warm welcome to me when I delivered a talk on the Cherokee Freedmen through the Philip Jones Lectureship in Ethics. I'd also like to thank many good folks at Northeastern State University in Tahlequah for their interest, time, and support: Terri Baker, Wyman Kirk, Harry Oosahwee, Special Collections librarian Delores Sumner, and Phyllis Fife and Melissa Strong, who also helped me find good opportunities to present from my work. A big ᏩᏙ to Sequoyah Guess, and also to Steve Osage and Victor Cope. Craig Womack, Robert Warrior, and Jace Weaver moved me along in both in my thinking and my career, and better examples of challenging, compassionate scholars I could not hope to find. I appreciate, too, the conversations I've been lucky to have with fantastic scholars like Amanda Cobb-Greetham, Jim Cox, Tol Foster, Joanna Hearne, Danika Medak-Saltzman, Dustin Tahmahkera, and Ted Van Alst.

ᏩᏙ ᎠᏂᎨᏳᎶ, ᎤᎬᏫᏳᎯ ᎠᎴ ᏦᎩᏫᏢ. My mother, Jeanie Nelson, has always been my best reader, editor, encourager, and model of hard work and service. Ronnie Roberts, the Hardys, Paddyakers, Tidmores, and Nelsons all offered unflagging support. Above all, thanks to Tiffany for her sacrifice, her support, and her love.

Progressive Traditions

ᏌᏊ

Introduction

Progressive Traditions centers itself in the specific field of Cherokee culture and argues that the broader study of American Indian culture and literature could profit by a more detailed view of what forms Indian identity. It critiques a pervasive tendency to describe American Indian identities, cultures, and literatures by oppositions—those who press to assimilate into the mainstream United States against those who maintain Indian traditions—a construction that proves far more limiting than descriptive. For decades, however, this binary has been deployed to chart the arcs of American Indian tribal histories from the Atlantic to the Pacific, from the Arctic to the Gulf of Mexico. Intentionally or not, it has also had the insidious effect of dismissing more than a few Indian thinkers and writers whose ideas have not seemed "Indian" enough to conventional wisdom. In this way, colonialist categories divide and conquer Indian groups by directly opposing traditionalism, at least when it most poses a threat, and by indirectly disempowering assimilationism as nothing but a dilution, not quite white and not quite Indian. It may be no accident that intellectual figures are among those whose ideas are often defanged by accusations of assimilationism. This strategy works best when at its worst—when it insinuates its either-or logic into the minds of American Indian people ourselves, convincing us that there is only one authentic way of being Indian, a way that doesn't allow for change in the modern world. *Progressive Traditions* sets about dismantling this opposition by using several disciplinary perspectives to examine a range of linked cultural practices and beliefs—"dispositions," in sociologist Pierre Bourdieu's term. It finds ample evidence of traditional dispositions' survival through times of radical change, together with the ongoing and healthy ambiguity of seeing progress in tradition and tradition in progress. The discovery of a wealth of characteristically Indian cultural concepts among writers formerly thought too pro-assimilation to be authentically Indian demonstrates an advantage of this critical model, attuned as it is to habits of thinking and doing that have not been thoroughly understood. Throughout, the habits or "progressive traditions" that I describe characterize an indigenous anarchism as a pluralist, community-centered political philosophy that looks to practices that preceded and surpass the nation-state as ways of helping Cherokee people prosper.

A problem attending several questions I take up in this book concerns the long-running debate over whether some essential, timeless feature distinguishes identities or, instead, the circumstances of time and place separate one group from another. That is, we're often concerned with whether differences are natural or constructed, essential or made up. At stake are communities' boundaries, which in the first case would be more cut-and-dried and in the latter more nebulous and open. Control over boundaries also means control over resources and representation—no small matters. But here, too, I'd like to look at this quandary from another angle in order to open the way for explorations of how Cherokee people managed less philosophically grandiose but more humanly imperative problems, such as changes to religious practices or to governmental organization brought on by settler colonialism. Intriguingly enough, however, their maneuvers might suggest ways in which essentialism and constructionism might be reconciled. The Cherokee authors I'll discuss rarely advocate context-free and eternal solutions; rather, they are precisely and inescapably historically and culturally situated, but they also draw on traditions that are deeply ingrained and reach far enough into the past to give them the character of things essential. Through various ways of learning—from families, friends, neighbors, schools, churches, and other social interactions—practices and beliefs get literally incorporated, worked into our very bodies, as unconscious habits of a particular culture, and so become embodied inventions. While the values and practices that shape communities' strategies extend from conservative traditions, culture and belief in their constituents' lived lives are still not immutable. Not often do we find authors trying to pinpoint defining and abiding ethnological features of Cherokee identity's essential difference as they write on often very narrow problems. Their works are instead efforts to persuade audiences to try out novel connections across already existing traditional beliefs and practices.

The literary works examined include the understudied memoirs of Catharine Brown, a nineteenth-century Cherokee convert to Christianity; the novel *Kholvn* by contemporary traditionalist Sequoyah Guess, a writer of a peculiarly Cherokee science fiction; and the political rhetoric of Elias Boudinot, a forefather of American Indian literature, and of John Ross, the principal chief during the removal years. Across several genres—autobiography, fiction, speeches, laws, letters, and more—we find these authors over and over again advocating for the continued political and cultural sovereignty of Cherokee people. While their advocacy for education, civilization, or cooperation might appear complicit with assimilation, their innovative responses to social, religious, and political dilemmas upend the common view that conservative and progressive tensions can describe the entire course of tribal histories.

In relation to debates over whether theories of non-Native origin can or should be applied to Native literature and culture, I concern myself less with origins than with results, gladly adopting positions that seem richest in accuracy and responsiveness. I try to be careful, however, to put mainstream theories into conversation with American Indian studies, not just over the primary material—the literature, practices, and beliefs of Cherokee people—but also over the theories' own strengths and weaknesses, with the goal of widening the scope and sharpening the focus of each position. In American Indian literary criticism, debates between two major camps, known as nationalists and cosmopolitanists in shorthand, have unproductively dominated the field. *Progressive Traditions* raises questions that neither camp has asked and critiques certain assumptions they share, especially concerning their too-ready conflation of tribal people with the tribal nation-state. As an anarchist by calling, I'm more excited by celebrating times and places where local communities managed their own affairs than I am by heralding the successes, genuine or dubious, of a coercive, centralized state.

In its attempt to refocus critical attention on cultural practices that I believe should be shaping political institutions rather than serving them, *Progressive Traditions* looks to strike a balance among several connected dispositions. It sets about this structurally by presenting the practice-based theoretical framework later in the introduction. In chapters 1 through 5, split into two parts, I take the methodology for a test drive. The first part concerns religion and the second, politics. The first chapter of each part examines cultural beliefs and practices that frame the literary readings that follow. A critique of gender runs through and further unites the sections. Their sequential focus on religion and politics, two key sites where the bankrupt traditional/assimilated dichotomy most confines our understanding, leads to the conclusion that attempts a synthesis of the two ethics.

The theoretical perspective elaborated later in the introduction develops Pierre Bourdieu's concept of the habitus, what he calls the sum of a given culture's principles and practices. Rather than attempt to isolate a timeless, differentiating feature of Cherokee or American Indian identity, I suggest that what makes many different sorts of Cherokees "Cherokee" issues from a measure of many potential dispositions. These include commonly understood affiliations and beliefs that inform behaviors, such as kinship, geographic residence, participation in traditions, language use, and more. But crucially, they encompass, perhaps infinitely, several more. Borrowing from Bourdieu, I find it helpful to think of culture as a web of collected dispositions and practices, each resonantly connected with all others, at least to some degree. Speaking in Cherokee inflects praying in Cherokee, just as religious beliefs influence political structures. In this dispositional perspective, essential difference, or that idea of a fundamental element not possessed by others that makes a group what it is, gets constructed on the move. The essence changes with the moment. In this same contradictory sense in which cultures retain and employ traditions as they manage progress, my critical perspective takes advantage of a pragmatic shiftiness to be responsive to future challenges. This approach to situating literature and other social practices within a closely described cultural context uncovers themes, motifs, and imagery invisible to positions less rooted in American Indian worlds.

As an initial step in breaking up the assimilated/traditional dichotomy plaguing American Indian literary criticism, the book's first part examines select traditional religious practices and theorizes religious innovations in works by two nearly unknown Cherokee authors: the memoirs of Catharine Brown, a nineteenth-century convert to Christianity, and *Kholvn*, a novel by contemporary traditionalist Sequoyah Guess. In these works Brown and Guess narrate forms of traditional practices like "gaining knowledge," a process of community edification through education in which groups of people vet new ways of knowing and potential solutions against inherited beliefs and traditions. The historical course of alterations to spiritual and religious principles and practices, though often maligned as a sinking of tradition, instead follows a gendered trajectory tending always toward the habitus's perpetuation, and as such charts both male and female culturally preservative agency, even as it sometimes entails changes more drastic than expected.

Chapter 1 surveys key religious concepts, such as harmony, cooperation, righteousness, education, and purity, which Brown and Guess literarily interpret. Of particular interest are social and religious developments ignored by most scholarship on Cherokee religion, which has more often been interested in an idealized, harmonious relationship with nature. This fixation can too easily degenerate into a vague "Indians communing with nature" motif. The authors I look at here thankfully don't take us to this Disney version of spirituality, but neither do they treat Cherokee religious tenets with the detail they demand. The often-celebrated concept of balance comes under scrutiny in this chapter for its potential complicity with limiting, binary constructions. My argument stresses Cherokee spiritual beliefs' insistence on right relationships to other humans, not as part of a loose-knit spirituality but as concrete religious edicts, even as I question the hallowed status critics have lately afforded community, too broadly defined. It is not enough to declare that reverence for community makes Indian people special. We need to detail communities' characteristics, their historical circumstances, and the kind of reverence we're discussing. What I call a Cherokee sacred humanism appears most clearly at pivotal historical moments—the decline of the traditional priesthood, the secularization of the government, the introduction of Christianity, and the masculinization of politics—moments when established ways of doing things *pivoted* toward a new historical course. This is not the same thing as complete redefinition. For instance, Cherokee women long held prominent social roles but were politically disempowered under centralized government. Some women shifted their leadership roles toward religious communities, offering an example of innovation and continuation in caring for others.

Among these women was Catharine Brown, one of the first Cherokee converts to Christianity. Her memoirs, discussed in chapter 2, have slowly gained critical attention for the firsthand glimpses they provide into the Cherokees' daily lives in a crucial historical period. Scholarship on Brown and her *Memoir*, however, has only glimpsed the potential strategies for culturally specific power suggested by her innovations to Cherokee religious traditions, in matters like dreaming, "gaining knowledge," communal vetting, and purifying ceremonies. Situating her writing and conversion in a tribal social history reveals far stronger attachments to Cherokee people *as* Cherokee people in multiple communities, such as those organized by gender, religion, and race, than her critics have yet been able to see. Her theology blends, modifies, adopts, and refashions Christian and Cherokee religious beliefs and practices into an intricately spun web, both complicated in its cultural distinctions and simple in its controlling tenet of proving "useful for her people." The important connections she initiated, along with other changes brought on by change, illustrate the powerful agency of Cherokee women.

A similar pluralism develops in the contemporary science fiction novel *Kholvn* by Sequoyah Guess, a self-published Keetoowah Cherokee author. Chapter 3 finds traditional and progressive religious practices continuing to develop in Guess's fantastical work, which confronts contemporary issues facing characters who stand in for several groups to be found in today's Cherokee country, such as Cherokee Nation and United Keetoowah Band citizens, Cherokee traditionalists, white and Indian Christians, and nonbelievers. The cooperative attitudes these characters must adopt, initially functioning as a plot device, develop thematically into a potent political statement on the necessity of diversity. In a very active sense, the hospitality Guess depicts among groups connected to Cherokee religious, political, and cultural communities urges awareness of, respect for, and adoption of multiple principled practices as strong expressions of tradition. This chapter positions Guess's work in a social-religious history of Cherokees who affiliated with Nighthawk Keetoowah traditionalists, Christians, and assorted political factions, primarily around the turn of the twentieth century. I argue that Guess's work models a progressively traditional means of mediating the tensions between today's Oklahoma Cherokee tribes, tensions that create immediate, unfortunate consequences for Cherokee people. As the Cherokee Nation and the United Keetoowah Band fight over jurisdiction and who can own a casino where, citizens forced to choose to whom they belong are denied access to resources that belong by rights to them, not to the contentious tribal states, despite Cherokee people's common declaration that they are one people.

But, of course, it's not like factionalism didn't appear until the twentieth century. The book's second part looks at a particularly devastating transitional time through Elias Boudinot's and Chief John Ross's political rhetoric of civilization during the removal crisis of the 1830s, read against a centralizing and gendered movement away from traditional indigenous anarchist political dispositions of consensus-building and debate. A key problem for the combined chapters of this part is the linkage of dissent with assimilatedness, a correlation that discourages discussion of nonconformist sentiments. Vesting cultural authority with the nation-state created a problem that is still very much with us, as it contrives its own self-serving version of tradition and marginalizes those who do not subscribe to it. Over and against the division into assimilated and traditional categories, the debates between Ross and Boudinot are more productively considered within the (de)structure of the centralization of power. When we moved governance from town council houses to the chief's office, we vacated the discursive spaces where dissent and debate forged consensus. Considering the removal crisis in the context of Cherokee governance's central gravitation, parts of Boudinot's public disagreement ironically emerge as more traditional than Ross's unilaterality as he struggled to accommodate the needs for authoritative rule of the nascent nation within the traditional political structure. As Theda Perdue has argued, a key group systematically divested of political and economic power by many of the political transformations of the early nineteenth century was Cherokee women. Such disempowering maneuvers directed at internal subgroups contributed to the disempowerment of the population as a whole.

Chapter 4 summarizes practices, beliefs, and structures connected with early anarchistic methods of deliberation and governance by consensus, following the changes they underwent in the transition from socially to politically based rule. This chapter concentrates on the period of national organization in the early nineteenth century, moving into the removal era, when Elias Boudinot and John Ross tried to forestall Andrew Jackson's removal policy. The overriding concern with remaining in the southeastern homelands led to a policy of ever-increasing centralization of government power that brought about a series of unforeseen changes to Cherokee culture, by no means all good. Specifically, this centripetal force worked to divest women of their historic social and political powers and generally constricted more democratic and inclusive ways of governing. Given many Cherokee officials' persistent efforts to kick out one group or another (outlanders, Freedmen, and others), we shouldn't pretend we've left such problems behind us. To set the stage for the next chapter's reading of the debates over removal, this chapter also offers brief biographies of Ross and Boudinot, together with an overview of the events leading up to the Trail of Tears.

The fifth chapter looks directly at Boudinot's and Ross's rhetoric in speeches, letters, and pamphlets giving their takes on civilization, education, removal, and political dissent. Most criticism and historical scholarship puts Boudinot and Ross on opposite sides of the assimilated/traditional dichotomy, and Cherokee people continue today to argue the controversy in the same terms. The ideas the men advanced, however—such as Ross urging the sale of Cherokee land to start a school and Boudinot practicing traditions of dissent—hopelessly confound those reductive categories. Though they bitterly disagreed on removal, they shared the desire to protect and enable Cherokee autonomy. Their championing of civilization programs reflects less a desire for assimilation into American society than a consistent dedication to self-determination. The debates between them proceed from this mutual principle, but in the context of centralized governance they inhabit polarized positions, increasingly less able and less willing to negotiate consensus. American Indian people could rededicate ourselves to consensus building, a radically democratic principle, as a means not only of fostering inclusive governance but also of combating the divisiveness engendered by colonialism and encapsulated in this long-running feud. Practically speaking, the argument aims to resuscitate the cultural history of political dissent against the nation-state, the urgent need for which the conclusion takes up.

The conclusion tests the dispositional theoretical strategy against the current controversy over the Cherokee Nation's disenfranchisement of the Cherokee Freedmen, who are descendants of former slaves. Their citizenship was mandated by treaty at the close of the Civil War and since then has been a controversial topic, with some inveterate nationalists (politicos, mostly) insisting that the tribal state's right to determine citizenship criteria trumps all other concerns, regardless of racism, greed, or any other potential motive behind forcing a group of people out of the nation. Against this position, I offer personal and historical examples of adoption and naturalization, long-practiced traditions informed by a socially compassionate ethic of inclusivity. Knowing that compassion and responsibility have played more prominent political roles in the past, I like to imagine that they could help shape Cherokee governance again. One aim of this concluding chapter is to help the Cherokee Nation reconsider its politically and morally problematic position in ways consistent with traditional culture, political expedience, and critical theory's philosophy of political and cultural hospitality. In other words, this chapter—and *Progressive Traditions* as a whole—attempts to bring together scholarship and politics, traditionalism and progressivism, and the past and the present, so that our cultural history can help clarify and shape practices and values that can contribute to the continuing life of Cherokee people. I'll close the chapter by looking at how cultural principles and practices mediate tradition and progress in ways that resonate with anarchistic dispositions of local community organization.

AMERICAN INDIAN IDENTITY AND AMERICAN INDIAN NATIONALISM

Maybe it reveals a bias, but I'm happy to admit that one of the things that most excites me about nationalists' contributions to American Indian critical theory is that the contributions largely come from Indians. Let me quickly explore why this might matter against some objections to why it should. First, the idea that Indians could speak with authority about Indian matters was not always subscribed to. In the decades around the turn of the twentieth century, scholars of the American Indian, in anthropology and ethnology, for instance, took on the roles of interpreter and translator, attempting to show how Indians' stories played out universal patterns, which explained what the stories were "really" about more than whatever ideas Indian people had about them. Though the disciplines moved past this paternalism, a fresh challenge arose from postmodernist critiques of ideas—about philosophy, history, identity, and everything else—that attempted to pass the ideas off as "natural," or objective, when it turns out they were often put together by a set of cultural and historical circumstances. These constructions tended to privilege the haves, punish the have-nots, and leave others out entirely. Because racial identities ranked high among these abused and misused socially contrived categories, postmodernists sometimes want to see them done away with, given that they're not real in an objective, outside-the-human-mind sense. Many postmodernists remain skeptical of affirmations of race, finding that such claims reaffirm a corrupt way of manipulating people into limiting their thinking, even when members of disadvantaged racial groups celebrate their social belonging. For the postmodernists, no special insight comes from the deceptions played by identities.

On problems like these, I tend to agree with identity theorists like Cherokee literary critic Sean Teuton, who aligns with a school of thought called postpositivist realism. These thinkers make the compelling argument that experience is relevant to how we are treated in the world, what we wind up empirically knowing about the world, and how we come to interpret it. Experience thus lends a *real* and certainly pertinent dimension to identities, even though identities are also constructed by social, cultural, and historical circumstances.[1]

How accurately identity-based interpretations describe experiences in the world is a common theme for postpositivist realists, though I favor a more pragmatic emphasis on efficacy. If we emphasize efficacy over accuracy, objectivity, or truth, we can admit that we will often be wrong about what we know or think we know, subject as we are to the vagaries of history or subjectivity itself, but we can also move more swiftly to the business of correcting error and identifying and working through problems to the best of our current abilities. If we buy this mediation of the essential/constructed debate, then we can begin to hear the insights of American Indian voices that have been marginalized, if not wholly ignored, in mainstream discourse. Their insights derive not from some genetic access provided by Indian blood but because culture matters to the ways people behave with and understand each other and their worlds. As Teuton argues, metaphysical or religious modes of understanding experience can empower people, just as historical consciousness of the influence of colonialism can empower political identities.[2] We don't have to claim that identities belong to some objective, eternal order to admit the practical difference they make in the world as people experience it; though crucially, those differences can be both positive and negative, in the short and long term. Indian critics, many of us anyway, have been exposed to the differences that being Indian makes, and that knowledge of how we live with each other and how we live with others can make for exciting revelations, including arguments that confront and actively seek to improve the all-too-real and too-often-deplorable conditions of Indian people's lives.

American Indian nationalists' novel, empowering analyses of Indian and other literature testify to the importance of their perspectives for all literary critics but particularly for Indian readers, like myself, who before the Native nationalists were largely without visible academic role models. Even though I disagree with some of their central points, I owe many nationalist scholars an enormous intellectual debt. Craig Womack and Robert Warrior taught me much of what I know about American Indian literature when I was a graduate student at the University of Oklahoma. Womack created the template for the tribalist critical mode I'll try to fill in, and Jace Weaver's work on Cherokee literature also set me on my path. All have been supportive mentors. They helped inaugurate a discourse among Indian thinkers familiar with intellectual and cultural particularities, ready to move beyond introductory matter, and prepared to engage in concrete political action. Although the early wave of criticism in the 1970s and 1980s attempted to situate the major texts and authors of the American Indian literary renaissance culturally and historically, it was largely a project of discovery, frequently limited to the anthropological or ethnological records and positioned on the outside of the tribes the critics investigated. The inner workings of every tribal community are not available to every Native critic, but the critics' affiliation with one or more tribe can open them to knowledge absent from official archives. Together with their attention to internal politics, nationalists' interests have often led them to turn their attention to the marginalized, intratribal voices of two-spirited, lower class, traditionalist, and other groups, which certainly makes for a more varied than usual version of nationalism.[3]

Nevertheless, Native nationalism retains a certain cohesion. Womack outlines his concept of nationalism: "The concept of nationhood itself is an intermingling of politics, imagination, and spirituality. Nationhood encompasses ongoing treaty relationships with the U.S. government. Nationhood has to do with federal Indian law, and tribes' testing of the sovereignty waters through new economic developments and other practices."[4] Here, culture gives place to politics in nationalism's operation. For Daniel Heath Justice, the tribal state looks very much like a natural extension of the tribal people: "Tribal nationhood is . . . distinguished from state-focused nationalism by its central focus on *peoplehood*, the relational system that keeps the people in balance with one another, with other peoples and realities, and with the world. Nationhood, then, is the political extension of the social rights and responsibilities of peoplehood."[5] In *American Indian Literary Nationalism*, a volume coauthored by Weaver, Womack, and Warrior that elaborates their perspectives, Weaver asserts that Native nationalism "sees itself as attempting to serve the interests of indigenes and their communities, in particular the support of Native nations and their own separate sovereignties."[6] This paramount political advocacy—for the increase of tribal nations' sovereignty—appears from one perspective their most attractive program, especially in its issue from a cultural campaign that, following

Warrior, they have dubbed "intellectual sovereignty."[7] Warrior, Womack, and Weaver each define the term differently, but each would seemingly agree it encompasses the self-determined intellectual, cultural, artistic, and political expression of the nation-people.

Nationalism, whether colonial or anti-, is the insinuation of the political sphere into the personal through narratives of commonality. In Benedict Anderson's terms, nationalism shapes how communities imagine themselves through various strategies, structures, and epistemologies.[8] A key strategy by which it persuades people that the nation's political interests align with their personal interests is through laying claim to cultural histories they treasure. Recounting ancestral forefathers' creation of the political structure in an imagined, shared heritage tries to demonstrate how the nation and the people were coextensive in the past, and so are now (or ought to be), and shall be into the future. Cleanly narrated histories in which the winners are heroes and rightful heirs of an interwoven cultural and political legacy not only serve as rallying national myths but also usurp authority over tradition. States are hardly above invoking tradition as they have reshaped it to authorize particular positions, such as on the question of the Cherokee Freedmen, and both tacit and overt condemnation of alternative perspectives as a product of assimilationist thinking often accompanies such posturing. It should go without saying that not everyone's cultural story makes it into these nationalist tellings. Notwithstanding claims that the political is the natural executor of the cultural, nationalism is foremost about politicism, which propagates uniformity, and not about heterogeneity, which instead complicates the solidarity under which nationalism operates most expeditiously. By urging citizens to get with the program, nationalism tries to present a front unified in a political course of action and in cultural outlook, which in the American Indian nations' case typically means veneration of tradition. But automatic acquiescence to a central state authority is, I believe, antithetical to tradition.

Insofar as nationalists support the increased sovereignty of the nation-people, including over the nation-state, theirs is a compelling project, but if we find a willingness to authorize the state as uncomplicatedly representative of the people, we run into serious problems. Nationalists may well mean to strengthen tribal-state power, specifically against U.S. and state governments, and intend only to remind their self-professed primary audience of Indian readers that resistance to fourth-world colonialism requires their attention. As contradictory as it may be with an anarchist position, I have to agree with them: strengthening the tribal nation-state is far and away the best organizational strategy for contending with external powers, but we cannot set aside discussion over why and how to limit the nation-state's coercive powers internally. Upon objection to any given tribal-state policy, nationalists can admit that governments make errors and do things that not all the represented people agree with, but these cases show up only as isolated exceptions insufficient to warrant reevaluation of the rule. Nationalists have claimed in several places that theirs is not a closed discussion, that they are only sketching the outlines of a discourse about political and cultural nationalism, but seldom in their advocacy for the strengthening of sovereignty have they suggested what limits they would impose on tribal-state power or according to what principles or processes it should be supervened.

Thankfully, there is movement on this front. Weaver, Womack, and Warrior have each written on the misapplication of state power in cases involving the Freedmen, and they have expressed reservations over the limitations that could result from tribal agencies or research councils having veto power over research agendas.[9] Womack, Justice, and others aligned with nationalism have also noted that tribal-statist campaigns against same-sex marriage are neither geared toward strengthening nations in their inclusivity nor are they very traditionalist. As nationalists have refined their agendas by confronting cases where tribal nation-states have betrayed their responsibilities by constraining the liberties of their constituents rather than protecting them by limiting the intrusions of outside forces, many of them have in fact moved toward wonderfully anarchist positions. Weaver in his book *Turtle Goes to War*, on the U.S. response to the September 11, 2001, terrorist attacks, makes powerful cases for both the defense of civil liberties against federal intrusions on basic rights and for dissent as an integral part of public debate.[10] He relates this position to his work in Native studies, which is necessarily familiar with the hundreds of federally recognized tribes and their relationships with the federal government. Supporting their national standing lends itself to what Weaver calls "pluralist separatism," by which he suggests recognition and respect for the distinctiveness of the many nations within a nation or, as he clarifies, "nations within a nation-state."[11] This qualification implies a difference between Native nations and the U.S. nation on the absence of a state with the former—a difference with which I disagree and discuss in detail in the next section. As in these cases, where nationalists suspiciously eye the nation, and in many more waiting in the wings, a too-rigid union of the cultural and political jeopardizes the personal and communal sovereignty of the nation-people in its a priori authorization of supposedly natural or fully consented-to cultural representation by the nation-state.

Cosmopolitan critics mount another objection to nationalism in their critique of a perceived antitheoretical rhetorical posture in nationalist separatism.[12] Womack defends his approach by arguing, "I do not bother much in this book with the skepticism of postmodernism in relation to history. It is way too premature for Native scholars to deconstruct history when we haven't yet constructed it."[13] Deconstruction can be pretty constructive, though. I'm perfectly happy to deconstruct our histories when they've been told using binaries we've taken on from mainstream methodologies. For their part, nationalists have demurred at cosmopolitans' point, agreeing that they do in fact use non-Native theory but asserting that their goal of fostering discourse among American Indian voices requires that those theories be privileged.[14] For nationalists, their eschewal more accurately reflects distaste for postmodern and postcolonial theories of hybridity and mediation rather than unawareness or incomprehension of them, believing these approaches poorly accommodate Natives' fourth-world conditions and do not confront Native material realities, when they have deigned to examine Native peoples and their literatures at all.[15]

COSMOPOLITANISM

Cosmopolitanism, the other leading contender in the field, argues that what is needed instead of insistence on difference is exploration of similarity, especially among peoples allied in anti-imperial resistance. Cosmopolitans believe with their philosophical forebears that, armed with a sympathetic intellect, they may find themselves at home anywhere, literally as citizens of the cosmos. With a perspective favoring general rather than specific investigations, they understand source material in relation to broad patterns in American Indian, pan-Indian, and global indigenous literature. Their familiarity with continental and postcolonial theory has brought sophisticated inquiry into the study of American Indian literature, and in facilitating its visibility they have generated widespread academic interest. The anticolonialist, subversive spirit of American Indian literature draws many cosmopolitans, who may then act as translators or mediators, as Arnold Krupat envisions the role, helping to introduce other audiences to an unfamiliar body of work.[16] Cosmopolitanism extends a liberal, humanist optimism for the potential of the nation-state to foster human development, a position with a long and respectable philosophical genealogy. It is not one without problems for Indian people, however, particularly in its secularism and its long-term goal of the replacement of tribal or other local identities with a utopian vision of affiliation-at-will.

Allied with nationalism by the common enemy of colonialism, cosmopolitanism by no means opposes nationalism at every turn, and in fact several leading figures of each camp have made collegial overtures to engage in productive conversation. Krupat, the chief proponent of a cosmopolitan critical position in American Indian literary criticism, however, hesitates regarding possible nationalist misrepresentations: "For Womack, the most important thing in any approach to Native literatures 'should be a study of the primary culture that produces them' [*Red on Red* 25]. Here, one might ask—as also with [Elizabeth] Cook-Lynn—whether culture and nation are synonymous."[17] Krupat points out parenthetically, "There are dangers, as a number of writers have pointed out, in treating the 'people' or the 'nation' as a unitary force or indivisible essence."[18] The dangers to which Krupat alludes might include the absence of administrative transparency and accountability, suppression of dissent, and the disenfranchisement of citizens. Krupat explains that the nationalist goal of expansion of sovereignty "means a decrease in the 'dependency' of Native nations on the federal government and a greater degree of 'autonomy.' But it is not clear just what political *forms* expanded sovereignty for the people—as the 'agency that lays claim to a monopoly of decision-making power' . . . and the sole possessor of 'legitimate force' (Ree 87)—might actually take."[19] Krupat rightly critiques nationalism's failure to articulate its ideal political forms, that is, to offer a definite statement of program, but he himself, along with other cosmopolitans, doesn't exactly meet this burden of proof, either.

If nationalists or quasi-nationalist cosmopolitan supporters advocate a dramatic reformulation or just an alternative structural design of the tribal political apparatus, they have not said as much. Whatever misgivings they may have, cosmopolitans gloss over the de facto problems of state power and remain dedicated to the enhancement of Native nations' sovereignty—especially as a thorn in colonialism's side—but not strictly because they support the nationalist goals of Native peoples or governments.[20] They see nationalism and its generative consciousness as a necessary evil, an intermediate point in materialist history's progress toward a higher loyalty to a "new humanism" or an "internationalist" consciousness, in Frantz Fanon's language in *The Wretched of the Earth*, approvingly cited by Krupat.[21] It's worth a look back at what Fanon has to say. He anticipates what he calls an "occult instability" in this novel identity, the characteristics of which he declines to clarify, although he hints at its enabling structure:[22] "As we see it, a program is necessary for a government which really wants to free the people politically and socially. There must be an economic program; there must also be a doctrine concerning the division of wealth and social relations. . . . What can be dangerous is when they ['African people and indeed all underdeveloped peoples'] reach the stage of social consciousness before the stage of nationalism. If this happens, we find in underdeveloped countries fierce demands for social justice which paradoxically are allied with often primitive tribalism."[23] For Fanon, nations must first buy into Marxist ideology (and perhaps Leninist statism—the "program" that will ensure compliance with the "doctrine") before they can develop the capacity to understand their local concerns' rightful, secondary place. Further, subscribing to a materialist historical model, Fanon and his cosmopolitan followers come off as assured of their proper place as the chief representatives of civilization and progress as did nineteenth-century imperialists. Even the language, with its jabs at "primitive" and "underdeveloped" peoples presuming to mimic their betters, uncannily reminds us of the epistemic abuses of savagism. There may be progress here, in a philosophical line that runs from Louis Henry Morgan to Karl Marx to Frantz Fanon, and that assumes universal development, but when it comes to respecting the ideas of indigenous peoples ourselves concerning where we are and where we'd like to go, how far has it really come?

Besides their contempt for tribalism, many cosmopolitans have inherited Fanon's general philosophic sympathy for the state as a civilized institution and administrator of the "programs" charged with advancing humanist goals.[24] Cosmopolitan theorist Kwame Anthony Appiah philosophically grounds his version of cosmopolitanism in the principles and practices of Western liberalism.[25] Classical liberalism, in its search for new forms of democratic political organization and authorization, calls for regular justification and careful scrutiny of state institutions, Appiah writes, "because they are both necessary to so many modern human purposes and because they have so great a potential for abuse. As Hobbes famously saw, the state, to do its job, has to have a monopoly of certain forms of authorized coercion; and the exercise of that authority cries out for (but often does not deserve) justification."[26] While Appiah maintains humanism's focus on basic human rights, he subtly eases the call for ongoing review of the structures intended to enable their protection when he asserts, "the primary mechanism for ensuring these entitlements *remains* the nation state."[27] Taking the nation-state's existence as authorization for the state nullifies the need for critique that should be continual, not formulated once and forever. As liberalism increasingly aligned itself with state-sympathetic politics, insistence on regulation of the state became state regulation. The authority of the nation-state to carry on its wide range of functions thus became vested. As for whether Appiah has proven the nation-state is indeed the "primary mechanism for ensuring" human rights—much less whether it *ought* to be—I am not persuaded, given the vagaries of national and tribal-national politics.

Krupat is in fact more suspicious of the state than Appiah, though both share the progressive vision of internationalist humanism against colonialism and late capitalism.[28] Krupat writes, "In my view, cosmopolitans will probably find themselves supporting not only nationalitarian [internationalist] forms of nationalism, but also—if warily—most nationalisms directed against an oppressive colonial order."[29] Diverging from Appiah and angling away from statist sympathy, Krupat enters a dilemma: how to support the Native nations' pitch for greater political sovereignty while maintaining scrutiny over the nation-state. He redeems Native nationalism by making a motion, seconded by Weaver and Justice, that its conception of the nation is premised upon a cultural formulation of the people rather than of the state—and the resulting organization, though it calls itself a state, is apparently something of a different order. He writes in *Red Matters*, "Native American nationalisms . . . differ from other nationalisms . . . in that they do not seek the creation of postcolonial states," news that may surprise tribal nation-state politicians.[30] According to Krupat, not only do Native people not desire an autonomous state, "The 'sovereign political entities' that Native nations were and continue to be were not and are not *states*."[31] He does not define "state" in *Red Matters*, or anywhere else that I can find. Rather than working through a challenging contradiction, Krupat simply denies it exists because we're somehow comparing apples and oranges. I'm happy to admit that *I* for one don't seek a more statist state, and I hope other Native people share this hesitance, but we can't pretend that Native nations aren't headed down this road as fast as they can travel.

In his equation of peoplehood with nationhood, nationalist Daniel Heath Justice also avails himself of this dismissal of the connection between tribal people and ugly versions of the state, claiming, "Indigenous nationhood should not, however, be conflated with the nationalism that has given birth to industrialized nation-states."[32] Whether the tribal nation-state conforms to Cherokees' ideal political structure is worth careful inquiry, but if tribal nations born of indigenous nationhood differ from other nations in some ways, in others, they are eerily familiar. Ernest Gellner, a scholar of nationalism, offers several criteria that characterize a nation against which we might measure tribal nations. Whether understood as an authority possessed of legitimized violence, a centralized political structure with a monopoly on decision-making power, a body of legislators, the arbiter of justice, a standing bureaucracy subject to codified legislation and regulation, the administrator of education, promoter of welfare, maintainer of order, or any other common standard, the Cherokee Nation and many other tribal nations meet the qualifications.[33] The Cherokee Nation, which began as a centralized body in the 1820s, administers a police force, whose officers are trained by federal law enforcement agencies, have the authority to use (and have used) deadly force, and are cross-deputized with county and municipal entities; it maintains headquarters; it employs administrative, legislative, judicial, and bureaucratic officials; it operates schools, child welfare offices, and health clinics, among other governmental responsibilities under the rule of law.

The Cherokee nation-state now also oversees the business entity Cherokee Nation Industries, an electronics company that manufactures, among other things, wiring harnesses for the Bell Boeing V-22 Osprey combat-troop carrier helicopter, under a federal Department of Defense contract. The Osprey, originally designed for use in combat situations, crashed several times in testing and was used in the Iraq war primarily to transport troops and supplies close to the fighting front.[34] (The wiring harness has in no way been implicated in the Osprey's design troubles.) I can only understand such national activities as part and parcel of an "industrialized nation-state."

In his book *X-Marks*, Scott Lyons pointedly critiques tribal nations' disenfranchising and banishing of citizens, demonstrating he does not need to be disabused of the notion that tribal nation-states can do no wrong, although he does stake out ground roughly similar to Krupat's in a qualified endorsement of nationalism. Much as I hope to do, Lyons looks to break away from incarnations of traditionalism that reject beliefs, practices, and identities as too progressive or assimilated to count as Indian, based on too narrow an idea of how much Indian peoples can change and retain their character as Indians. He urges understanding many changes, such as the development of nations, as modernization or volitional assent to changing historical circumstances, albeit in frequently exploitative circumstances, rather than as plain acquiescence to purely non-Native modes of living. One of the few scholars in American Indian studies to look at mainstream scholarship on nationalism, Lyons borrows from Anthony Smith the concept of the "ethnie," or premodern ethnic groups that in the nineteenth century established the rough demographic and cultural boundaries of the nations to which they gave way.

While he finds tribal nationhood an effective political structure that arose in opposition to colonialism, Lyons sees it as hampered because it retains too much of its premodern character, and he encourages its continued modernization and development. Even though he declares, "my call for more modernization is simultaneously a demand for greater nationalization," he would like to see American Indian nations curtail their normalizing and marginalizing tendencies.[35] These have led to, for instance, the disenfranchisement of Freedmen, the banishment of law violators, eviction of non-Native spouses from tribal lands, and more recently to the disenrollment of large numbers of tribal members contending over casino profits. Despite these critiques, Lyons argues that the state itself is key among the strengths of modernization, and going even farther than many cultural nationalists, he wants to see Native nations grow to resemble their larger, more powerful state counterparts. He approves the movement of the nation-people toward becoming a nation-state, writing, "the nation is always shifting 'away from kinship and cultural dimensions to territorial, educational and legal aspects' of community."[36] This may be the case, but it is not *necessarily* the case. I am less optimistic than Lyons that the state's benevolence will grow proportionately with its power, especially as it "leaves behind" matters of kinship and culture. For premodern concepts, these did a respectable job of binding communities together, and they still have much to teach us about responsibility, compassion, and justice. But Lyons is pushing for a larger, wider degree of affiliation when he writes of "new societies," "prophetic discourse," and "uttering the universal."[37] His is a vision of an anticapitalist, panhuman identity shared by many cosmopolitans from Fanon to Krupat, and how it fits into American Indian worlds bears a closer look.

In addition to the automatic authorization of state authority, the humanist position undergirding cosmopolitanism advocates two features that impede its acceptance among many Cherokee people: (1) the dissolution of community boundaries and subsequent birth of Fanon's aforementioned "new humanity" (like Lyons's "new societies") that will "define a new humanism" and (2) an associated secularist privilege.[38] This new model of affiliation, liberated from narrowness and born of "occult instability," is couched as an inevitable historical outcome but also something that we should not try to describe using our current vocabularies so that we don't limit it by our present deficiencies. Fanon promises it will be an unencumbered future, but there may be some strings attached.

The vision for the new humanity precludes loyalty to any of the internationalist collective's national or tribal forerunners, supplanted by a humanity-wide imperative to be enforced by what cosmopolitanist scholar Pheng Cheah calls "an ideal institutional framework for regulating the anarchic behavior of states."[39] If I read him right, this sounds like a utopian description of a state without coercive powers or the need for them (although it also sounds much like a superstate). In this new world order, earlier, "primitive" ways of belonging will be set aside. The postcolonial theoretical giant Edward Said concurs with Fanon's value-laden indictment of tribalism cited above, which I believe is more or less synonymous with what Said calls "nativism": "The tremendous *ressentiment* in nativism aside . . . there are two reasons for rejecting, or at least reconceiving, the nativist enterprise." The first is that it is not "the only choice for a resisting, decolonizing nationalism." More importantly for Said, "To accept nativism is to accept the consequences of imperialism, the racial, religious, and political divisions imposed by imperialism itself. To leave the historical world for the metaphysics of essences like *négritude*, Irishness, Islam, or Catholicism is to abandon history for essentializations that have the power to turn human beings against each other; often this abandonment of the secular world has led to a sort of millenarianism if the movement has had a mass base, or it has degenerated into small-scale private craziness."[40] The disregard for so many groups' own ideas of themselves and the communities they proudly belong to in the shadow of this new-humanist opacity might well alarm American Indian communities. One major problem is the disregard's genesis in the proposition—perhaps accurate in its description of some African or Middle Eastern groups but largely untenable among American Indians—that imperialism created tribal divisions; another is the pejorative description of those divisions as coming from an irrationality approaching lunacy, and still another is the disingenuous equation of religiosity with fanaticism. If tribal peoples do indeed turn toward history, as Said calls for, we are likely to find he doesn't mean our shared languages, our genealogies, our philosophies, our occupations of places from time immemorial—none of which are necessarily essentializations, let me add—but something more like Marxist historicism. In this, we know where tribal peoples stand: as primitives in need of patronage and civilization. We've seen the good that's done. If the uncharacteristic vitriol in Said's quote is characteristic of humanist adherents, it is unclear if antitribalist theorists would reexamine their hard-thought stance in light of American Indian historical and cultural contexts. And once again, Indian ideas about our selves and our futures would go ignored.

Writing about American Indian literature, Krupat marshals an auspicious intellectual genealogy in Fanon, Appiah, and Jean-Paul Sartre, to whom we could add Said, Homi Bhabha, and more. Krupat wonders with them if "we"—humanity, presumably—are ready for the "transcendence of racism and an end to violence" through internationalist affiliation.[41] But writing as he is about Native literature, the real question for him seems to be if *Indians* are ready for the new humanism. To American Indian communities looking to preserve their religions, cultural practices, epistemologies, and everyday comings and goings, many practical effects of old evangelical and new humanist interests in their communities bear an uncanny resemblance to each other. Both relegate Native interests to a subordinate status and see in their final goals a nullification of tribalism: its cultural differences, political traditions, religious beliefs—any loyalty below a transcendent humanity.[42] Before deigning to wonder if Indians are "ready" for progress in this particular course, perhaps someone should first ask if indeed we even *want* it. Cosmopolitanism and humanism offer insights for American Indian literary criticism to be sure, especially in their work on the effectiveness of human rights-based claims against colonial states. We should approach them, however, well informed of their goals, of Indian groups' relationship to them, and of our own capacity and right to reshape them to suit our own needs, should we want to do something primitive like hanging on to, maybe even critically privileging, the time-immemorial idea of ourselves as Cherokee people.

PROGRESSIVE TRADITIONS

That idea, however, of what makes a Cherokee "Cherokee" has indeed developed over time and will surely continue to change in the future. Reluctant as we are to abandon our identity as Cherokee people—whether for allegiances hereditary or imagined, benefits material or psychosociological, or for whatever reason—we might ask ourselves some questions about the directions we want to take our ideas of ourselves into the future. These might look at problems with our nation-state, what we could do to mitigate them, and where and how to develop alliances with others. As we think of our future selves, we should be leery of establishing a single distinguishing feature, for such an attempt is ultimately an invitation to buy into an idea of never-changing traditions—an invitation to fall into the same dichotomy that ossifies identities and limits our imagining what Indian people can do and believe. This section will discuss some of the problems with trying to cram all our eggs into a basket too small and will offer an outline of a theoretical approach to understanding collective identity organized outside the auspices of the nation-state, which I think holds greater promise.

It is not necessary to belabor the theoretical problems with the kind of binary reasoning that credits one category with authenticity and the other with contamination, especially after Jacques Derrida reverse-engineered the dichotomies in the philosophy of Jean-Jacques Rousseau and the structuralism of Claude Lévi-Strauss. With his concept of the "supplement," Derrida shows how apparently opposed terms in fact often depend on and mutually constitute one another.[43] He famously demonstrates, for example, the affinities between writing and speaking in their shared processes of articulation, differentiation, and spacing. If we look at traditionalism and assimilation as they play out within tribal groups, we can see that tradition is not an unadulterated force of unalterable conservatism nor is assimilation one of unrestrained avant-garde progress, but that both are oriented toward the support of community cohesion, collective values, and basically making people's lives better. They plainly differ in mode, just as writing differs from speaking, but they similarly respond to ongoing change by drawing from various existing strategies, borrowing strategies from other groups, or inventing new ones. More pointedly, assimilation names one method, by degrees more open to outside influence in adapting to changing circumstances, whether introduced by outside forces or arising from within.

When, however, could there have been a time that cultures did not face change, did not grow, did not have to adapt to their neighbors' actions or their members' new ideas? When could cultures not have assimilated innovation into tradition? Too, just as it's fair to admit that the United States' assimilationist strategies have damaged existing tribal institutions far more than they have maintained them, so too should we be prepared to admit that traditionalist strategies have at least sometimes had similar effects. For example, when traditional Cherokee groups withdrew from political contention over land allotment under the Dawes and Curtis Acts, assimilation proponents (willfully) misinterpreted their traditional mode of protest as assent, allowing the advocates to downplay opposition to the policy. This focus on interplay in supplementarity is not to say that no differences exist between the new and the old, but that in the dependence binding assimilation and tradition we can spy far more complicated actions and reactions than simple paired conflict.

Deconstructionists can help us see *how* the traditional/assimilated split goes wrong, but to understand *why* scholars of American Indian history and culture created and continue to invoke the split to organize the broadest of analyses requires examining what's at stake in its use and how it profits its proponents. Near the turn of the twentieth century, when major histories began appearing, the dichotomy likely owed something to eugenicist anxieties over the mixing of races, which many feared would lead to the degeneration of the supposedly superior white bloodline and the creation of a shiftless but dangerously educated group interested not in joining American society on a second-class basis but in opposing it for the benefit of Indian people. Having learned something of American law, politics, and literacy, the group's members could mount formidable opposition and also publicly challenge and reveal the duplicity and violence of American Indian policies and, by extension, American civilization. Desirous of claiming the Indian problem over through the unfortunate but necessary march of progress, many Americans found that Natives who pressed for their rights, who wrote books calling the United States to account, and who refused to die off amounted to the wrong kind of Indians. Better were those who, belonging to the past only, could be nostalgized as worthy but firmly defeated enemies.[44] If Indians had to linger, they should be docile, containable, and less apt to reflect an image of the American self more uncanny and darker in skin and tone than the United States was prepared to countenance.

Similar reasons could account for the traditional/assimilated binary's staying power among inveterate anti-Indian opposition arguments, but in pro-Indian academic circles, it may pay off in certain less obvious ways, too (if I can indulge in a little psychosocial speculation). In continuing to blame assimilationist Indians for their complicity in exploitation, for their failure to represent the wishes of the conservative majority of their people, for their alienation by virtue of their wealth and education, could progressive academics today be revealing as much about contemporary anxieties as about scores of tribal histories across hundreds of years? Maybe so, and I get a kick out of thinking about the possibility, but more plausibly, the binary's use today likely owes more to its longstanding prevalence than to biological fears of mixing races or collective unconscious projection. The story of mixed-bloods adopting white dispositions and betraying traditional interests for the sake of profit has become so ensconced that it can be taken as a factual given rather than as a historicist construct to be interrogated. Too, it's a story told by authoritative, discerning, and requisite histories, from James Mooney at the turn of the twentieth century to William McLoughlin in the mid-1980s and Theda Perdue a decade later, so it's easy to see why even so keen a contemporary critic as Mark Rifkin adopts it, albeit in modified form. I discuss the shape he gives it in chapter 4.

To be fair, neither progressivism nor mixed-bloodedness has everywhere or always been devalued. During the American Progressive era, the decades around the turn of the twentieth century, many American Indian intellectuals, activists, and writers successfully lobbied for positive change at local and national levels, allied with groups such as the Society of American Indians to advocate for causes like universal American citizenship for Natives, and wrote novels like Mourning Dove's *Cogewea* that found strength in mixed-bloodedness. More recently, the work of Gerald Vizenor, beginning with his 1978 novel, *Darkness in Saint Louis: Bearheart*, and of Louis Owens, especially his 1998 book of literary criticism, *Mixedblood Messages*, reconfigured how mixed-bloodedness is understood not just in literature but in thinking about American Indians generally. Vizenor's wild "crossblood" trickster characters signaled a turn toward subversive resistance to colonialist attitudes and pointedly made their lack of purity a positive strength. In *Mixedblood Messages* and elsewhere, Owens demonstrates how the instability that results from the indeterminate space between white and Indian, which he spatially represents as the unruly "frontier" as opposed to the demarcated and limited "territory," generates hybridist energy and agency that resists the controls of hard-and-fast boundaries.[45] These authors' positive coding of mixed-bloodedness effectively turned the traditional/assimilated dichotomy on its head. One caveat to bear in mind with this movement, however, is Derrida's caution against a simple reversal of a binary's favored terms. While neither Owens nor his intellectual allies like Pulitano devalue full-bloods or traditionalists, they do caution against identification that veers too closely toward homogeneity or essentialism, as I discuss above.[46] The ideas of mixed-bloodedness and full-bloodedness and of progressivism and traditionalism have gone through several historical permutations and will continue to be reworked in connection with topical trends, but their dichotomous pairing is likely to continue, as is their serving as a reductive point of reference. Another caveat to consider, of course, is that despite this and similar revaluations, far too many still hold to the negative account of mixed-blooded progressivism.

A shift in critical focus away from these binaries, which define traditionalism in particular by singular markers of culture and toward a range of the practices by which cultures manage to survive all that history has thrown at them, can mitigate some of these deficiencies. In thinking through what such an approach might look like, I'm helped along by Pierre Bourdieu's concept of the habitus. Although exploration of that range of practices must be partial, we can nevertheless more thoroughly describe Cherokee culture and its capacity to simultaneously innovate and maintain itself than we have so far. We can do so at least to the extent that we can link up shared principled practices with groups of people who call themselves and are called by others "Cherokee." What I mean by this qualification is that self-identification and social identification are reasonable and pragmatic ways, if contestable and impermanent ways, of defining whom I'm calling "Cherokee." These principled practices are formed in conversation with cultural values and the histories of those values, in which they both shape and are shaped by those values. Principled practices might or might not operate consciously, which means we could be using strategies that we don't even think of as strategies. Among the multitude of principled practices, some manage alteration to the social structure in terms of beliefs, habits, and practices. The way they regulate development tends to perpetuate both the practices and the matrix of conditions under which they're used to operating.

This is the culturally conservative, even the traditionalist, nature of what Bourdieu calls habitus: "The conditionings associated with a particular class of conditions of existence produce *habitus*, systems of durable, transposable dispositions, structured structures predisposed to function as structuring structures, that is, as principles which generate and organize practices and representations that can be objectively adapted to their outcomes without presupposing a conscious aiming at ends or an express mastery of the operations necessary in order to attain them."[47] The "outcomes" of these practices are as important as their mode of operation inasmuch as the habitus "is always oriented towards practical functions."[48] Such goals may be either concretely social, such as accumulating economic or symbolic capital, as Bourdieu discusses in his analysis of marriage strategies, or they may be metasocial, such as maintaining the value of that capital and the economic or social conditions that determine and support the goals. Bourdieu understands "durability" as intrinsic to the dispositions constituting the habitus, claiming it "tends to ensure its own constancy and its defence against change through the selection it makes within new information by rejecting information capable of calling into question its accumulated information." It further "tends to protect itself from crises and critical challenges by providing itself with a milieu to which it is as pre-adapted as possible."[49] It achieves this largely through socialization—members of a given community internalize existing social scripts, or schema, simply by modeling what they see parents, teachers, and others doing. Though Bourdieu makes much of the habitus's traditionalist refusal to alter when it alteration finds, his emphasis on its conservative tendencies results from his attention to its everyday operation.

It is just as present, however, in moments of inescapable crisis and rupture, and here, too, I believe we can see it still alters conditions only parsimoniously, at least when it is able, preserving categorical form if not exact pieces of culture. There are undeniably times and cases characterized by absolute upheaval and erasure, such as a trauma like removal would effect on relationships to specific places, but insofar as we still see observable differences that we account "Cherokee" in form and content, the habitus helps us make sense of how that is so. The degree of change to both form and content is an important consideration, and in measuring it we should take into account how sweeping the change is to particulars and to their place in the broader habitus. We should also bear in mind that, while some changes come from rupture, others come from modernization that Cherokees volitionally participated in. This is all to illustrate a fairly simple point: change doesn't always change as many things as it appears to. While many changes in Cherokee culture, too many of them radical, came about through colonialist coercion, the story of loss and decline has been told many times. I'd like to explore some continuances, not necessarily because they are sweepingly more prevalent in terms of Cherokee history but because they also matter, even if they are anomalous.

Though the habitus has limits, it can still accomplish an enormous amount of innovation. Because dispositions are found throughout the matrix of the social structure, Bourdieu writes, "the *habitus* is an infinite capacity for generating products—thoughts, perceptions, expressions and actions—whose limits are set by the historically and socially situated conditions of its production."[50] The habitus's situation in time—that is, its social and historical contexts—thus shapes dispositions, but it still manages to come up with effective, novel combinations with the tools at its disposal. This "infinite capacity" Bourdieu invokes I find an incredibly exciting avenue when it comes to exploring the ways that Indian communities have responded to unfamiliar challenges by refashioning already existing pieces of their cultures. It also helps respond to what some have seen as a totalizing tendency: bearing in mind the emphasis on innovation, albeit constrained by context and circumstance, the habitus reveals the strategizing that goes into a course of action proceeding from traditions. To say that practices, dispositions, or traditions belong to the Cherokee habitus is not necessarily an endorsement of them, and they will often be in conflict. In the cases of the progressive traditions I discuss, it is important that we broaden the scope of our understanding of traditions so that we can better and more comprehensively evaluate the tactics that principled practices like consensus-based governance or adoption represent in their social and historical settings. Again, because these components may not be consciously or overtly theorized, seeing their traces in either old or new forms can require thorough cultural familiarity.

I use the term "principled practices" more or less synonymously with Bourdieu's "dispositions" to reiterate their interdependent relationship, which seems to me so close that I understand the habitus itself more as a dynamic process than as a static collection. Bourdieu inclines more toward reifying the habitus, but given that practices are what it generates, conceiving of it as process does not fundamentally alter our understanding of its functions: offering a set of combinatory strategies, perpetuating the practices and conditions constituting it, and regulating change. These actions born in multiplicity can help clarify the pieces and strategies subsumed under the appellations "traditional" and "progressive" and help trace how they work toward similar ends, and these are the functions I connect with "progressive traditions."

Several attempts have been made to identify single necessary and sufficient markers of essential American Indian difference. The leading contenders are philosophical or spiritual beliefs about land, kinship or blood ties, indigenous language use, retention of mythical stories, self-identification, community recognition, ceremonial participation, religious beliefs, a history of treaty-making, geographic residence, and historical or cultural awareness. For some, phenotype undoubtedly remains an indication of Indianness; for others, Indianness might well be precluded by membership in too high an economic class. Over time, all of these have waxed and waned in importance in the critical literature. I don't dispute that any of these practically function as boundaries for some groups. The numerous contradictions in the historical record and common experience to each of the proposed limiters, however—people(s) who are almost universally regarded as Indian but fail to conform to one or more of the theoretical standards—point up the need for theories better attuned to anomaly and complexity. If there is a locus of cultural difference, perhaps it resides not in any singular, discrete feature but gathers together and migrates across the infinite combinations of thought and unthought beliefs and practices.

I question the practicality of using many of these characteristics as wholesale markers of identity, or more to the point, I worry about the rhetoric used to advance them, which circulates not just in academic discourse but also in local Indian communities. In arguing that Indian culture depends on its connection with ancestral land, as many cosmopolitanist, nationalist, and indigenist critics do, how are we to make sense of tribes that have been relocated? How many tribes were not? As for those living on the lands where they were before European invasion, if their country has on average been constricted by, say, a conservative 75 percent—are they one-quarter the Indians they once were? What is gained by arguing that loss of indigenous languages heralds the loss of identity entirely, as I have heard several language instructors, students, and members of stomp dance grounds argue? Is interest in learning the languages increased, or are nonspeakers alienated and discouraged? Too often the rhetoric of imminent demise that advocates use to make their case for urgency reinforces the myth of the vanishing Indian, and where that dominant discourse once fixated us in the past, I worry we are now writing ourselves out of the future.

This is not to say that boundary-drawing practices are not important (although we would surely like to see some left in the past); quite the contrary—they are of enormous importance and are made yet more so and made more powerful through their interrelationships with each other and with the innumerable other principles and practices that constitute the tribal habitus. The strength accruing in the connections between principled practices dispersed in the habitus also mandates a responsibility on the part of community members to maintain others that lend each their salience and force. No one wants to see old ways fade, but by declaring Indian identity as entirely tied to a single measure, we could be providing those antagonistic to Indian interests a road map to proving our cultural extinction. We don't need to help them with this.

Recognizing the catch with such hard-and-fast identity measures but also committed to their preservation, Lyons suggests the nation—specifically, the criteria it establishes for citizenship and belonging—can play a key role in maintaining values and practices. Simply put, he suggests that Indian nations should *"require what you want to produce.* If your heritage language is dying, then make fluency a requirement for citizenship. If your territory suffers from brain drain, make residency a requirement for citizenship. If you need capital, make commitment to the nation's laws a requirement for citizenship and level a progressive income tax."[51] Despite the optimism Lyons inspires, I'm not sure that results are so easily accomplished by bureaucratic, top-down solutions. A host of circumstances and reactions limits the productive scope of boundaries like blood quantum, for instance. Lyons admits, "If you wish to produce a nation of lineal descendants with a certain blood quantum and little else, you are probably well on your way," but at this point in his text, he fails to mention a crucial problem with blood quantum: besides producing a population of lineal descendants, it also produces a rapidly dwindling population.[52] As long as Indians insist on marrying people for reasons besides race, enrollment, or Certificate Degree of Indian Blood fractions, citizenries will continue to be legislated out of existence. Lyons knows this, aptly calling blood quantum "statistical extermination" just a few pages earlier.[53]

The other criteria he offers could well bring about similar precipitous drops in numbers. How many people currently living outside geographic boundaries would be able to pack up and move their families, jobs, and lives for the sake of maintaining tribal citizenship? Would they be able to find jobs at all, or isn't the lack of employment opportunities already a primary cause for the brain drain Lyons notes? Imposing a language requirement, too, even if phased in, would likely prove dicey. Working people do not often have several hours a week to devote to language lessons or money to spend on tuition, and as language teachers can tell us, the curriculum for upper-level learners is often still in the development phases. Making citizenship contingent on such characteristics or skills, valuable as they are, could prove disastrous. We need to constantly bear in mind a key condition of Lyons's "require what you want to produce" formula: one thing we want to produce is a population that isn't vanishing.

So long as we've got nations, I'll go along with the idea that we should put them to good use, and working for the "survivance" of traditions, to borrow Gerald Vizenor's term, is a reasonable enough use. But healthier relations would develop if nations were to focus on providing incentives for or demonstrating the benefits of the practices they want to foster rather than coming down on their people for suffering the effects of colonialism, sometimes to the point that they might even cease to *be* the people. If we want to preserve indigenous languages, for instance, we should demonstrate the insights they provide and their beauty. To get people living in tribal areas, we should focus on making those places viable, attractive, and welcoming—places that provide more carrot and less stick. Stridently exclusionary citizenship criteria, however well intentioned, run a serious risk of weakening rather than strengthening nations, and mandating a handful of similarities won't take us very far forward. Nations like the Cherokee need people with varied talents, as many as they can bring: people who speak Cherokee, who speak English, Spanish, and Quechua; people who understand politics in Tahlequah, Oklahoma City, Washington, D.C., and the United Nations; people who make art, crafts, medicine, machines, and money. In short, people who can capitalize on the numberless possibilities contained in the habitus.

AMERICAN INDIAN ANARCHISM

Having critiqued nationalism and cosmopolitanism for their statism, I nevertheless find myself using the vocabulary of nations to talk about people (as in the preceding paragraph) without giving it a second thought—but a second thought is in order. The case for progressive traditions is anchored in heterogeneity, and nationalism is not the paradigm best suited to celebrating the advantages of difference. Anarchism offers a more fruitful outlook, and pairing it with a methodology concerned with progressive traditions reveals many enduring Cherokee communities structured not around the state and its unilateral authority but on local principles and practices that are no less Cherokee for having fallen out of favor in the centralization of Cherokee governance. American Indian literary nationalists like Weaver, Womack, and Warrior in *American Indian Literary Nationalism,* their forerunner Elizabeth Cook-Lynn, and others have proposed theories grounded in autonomous Native intellectual traditions and practices directed toward greater political and intellectual sovereignty for tribal nations. Cosmopolitanists have largely backed them up. Both theories, however, have imprecisely articulated the relationship between the national political apparatus, the nation-state, and the national cultural body, the nation-people.[54]

Rather than trying to stretch one or another of these theories to accommodate the infinite array of strategies and values that shape dynamic identities in the Cherokee world, my reading of Cherokee practices argues for multiplicity and closer description. It opposes neither nationalism nor cosmopolitanism totally, joining with both in the support of Indian peoples' right to self-determination. As a practical (weak-kneed?) anarchist, I also appreciate Noam Chomsky's distinction between long-term visions and short-term goals, which means accepting the necessary evil of the state as a periodic or temporary means of effecting immediate positive change, something the orphanage founder W. T. Whitaker clearly understood.[55] I depart from them, however, insofar as they fail to confront the depredatory, coercive powers available to tribal nation-states that even now centralize power, hamper public discourse, segregate populations, and disenfranchise groups considered refractory or simply distasteful. Nationalists might counter that the force of colonialism necessitated their turn to and faith in statist political institutions, but to address Indian audiences familiar with the real and potential abuses of tribal states and to omit discussion of effective means of resisting their power does little to empower agency at its root.

The anarchism that I'm describing I understand not as anarchy in the pipe-bomb-throwing sense but as a temperate philosophy of how people might live together and govern themselves without a state. In local, nonhierarchical communities, traditional Indian communities and intratribal groups resemble the small, voluntary collectives envisioned by anarchistic writers from Chomsky back to Mikhail Bakunin. As decentralized, regionalist, and confederalist collectives, they embody the principles of anarchist organizations that Colin Ward describes: "they should be (1) voluntary, (2) functional, (3) temporary, and (4) small."[56] The point of these principles in anarchistic thinking is "the free development of human beings whose values are not accumulation and domination, but independence of mind and action, free association on terms of equality, and cooperation to achieve common goals," as Chomsky puts it.[57] To my mind, these characteristics and goals resonate powerfully with American Indian traditions. Politically, voluntary association and consensus-based decision making stood in for coercion. In terms of functionality, communities addressed all sorts of social, religious, political, and other goals by affiliating in groups small enough to recognize and appreciate the members' natural connections to each other. As for Ward's suggestion that an anarchist organization be temporary, he explains that the group might remain constituted so long as it is fulfilling its function. The key for him is that such an organization should not take on a life of its own once it outlives its original purpose.

Historically, anarchism has organized in various models and emphasized various principles in the different contexts in which it has appeared. The key progressive traditions that I describe in the following chapters—such as localized communities based on ethical consensus, embrace of diversity, decentralized governance, principles of dissent, and hospitality—themselves constitute anarchistic dispositions that mediate change and continuity. Against the exclusions of either/or dichotomies, the indigenous anarchism I discern based on my investigation of Cherokee culture and literature embraces paradox and pluralism as it simultaneously adapts to new circumstances and conserves inherited values and practices—anarchism does these things, just as progressive traditions do these things. This book points to many places where the two are synonymous. Where I discuss, for instance, pluralism, local independence, decentralization, consensus, noncoercion, and dissent from nation, state, and hierarchy, I am also detailing indigenist anarchism.

The ideas of anarchism Ward describes don't just strike me as similar to tribal philosophies—in fact, if we trace the influences of the ideas, we can see that American Indian people inspired many of the ideas, which helps make the case for bringing the two together.[58] A key historical link in this chain is Lewis Henry Morgan's early anthropological work on Haudenosaunee people, which Karl Marx studied at length in his ethnological notebooks. Friedrich Engels reworked Marx's thoughts on Morgan in *The Origin of the Family, Private Property and the State*, and Morgan's model later directly influenced the work of one of anarchism's foundational figures, Russian anarchist Petr Kropotkin, particularly his *Mutual Aid*. Anarchistic writers' work on the possibilities for localized self-rule—where they harmonize with tribal peoples' own goals—can help communities make the case for the desirability and feasibility of nonstatist organization.

I'll mention these thinkers here, but theirs is not the discussion *Progressive Traditions* wants to join. It's true that "anarchism" is a loaded term, alarming to some, and perhaps overburdened with historical and theoretical baggage, maybe irrecoverably so. So if it's not mainstream anarchism I'm talking about, why use the term? On one hand, I think there's room, even need, for an Indian version of anarchism, given the affinities between the mainstream and indigenist philosophies. On the other hand, while the substance of the ideas of sovereignty and communal self-determination, the most prominent concepts in American Indian critical theory, dovetail with the anarchistic progressive traditions I discuss, this vocabulary is no less laden, here with connections to the legacies of the hierarchical concept of political sovereignty and to federal Indian policy (the Indian Self-Determination and Education Assistance Act of 1975, for example). Both sovereignty and self-determination and their connotations serve to reify the nation-state as the epicenter of Indian collectivity. "Anarchism" jars us into thinking about what communities might look like outside the nation's borders and bureaucratic structures.

The version of anarchism I favor blends more or less smoothly with the "anarcho-indigenism" that Taiaiake Alfred advocates in *Wasáse*, where he, too, sees fruitful connections between anarchist and indigenous ways of thinking about paths forward. In an exciting but brief overture, he gestures toward the possible features of an anarcho-indigenist intellectual alliance: "This philosophical outlook is close to what Vaclav Havel described as his utopia—in his terms, a decentralized economy, local decision-making, government based on direct election of political leaders, and the elimination of political parties as governing institutions, a sort of spiritual socialism."[59] I am more interested in these elements and other positive steps communities can take to commandeer control over their lives than in the reactionary, confrontational "warrior ethic" Alfred focuses on as a spiritual antidote to colonialism elsewhere in his volume. The aggressive action against the state that he calls for, however, adds an imperative dimension to this burgeoning and promising theoretical position. Jacqueline Lasky further develops the field in adding a feminist emphasis, echoed in her alternative spelling "anarch@indigenism." Among the major characteristics that she describes are veneration for tradition (an emphasis of hers I'll reiterate) and privileging of local connections, but at the same time, she hastens to recognize globality in the unifying efforts of indigenous and feminist positions, an expansion that also points up the need to respect the accommodations that traditions must make in modern circumstances.[60] Mainstream anarchism, too, could profit by emulating this balancing between progressivism and traditionalism. As it has tended to favor progressivism, the contempt with which it often regards spirituality has hampered its acceptance among people weary of outsiders telling them that their beliefs are primitive. By engaging with indigenous histories and contemporary cultures, it could also find several much-needed models of effectively run, nonstatist communities.

For an example of local, anarch@indigenist autonomy in action, Lasky points to Hawaiian women's taro-farming collectives, where by reclaiming state lands the women powerfully "take back resources previously monopolized by colonial powers for traditional uses, recreate their own material and cultural economies . . . and articulate a consciousness of themselves rooted within renewed indigenous intersubjectivities."[61] Maybe such small communities, or the religious groups like those I'll be discussing, seem like small potatoes to nationalists or cosmopolitanists interested in the grander human-development projects of the state. To them, questioning the expansion of political sovereignty may seem retrograde, but a moment's reflection on the history of imperialism should check this expectation of support for government on the part of many American Indian people. The statist campaign against American Indians hardly belongs to the remote past, either; in the 1970s the Indian Health Service was sterilizing Indian women without their consent, and not long ago, in opposition to the Cherokee Nation's bid to disenfranchise the Cherokee Freedmen, members of the Congressional Black Caucus introduced a series of bills threatening to terminate the trust relationship between the United States and the Cherokee Nation.[62] These are just a couple of recent attempts the U.S. state has made that endanger Indian people's welfare. We know only too well how long and ugly that history is. That American Indian tribes would oppose U.S. statism seems obvious; more complicated is the attitude toward tribal statism, which as it consolidates power moves away from rule by consensus and restricts the sphere of debate.

Following the political breakup under allotment, the Cherokee nation-state reincorporated through the Indian Reorganization Act and the Oklahoma Indian Welfare Act, survived the termination era, and has in many ways prospered under the current self-determination policy, and many have celebrated the advances made in tribal sovereignty. The distance between the Cherokee bureaucracy and the Cherokee people, however, is widening—a point that Cherokee legal scholar Steve Russell compellingly makes in discussing what he calls the "adversarial relationship between tribal governments and tribal citizens."[63] The nationally owned Cherokee Nation Industries manufactures military helicopter components, the executive branch enables the disenfranchisement of Freedmen, the judicial branch denies the right of same-sex marriage, and the legislative branch conspires to undermine the validity of the United Keetoowah Band of Cherokee Indians, yet literary critics largely remain silent about how national rule might be at odds with the interests of Cherokee people, how their opinions might be better solicited, or how they might manage their affairs with greater independence. A rigid nationalist position might argue that whatever objections tribal people have to the tribal nation-state should be preempted by their loyalty to the centralized political body. The literature of many Cherokee authors tells another story, however, one with deep-seated doubts about centralized power in the hands of anyone, including other Cherokees. Traditional stories about the people's revolt against and destruction of the power-hungry *anikutani*, the historic priestly caste, attest to this distaste for undemocratic rule.[64] Throughout our history, demand for local control and accounting of the state's responsibilities in representation, justice, and restraint offer examples of traditions we would do well to recover.

At least since the 1997 constitutional crisis, when then-principal chief Joe Byrd and his Tribal Council allies battled with law enforcement officials and other members of the legislative and judicial branches over misappropriated funds, transparency, and power in general, factionalism has multiplied many of the troubles that plague the Cherokee Nation. In this case, the government all but fell apart as the chief, resisting investigations into missing monies, fired several law enforcement marshals (and later several employees of the national newspaper reporting on the debacles), the judicial branch overstepped its authority by declaring the fired marshals still employed, and without reaching a quorum the legislative branch proclaimed the high court justices fired. The Bureau of Indian Affairs (BIA) had to step in to pull the government from the brink of dissolution. Chad Smith defeated Byrd for the office of chief in 1999, but that did not bring an end to the troubles.[65]

As factions entrenched, the 2011 contest for chief between incumbent Chad Smith and former counselor Bill John Baker saw no fewer than three vote counts and two official elections, the first being tossed for mathematical uncertainty amid flying allegations of vote tampering, voter fraud, and more. Before the second election, the Cherokee Supreme Court happened to decide a years-long case on the eligibility of the Freedmen to vote. Four justices appointed by Smith assented to disenfranchising the Freedmen, with one justice, appointed by Byrd but reappointed by Smith, dissenting.[66] Many expected the ruling would favor Smith, given his opposition to Freedmen citizenship. Washington, D.C., was not pleased. The federal Housing and Urban Development office withheld $33 million in housing funds, and the BIA threatened not to recognize any election in which the Freedmen were not allowed to vote. The Cherokee executive branch, led at that point by the deputy chief, capitulated to the feds against the objections of the Cherokee Supreme Court and allowed the Freedmen to vote in the second election, which Baker won with 10,703 votes to Smith's 9,128.[67] After taking office, Baker fired several employees of the Cherokee Nation who had supported Smith in the election. Represented by Smith, they have since filed suit in tribal court for wrongful termination.[68]

What would a sovereignty-based response to such misuses of power look like? It would likely propose many reasonable and even necessary suggestions, such as a clearer delineation of the branches' responsibilities and restraints, greater transparency, stronger commitment to checks and balances, and more. But on fundamental principles, it would also likely call for bigger hammers, which is to say, more power for the government as it already exists, through expanding control over areas that appear insufficiently regulated. To my mind, a proposal at once more traditional and progressive, and healthier for the civic life of Cherokee people, would be to disperse and democratize representation, at the very least by dramatically increasing the number of council seats and/or districts and adding representative seats for nongeographic constituent groups such as women, elders, or students; decreasing the lucrative benefits attached to holding office; making voting easier by increasing the number of voting days and investigating Internet voting; increasing the number of issues on which citizens vote; and raising the minimum percentage of votes required for passing major legislation and perhaps for electing officials rather than bequeathing greater powers to government offices (and their dominant factions). Distributing responsibility for administering programs and resources to districts could also help decentralize governance, making factions harder to coalesce and rendering them less relevant. Most importantly, to these steps we could add a call for turning our political culture away from adversarial contest toward general consensus. Such changes would be difficult, without a doubt, but they could go a long way toward reinvigorating a traditional model of governance that would progressively respond to the increasing distance between the government and the governed.

In looking at historical moments when such conditions were more of a reality and thinking about how they suggest possibilities for our future, I borrow from cosmopolitanists and postcolonialists their celebration of diversity, from nationalists an insistence on tribal specificity, and from the Cherokee authors I study a delight in inconsistently considering any strategy that promises positive results, whatever quarter it comes from. A reading strategy attuned to an understanding of internal variety encourages swifter and more sustained discussion of theoretical issues than has been formerly possible, when critics were hampered by the expectation that readers required rudimentary instruction in who American Indian authors were, which made it difficult to broach focused critical problems surrounding them. The time has come to supplement underevaluated Indian generalities with local specifics. When we know that Cherokees organized towns in lines and squares and built cabins full of right angles, "Indians think in circles" no longer tells us all we need to know. While I hope a range of Indian and non-Indian thinkers will find this call for detail and consideration of anomalies a useful approach, I understand that other tribes' circumstances differ dramatically from those of the Cherokees. Few tribes, however, have not been accused of being "too assimilated" to count as Indian or have not had their duly elected governments choose to empower themselves at their citizens' expense.

Looking back at the progressive traditions that others have put together before can help us theorize not only historical agency but also approaches to present and future challenges. The principled practices related to worship, deliberation, diplomacy, and hospitality, only a few of many, are among those I would like to consider in Cherokee literary representations from the early nineteenth century up to the present, as authors not only mitigated the rupturing force of colonial history but also deliberately worked to preserve Cherokee culture. As a way of structuring this inquiry, I introduce the sections on religion and politics with preliminary overview chapters followed by chapters in which Cherokee writers' voices take primary place. In the overviews, I have tried to look into principles and practices as thoroughly as I know how. These may seem to some literary readers to spend an inordinate amount of time reviewing critical material originating outside literary scholarship, in anthropology, ethnology, sociology, religious studies, history, biography, and more. I'm trying with this approach to avoid a tendency in literary criticism to make generalized, unsupported allusions to Indian cultures without the support of either experience or comprehensive research into tribal specificities. Romanticizing the spiritual or religious value of harmony, for instance, keeps us from making sense of the important and extensive arguing that went into political debates that led to consensus. It pays to paint details like this into the picture. If this interdisciplinary, social-science approach to literary reading seems unorthodox, so once did arguing for literature's historical contextualization.

While this study is rooted most firmly in the tribally specific critical mode urged by Craig Womack, it also engages to some extent with the latest transnational movements in American Indian critical theory. Not entirely unlike cosmopolitanism, these take comparisons of similarities across groups as their raison d'être but are not incompatible with close attention to the local and specific. For Chadwick Allen, the point of his "trans-Indigenous" approach "is not to displace the necessary, invigorating study of specific traditions and contexts but rather to complement these by augmenting and expanding broader, globally Indigenous fields of inquiry."[69] In a similar vein, if the study of the local is to be politically realistic and relevant, it should also find a complement in looking broadly at the field in which it is situated. How Cherokee people treat non-Cherokee people, particularly those to whom we have significant connections, is of paramount concern to *Progressive Traditions*, and it takes up several instances, though my analyses undeniably center on Cherokee contexts. These include the adoption of non-Cherokees and/or their habits in religious communities, which I examine with Sequoyah Guess's work in chapter 3; in social circumstances, such as exogamous marriage; and in political situations in which individuals and sometimes entire tribes became naturalized Cherokees. In the last chapter, I will look at these two latter cases together with the Freedmen controversy, which I see as the most important contemporary Cherokee issue linked to questions of transculturalism.

I prefer "transculturalism" to "transnationalism" to avoid affirming the nation as the starting point of the exciting boundary crossing inquiries that "trans"-conscious perspectives enable. As Allen's opting for "trans-Indigenous" over "transnational" suggests, the field does admit more options than the nation. Given the postnationalist concerns shared by many working in "trans-" modes, my focus on indigenous anarchism may not be as novel as it seems, notwithstanding its slightly more aggressive stance. Shari Huhndorf, for instance, writes in *Mapping the Americas*, "Identifying national boundaries as colonial impositions, my cross-border analysis points to the challenges indigeneity poses to nation-states as it expands the range of Native studies."[70] James Cox, too, in *The Red Land to the South* finds along with Rachel Adams that several Native writers (including Cherokees Lynn Riggs and Thomas King, respectively) exhibit a "drive to form coalitions across the boundaries of tribal nations and nation-states. In their work, such coalitions are not simply a reaction to the fractious power of the nation-state, but rather the resumption of alliances and networks of filiation that were severed by the conquest and its aftermath."[71] Hearing these coalitions described by their resistance to states and by their affirmation of organic connections, I think of anarchistic communities voluntarily associating, pushing back against the nation-state, governing themselves, and venerating their traditions.

I want to admit that my own subjective position as a Cherokee grants me no supernatural insight into what makes something authentically Cherokee. I have taken a far more pedestrian route on these questions and tried to find corroboration of all of my references to experience or culture in publicly available resources; in this way I think I've avoided divulging any protected knowledge, which I don't think I even have. Even though individual experience is important, my own is not the kind that makes me a full-blown expert on Cherokee culture. Many marvelous and rewarding interactions with Cherokees infinitely more knowledgeable than I am about our traditions have shown me this only too clearly.

I can only scratch the surface of that knowledge here in investigating the various principled practices connected to areas like worship, argument, and compassion; the literary representations in memoirs, science fiction, and political diatribes; and the progressive traditions that reject others' concocted limits on Cherokee identity even as they work toward Cherokee people's autonomy and survival. Still, I hope it's worthwhile, and I hope, too, that from this, more avenues of investigation into many other ways of Cherokee being and doing might open up. The authors taken up in the ensuing chapters frequently bear the brunt of accusations of assimilatedness, of having crossed over to the Light Side, as it were, often for what are in fact traditional dispositions, though acted out in changed circumstances. These dispositions, though coming to us from a long time back, still have much to do with contemporary issues facing Cherokee and other tribal peoples. A fresh look at our traditions, beliefs, and practices, with an eye toward the full range of their application to the complexities of being Indian in America, can not only improve our political structure but can also embolden our communal imaginations as we carry our past into the present.

Part One

ᏁᏂᎳᎾᏍᏊᎪᎢ

We Worship

WP

CHAPTER 1

Paths of Righteousness

To help contextualize the next chapters' readings of Catharine Brown's memoirs and Sequoyah Guess's *Kholvn*, this chapter introduces traditional Cherokee religious beliefs and practices that pertain to some of the less conspicuous cultural presences in their works, particularly regarding harmony and cooperation, righteousness and charity, continuity and education, and purity and cleansing. I describe several other communal principled practices, such as gaining knowledge, which closely resemble those of anarchism and are found among religious communities (apparently unaware of the tensions between anarchism and religion). I specifically look to social and religious developments that have been underemphasized in much scholarship on Cherokee religion, which has instead been more often interested in exploration of an alternative, if not romanticized, harmonious relationship with the natural world. Without discounting such ecological worldviews or the insightful theorization that Cherokee cosmology extends kinship relations to the nonhuman world, I want to explore how spiritual beliefs also inform right relationships to other humans, not only as a feature of a loose-knit cultural spirituality but also as concrete religious edicts that kept local communities running smoothly. To keep things anchored, it is also important to position this Cherokee sacred humanism in relevant historical moments, especially during the decline of the traditional priesthood at separate times. These include the anarchistic rebellion against a priestly caste as recounted in oral history and priests' later separation from the polity. The introduction and spread of Christianity and the gendered transformation occasioned when men moved to political from religious leadership roles provide further context. In many ways women became religious leaders as Christianity spread, setting the stage for Brown's and Guess's narratives and offering an example of women's innovation mobilized out of the habitus.

This chapter's selection of principled practices by no means intends a comprehensive or even middling representation of Cherokee religion but only a map of a few routes through various dispositions at particular times. Despite my constricted scope—perhaps even because of it—I hope that the chapter might nevertheless illustrate the wealth of innovative intersections of traditional and progressive practices and beliefs available along even a single path through the frontier of the habitus. Much of the traditional Cherokee religion I discuss concerns stomp dance societies, which have their roots in oral histories that proclaim the ancient town of Kituhwah as the original nucleus of the Cherokee. The modern religious incarnations of the Keetoowah were developed near the turn of the twentieth century through Redbird Smith's direction of the communal recovery of ancient traditions. I offer nothing revelatory about Cherokee religion or the Keetoowah Society.[1] I have relied on sources long publicly available or offered publicly by religious leaders, for several reasons: (1) to respect traditional practitioners' right to privacy and the protected nature of much religious knowledge; (2) to acknowledge my own position as an outsider to these traditions, without authority to speak representatively or definitively; and (3) to keep the lines of discourse open, using the plentiful information already at general disposal. If traditional religious leaders want to gain more exposure or to make more information available, they will do so, as they have in the past. In the meantime, interpreting what they have already offered can keep us busy for some time, if we are open to new ways of approaching, understanding, and applying it.

THE WHITE PATH: HARMONY, RIGHTEOUSNESS, AND COMMUNITY

The traditional Cherokee principle that has received the most critical attention is that of harmony, according to which a Cherokee maintains positive "relationships with his fellow Cherokee by avoiding giving offense, on the negative side, and by giving of himself to his fellow Cherokee in regard to his time and his material goods, on the positive side," as anthropologist Robert Thomas has it in an early discussion.[2] Drawing on Thomas, Fred Gearing emphasizes the former injunctive dimension: "The single focus which created pattern in Cherokee moral thought was the value of harmony among men. . . . This principle of harmony appears to direct those Cherokees today, cautiously and virtually at all cost, to avoid discord. The emphasis in its application is negative—thou shalt not create disharmony—rather than positive." Gearing elevates harmony from a "basic principle" as in Thomas's formulation to a supreme, singular guiding principle, even as he admits, "This Cherokee ethos cannot be demonstrated directly by the historical record."[3] I understand this disclaimer to mean that, while Cherokee actors endeavored to maintain harmony, they did not enunciate it as a principle per se, and also that proving a negative like avoidance or nonaction, by showing how a disrupter of harmony might have been shunned, say, cannot be accomplished with the historical record.[4] These anthropological considerations of harmony mainly confined themselves to interpersonal relationships in a community. Theorists have begun to spot the harmony ethic's influence, first seen mainly in the social sphere, in literature, religion, politics, cosmology, epistemology, and elsewhere.

Mary Churchill's 1997 dissertation, *Walking the White Path*, offers an influential example of this expansion of the harmony principle to literary studies. For her, harmony exemplifies the socially oriented synthesis of forces in (typically) dialogic, nonantagonistic opposition, but the forces' equality results in a binary more durably static than in a Hegelian system of conflict and conquest of one element by another. This codependent tension defines for Churchill the concept of balance, which is connected to harmony but refers specifically to the opposition she identifies between, for instance, genders, directions, color symbology, war and peace, and other paired complements. Like harmony, the concept of balance has taken center stage in studies of Cherokee religion and features prominently in the literary theoretical perspectives of Churchill and Daniel Heath Justice.[5] Both also appear in the voluminous writings on American Indian religion not specifically focused on the religion of the Cherokees, although most authors tend to treat the two more synonymously than does Churchill, with harmony extending to relations with nonhuman realms. I will return to Churchill's formulation later in this chapter, following discussion of some of the other principles, practices, and historical circumstances impacting Cherokee traditionalism that will help contextualize the ideas of harmony and balance.

Without attempting to dislodge harmony from its privileged place in indigenous religious studies, I would like to suggest that it is not so original a concern in Cherokee morality as the critical literature suggests. Ample evidence in oral and written history and in literature testifies that harmony and balance are guiding principles, necessary dispositions for keeping the peace in an indigenist anarchist community to be sure, but overly focused attention to them as such seems relatively recent and may reflect internalization of a discourse concerned more with broad "Indian" questions rather than close study of Cherokee or other tribal cultures. Pan-Indian influence does not necessarily mean the Cherokee theorizing of Churchill, Justice, and others is contaminated or anything like that; if anything, it suggests that Cherokees have affirmed those values as broadly consonant with their other concerns. Locally oriented philosophies focused on other principles predate the obsession with harmony and balance, however, and these have received little scholarly treatment. While pervasive, dispositions maintaining harmony are inseparable from the broader conditions in which they arose and that get replicated by the habitus to keep the world recognizable and functioning. Those conditions are assessed not simply on the basis of an absence of discord but on the extent to which they provide the same sorts of happiness any people seek: some measure of love, liberty, security, creativity, and so on. The Cherokee religious concept of the White Path symbolizes some of the principled practices thought to enable these goals in conditions that make possible a harmony worth preserving.

Though the White Path, also called the Path of Peace, is discussed somewhat spottily in oral histories and secondary literature, several characteristics recur in speeches and writing that take it up explicitly or metaphorically. Thomas offers a useful summary: "[God's law] is the 'Law' or 'Rule' which God laid down for the Indian to follow. It consists not only of 'following the White Path,' that is being peaceful, friendly, and observing the rest of the moral virtues; but also of keeping up the old Cherokee customs, such as the fire, stomp dancing, etc."[6] He emphasizes here the White Path's social dimension, which is inseparable from its culturally preservative function. Foremost a religious concept, the idea of the White Path urges peace and harmony in social, natural, and cosmological relations through language, hunting, doctoring practices, and more, all governed by an idea of "righteousness" as a means of achieving "a good mind" or "becoming right-minded." Anthropologist Albert Wahrhaftig argues that harmony is more an effect of righteous living according to the law symbolized by the White Path than it is a causal force itself. This is because social and individual contentment work more like evidence, providing "the ultimate sign that [the Cherokees] are living according to sacred design."[7]

In more figurative terms, Keetoowah Society leader Crosslin Smith in a 1986 speech given at Northeastern State University in Tahlequah, Oklahoma, described the White Path as "a white righteous road" that connects the four peoples across the four corners of the earth via a "white road, the first cross of extreme, deep religious meaning. It is the same law that was passed on in to the Bible—this is pre-history time." He clarifies the law's fundamental precept: "'Love one another and love me': this was the first law. The same law gives full complemence [*sic*] to the new law called Ten Commandments."[8] Here and elsewhere, the connection between righteousness and divine law is made explicit. While the Keetoowah divine law is plainly not as codified as, say, the Bible, it similarly and foundationally concerns the proper attitude humans should have toward the Creator and toward each other. Ceremonies, dances, and prayers all reinforce these attitudes as do the instructions for living, which are related in oral histories.

Even as Smith emphasizes the injunctions to love the Creator and others, we see the law presupposes certain entities (you, one another, the divine "me") and right ways of treating them (with love, which may be of a different sort for the human and the deity) that are not explicitly defined and can only be understood by reference to other laws, habits, principles, beings, and so on. Upholding this law will require reference to a great deal else in order to find its own "complemence," to borrow Smith's word. If upholding the primary law, itself a social principle, may be taken as practicing righteousness, the plurality of the attitudes constituting it reinforces the sense that it, too, is not a monistic foundation of the Cherokee cosmology or worldview but rather another forceful principle among many in the web of the habitus, perhaps more influential or far-reaching than others but still not sufficient unto itself.

To help clarify the primary law, Keetoowah traditions retain and impart others—the laws of the Seven Clans. Citing Janet Jordan, Churchill recounts six:

> Be peaceful and loving, they say.
> Have a white, a pure and cleansed heart, they say.
> Do not falsely judge another, they say.
> Do not do people harm, they say.
> When people make demands upon you, fulfill them.
> Love thy neighbor as theyself [*sic*].[9]

In personal conversations with stomp grounds members, I have also been told of four other guidelines for interpersonal relations, here paraphrased: love each other unconditionally; treat every person as a sacred creation; cling to each other; and be stingy with one another (that is, don't use each other up). The categorical differentiation of humans and the attention focused on them specifically in these traditional religious teachings are often overlooked in scholarship on the Cherokees and other American Indians. Many scholars are attracted to the cultural components of Indian beliefs and practices that promote less consumptive environmental dispositions, but few investigators have seen—or they have declined to see—the religious connections that lend the beliefs and practices their force, divorcing ecological beliefs and behaviors from the spiritual, social, and material emphasis on taking care of other people that traditional practitioners themselves profess to be at the heart of their philosophies.

This concern for others shows itself in principled practices like charitable giving, ready hospitality, and community labor, all practices that give shape to an indigenous anarchism that requires compassion, inclusiveness, and widespread participation.

A focus on community takes center stage for two important Cherokee theorists of Indian identity and literature, sociologist Eva Marie Garroutte and Native American studies theologian/lawyer/literary critic Jace Weaver. Garroutte's *Real Indians: Identity and the Survival of Native America* surveys the most common ways American Indian identity is reckoned in legal, biological, cultural, and personal discourses and, in its latter chapters on defining community, proposes an alternative set of criteria based on kinship. Garroutte writes that "a definition of identity founded in kinship responds to at least two themes that one encounters across a range of tribal philosophies. One of these reflects a condition of *being*, which I call relationship to ancestry. The second involves a condition of *doing*, which I call responsibility to reciprocity."[10] The first may be seen in genealogical or ancestral connections, although Garroutte hastens to point out that those she imagines do not concern bloodedness or pedestrian, racialized identity markers. If this hereditary state of being still suggests an essentialism, it is a well-qualified, Native version open to alteration through adoption, communal vetting, and other processes.[11]

Garroutte's second criterion is more germane to consideration of traditional religious dispositions, both in its emphasis on doing, which I see as closely linked to principled practices, and in her insistence that others' social concerns are also of paramount concern to the individual's comportment and constitution, in voluntary behaviors that "contribute to tribal survival" through generosity of time, resources, and spirit.[12] The interview respondents she quotes severally underline the importance of helping behaviors that maintain "the People—those who understand themselves as bound together in spiritually faithful community," again emphasizing the religious aspects of community-mindedness.[13] The behavioral responsibilities they point to as embodying or enacting Garroutte's idea of reciprocity often concern the immediate, this-world, material well-being of the community by providing for others' food, safety, labor, or economic needs in accordance with spiritually understood "Original

Instructions . . . sacred stories, and historic practices."[14] Each of these, Garroutte argues, helps constitute *tradition,* which she defines as "fundamentally a *sacred* concept." She affirms a Cherokee/Choctaw respondent's definition: "Tradition is what is passed on orally, and it tells you the way you are *supposed* to be. It has to give us *good.* It has to give us *growth.* It is the lessons that were taught us by the ancient ones and the elders to help [each of] us be a better person, and closer to the Creator. And we have to use it in the way it is intended. . . . It's spiritual."[15] This progress-oriented expression of traditional values urges the development of good relationships (righteousness, perhaps) with the Creator, with the self, and with the "us" of community, which encompasses the present community and also the past-in-present community of elders and "the ancient ones."

Garroutte's identity theory recalls Jace Weaver's in *That the People Might Live,* where he writes, "Natives define their identity in terms of community and relate to ultimate reality through that community."[16] In his argument, community "is, in fact, the highest value to Native peoples, and fidelity to it is a primary responsibility," and he reiterates the religious foundation not just of social behavioral principles but also of a general, commonly held difference in American Indian thinking or consciousness.[17] He asserts, "Because of the failure of Native cultures to recognize any split between sacred and secular spheres, this worldview remains essentially religious, involving the Native's deepest sense of self and undergirding tribal life, existence, and identity, just as the Creator undergirds all the created order."[18] Like Garroutte, he asserts the relevance of the religious principle of righteousness to community interaction, arguing that "being *rightwised* . . . involves right relation not only between the human self and human others but between self and place."[19] Combining the phenomenological, ontological, moral, and social centrality of community with a "proactive commitment" to it—that is, actively working for its survivance—Weaver coins the term *communitism.* This fusing of *community* and *activism* describes what for him is "the single thing that most defines Indian literatures."[20] Literature, too, functions primarily to maintain community, but seeing in it no less diversity than in social communities, Weaver avoids casting Indian identity as homogeneous with his recognition that "today we exist in many different kinds of community—reservation, rural, urban, tribal, pan-Indian, traditional, Christian."[21]

Despite this important qualification on community diversity, I am reluctant to fully accept community preservation as the "single" most descriptive essence of the variety of the Cherokee (much less the Indian) world, not because I reject the pervasive significance of community—indeed, I am here endorsing just that and see a commitment to the well-being of others as foundational to how indigenist anarchist collectives work in cooperation—but because it becomes too encompassing a term in Weaver's and Garroutte's constructions. Weaver broadens the Indian idea of community to include what he calls "the 'wider community' that includes *all the created order,* which is also characterized in kinship terms. No sharp distinction is drawn between the human and nonhuman persons that make up the community."[22] Garroutte shares his general sense: "In tribal philosophies people take their place, or find their identity, within a kinship network that includes not only other humans but also animals, plants, minerals, geographic features, the earth itself, celestial bodies, and spirit beings."[23] Both here expand the argument, grounded in the evidence of traditional and contemporary oral histories extant in perhaps all tribes, that kinship relations extend beyond the human world and inform right relationships with those human, natural, and supernatural. But in generalized theories of identity, however, community becomes no less than *everything*—all the seen and unseen in the universe. In a limited case, Native identities and literatures, then, are ostensibly to be distinguished from those of non-Natives by virtue of being positioned within, well, the cosmos—and how then are they unlike those of non-Natives?—and they find their essential nature in their support for the universe or any given part of it. Native or not, what way of being is not supportive of some part of existence? Even nihilism works for *something.* Knowing that Indian peoples are not committed to everything under the sun in identical ways, a tautological definition of "community" does not say enough about distinctions—how they originate and function and to what purposes.

A narrower critique reveals other problems with the descriptive power of casting community as the essence of Indian identity and literary expression, at least as a, er, uh, blanket principle. Weaver and

Garroutte both stipulate that Indian communities may be urban and Christian, say, but dedication to the furtherance of such communities *alone* does not make them peculiarly Indian any more than advocacy for an Indian community makes the advocate Indian.[24] Further, relationships between communities, whether or not affiliated in kinship terms, are not everywhere governed by identical principles or practices—there *are* practical differences between humans and nonhumans. Cherokee clan names come from human, animal, and plant communities, for instance, but we do not interact with each of these forebears equally: we might, for instance, eat deer and potatoes, but we do not eat humans. And while we use kinship terms to speak of some entities in the natural world, like the thunders and rivers, we do not speak of dirt, say, as a relative. Besides, a number of Native and Cherokee people are in fact selfish and define their identities according to very individualistic agendas—and they are still *Native* people, who perhaps even deserve scholarly attention. If we were to consider these details on their own terms and explore the particular imaginative strengths they provide, we could understand how *this* culture's theorization of place or land or its principled practices concerning living and moving and exploring enable it to persevere and prosper in a transplanted locale.[25] Theories that while admirably seeking to offer communities a broadly applicable means of strengthening their cultural or political positions unfortunately obscure many unique, local ways of being and believing that generate enormous power in their own right.

Without understanding the specific nature of the relationships among communities predicated on traditional philosophies, our apprehension of the principle of communities as kin is imperfect. The clarification of the diversity of Indian lives that Weaver begins is crucial not least because the plurality it affirms complicates and vivifies what might otherwise seem a simple inversion of the individual versus society binary that fails to transcend binaristic thinking. That pluralism, however, is nearly undone by the monist insistence that "community for community's sake" sufficiently describes the values by which every possible community might justify its differentiation, regardless of its own interpretations of its central values. If (often, when) generalizations come to be reified as expected features of Indian communities or representations, particularities that might not accord with them can be discounted as assimilationist or, worse, as precluding an Indian identity. Without narrowly describing the parameters of the communities Indian writers seek to maintain or develop, readers might too easily lapse into quick and easy recapitulations of reified, externally produced characterizations (too often caricatures) of what makes an Indian community "Indian," disregarding or disparaging any traits or boundaries that smack of too much assimilation, do not harken far enough back, or seem to affirm the wrong kind of community. I fear that Weaver has done something like this in his analysis of Elias Boudinot, discussed in chapter 5, perhaps as a result of his willingness to identify, if circumspectly, an abiding essentialism.

Like Weaver, American Indian religious scholar George Tinker echoes Vine Deloria's generalizations about American Indian religious concepts as he posits a basic difference between Western thinking as fundamentally temporal and Indian thinking as spatial, a distinction that structures the association of community with land or place, which I worry is becoming critically fixed. To return for a moment to the value of harmony—when conceived spatially, it represents a static state of balance achieved through restraint and respect for other lives and forms of life.[26] Less rigid both temporally and spatially, the symbolism of the Cherokee White Path suggests rather a methodic dynamism operating in fluid circumstances, regulating change and mediating its impact in an ongoing process. As a "path," a combination of the spatial and temporal—a site for moving, a moving site—it maps the way to righteous relations rather than marks off a boundary to a discrete or unalterable space. As explained by Crosslin Smith, the White Path not only represents the laws of peace and righteousness universally shared by all peoples (in his words), but it also unites and connects them in processes that necessarily require some modification. Again, this does not, however, mean that one thing changed means all things have changed. Cherokees have exercised unique dispositions to manage development socially, culturally, and religiously to ensure that changes are made in accordance with the bulk of tradition, that they accord with accepted notions of what is right, and that they meet with general consensus. The practice of gaining knowledge is one such principled practice.

GAINING KNOWLEDGE: THE MAKING OF TRANSFORMATION

Gaining knowledge involves investigating a variety of potential problem solutions, not necessarily for the sole sake of learning but to address needs in accordance with values of communal harmony, among others. Appointed representatives are dispatched in some way to explore and report back on new knowledge or strategies that their communities believe might prove productive.[27] At times, such as during Redbird Smith's investigation into forgotten traditional practices, community outsiders were consulted to help address questions that group members were having trouble answering on their own.[28] Following this "fact-finding" mission, the communities effectively vetted proposed solutions, often through committees, to determine their compatibility with inherited beliefs and their potential effectiveness, resulting in only parsimonious alterations to tradition. Keetoowah traditions recount several instances of such communal interpretive management, from the earliest stories of the Cherokees' coalescence as a people to the recovery of religious traditions during the stomp dance revival in the twentieth century.[29] Keetoowah Society member Benny Smith describes his group's general process and several component practices:

> In times of crises, the Keetoowahs have a unique way of asking guidance for the action that should be taken. A Keetoowah council composed of seven medicine men from each clan is called upon to examine the threatening situations. These medicine men in the olden days were known as the wise men or elders of the tribe. The duties of medicine men are to work for peace, to work for the sake of humanity, and to keep the favor of God; therefore, on all major decisions, these men are called to examine, through spiritual consideration, the best course of action to take. This spiritual consideration might consist of fasting, following certain rituals, offering solemn prayers, or meditating while seeking God-sent visions or revelations. This procedure is used in all important decisions and sometimes during illnesses.[30]

The Keetoowah Society is not alone among Cherokees in regulating adaptation in this way, for there are several historical references to such counciled mediation. Calling it "a" way is perhaps a misnomer, however, for as Smith demonstrates, gaining knowledge (at least, as I am casting it here) gathers together many other practices, all in the service of yet another, the traveling of the White Path.[31] In a relatively short space, Smith here demonstrates what Bourdieu calls the habitus's "infinite capacity" to constellate dispositions from across the entire field of available beliefs and practices. A single disposition like community vetting brings together forces social and familial (in the clan representatives and council formations), symbolic (in specifying that the council should be formed of elders), scientific (through the medicine men's work); religious (more or less throughout); historical (invoked in the phrase "olden days," which the elders will best remember); and philosophical (materially humanist in its attention to, well, "the sake of humanity" and illness)—and this interpretation is far from exhaustive. Even though Smith's description is of relatively recent vintage, I imagine that gaining knowledge and community vetting were widely and long understood as a customary means of mediating debate. These largely untheorized practices perhaps also ferried goals not entirely their own, together with unintended consequences, some of which undoubtedly contributed to the erosion or erasure of some traditions. It is fair to say, however, that a primary function, conscious and unconscious at both individual and communal levels, of the pluralistic practices clustered together in gaining knowledge and deliberating in council is to edify the community spiritually and materially—to preserve by adaptation, to progress by conservation. The pluralistic practices also line right up with many anarchistic dispositions, especially consensus-based, localized decision making that looks to the strengths of plurality to aid in adaptation.

This developmental continuity recurs throughout the revolutions of Cherokee religion, in its earliest traditional incarnations led by what Rennard Strickland has called a "priestly class," a phrase with connotations suggesting too sharp a separation from others in society and too hierarchical a system of power.[32] It has some advantage over "medicine men," which when not hackneyed still fails to impart the religious connections to the medicine people's healing work. Though religious leaders' power once permeated the Cherokee world and they advised everyone from clan elders to war and peace chiefs to individuals, their power underwent a steady decline at least from the time of European contact—"at least" because oral histories tell of the people's tension with religious leaders some time before the Europeans arrived. Howard Tyner in his history of the Keetoowah Society records an account of an early group of medicine men's widespread misuse of their knowledge, which led to the imposition of the death penalty on any medicine man who caused the death of another by conjuring.[33]

In other stories found in several sources, a group of priests/medicine men called the anikutani had begun to think of themselves as above common people and above the laws of righteous behavior, especially in regard to sexual mores. Their abuses of their station generated resentment and indignation among the people that turned into disharmony and finally rebellion, when the anikutani were killed in great numbers.[34] To what degree oral histories of the anikutani narrate an actual, widespread execution is unclear. The revolt seems to me and to many other Cherokees with whom I have spoken to be largely allegorical, if perhaps based on historical events. I also see it as a thoroughly anarchistic admonishment to rulers not to lose sight of their responsibilities and their accountability. To be sure, however, some interpret it more literally. Whatever its source, like the story Tyner recounts, it establishes an affirmative precedent that the general populace is empowered with the ability to alter religious institutions as it sees fit and to assert final control over them—even through violent upheaval—to bring them in line with social expectations. At the risk of stating the obvious, it is worth reiterating that the oral tradition here itself documents *change*—to religion, a fundamentally stable sphere, and to religious authority that is invested with dangerous supernatural power—as a means of bringing about the continuance of the larger value of righteousness and antihierarchical equality for the larger body of the people.

In the written record, later events chart the further decline of religious leaders' power. Several historians cite medicine men's inability to treat smallpox as a chief cause of their waning influence, which they argue suggested to Cherokees their disfavor with the Creator and/or the medicine men's ineffectiveness. In his late eighteenth-century history, James Adair claims that the cold-water purification rites the medicine men prescribed hastened rather than checked the disease's course, leading them to an apostate despair in which "all the magi and prophetic tribe broke their old consecrated physic-pots, and threw away all the other pretended holy things they had for physical use, imagining they had lost their divine power by being polluted; and shared the common fate of their country."[35] According to anthropologist Raymond Fogelson, other potentially contributing factors included the Delawares' theft of a sacred medicine bundle and the extinguishing of the sacred fires in the Cherokee homelands with the linked, gradual abandonment of consecrated places. He points out that some believe the fires were moved as lands were lost and ultimately conveyed along the Trail of Tears, with new places of worship sanctified upon arrival in the West. The foregoing explanations share a somewhat synecdochic or inductive interpretation of the decline of the medicine men's power. By this I mean that they extrapolate the whole of the historical arc from specific moments or parts of the religious history, framing its changes in a narrative order that both attempts to make sequential sense of their complexity and affirms the Cherokees' volitional capacity to draw religious institutions into right relationships with social principles.

Other scholars have suggested more socially oriented causes for the dissolution of the traditional religious complex. Rennard Strickland accuses the priestly class of complicity in the shift toward a money economy in medicine men's acceptance of traders' and government officials' gifts and favors received in their roles as the de facto leaders and negotiators for the tribe. Their participation in secular politics, he argues, resulted in a "close identification of the ancient priestly class with the new commercialism," which contributed to their loss of spiritual authority, especially given the Cherokees' progressive implication in an economy in which they were becoming both dependent and disadvantageously positioned.[36] Other developments may also have exerted unforeseen effects. Robert Thomas identifies literacy as an unexpected detriment to the medicine men's institutional stability insofar as the formerly intensive training was relaxed with the introduction of a means of recording sacred formulas and prayers in Sequoyah's syllabary. Thomas also suggests that the writing down of easily reproduced religious knowledge democratized and diffused it, further weakening the "priesthood."[37]

Largely eschewing such explanations, historian William McLoughlin argues, "Often the greatest pressure for rapid cultural change came from that group of Cherokees who were of mixed ancestry, better-educated, wealthier, and who expected personal gains in power and prestige from new laws and institutions. . . . In accepting the ways of their conquerors, they overcame the insecurities of defeat. But by grasping at this new source of dignity and self-worth, they had to reject their identity with the values and customs of their own people."[38] Discussing here a relatively short span of time, McLoughlin attributes the centrality of major cultural change, including religious leaders' decline, to the catchall ascension of the self-aggrandizing "mixedblood elite," a demonizing trope that has been used to account for the decline of almost every traditional practice. Although McLoughlin admits that the members of the mixed-blood elite "were strongly committed to sustaining Cherokee control over their own affairs and skeptical about assimilation," he nevertheless affirms that their best efforts to assert their sovereignty tended ironically to whittle it away as an effect of an internalized, colonialist inferiority complex.[39]

This argument holds only if we accept the implicit assumption that "the ways of their conquerors" (never mind the implicit assumptions of this naming)—for example, practicing religion, education, diplomacy, and so on—were the exclusive provinces of whites, that precontact societies did not worship, teach their children, negotiate with other tribes. There may have been marked differences in the ways Cherokees and whites understood and enacted such practices, but they were not so alien as to be categorically distinct. Alternatively, we would have to assume that if Cherokees had such dispositions, mixed-bloods were able to excise and transplant them *completely*, a nearly impossible operation given the reticulation of dispositions. Replacing religion or any other metadisposition in an individual, much less in a corporate, body would be less like transplanting an organ than like replacing the central nervous system. While acute ruptures may potentially transform the habitus, the continued, subtle presences of traditional practices evidence a slower and more measured evolution.

To be sure, the sons and daughters of Cherokees and whites were more likely to be Christian and often aided missionaries in proselytizing, which was at times aggressive and insidious. But the Cherokees' democratic religious structure, the priests' inability to cope with smallpox, Cherokees' identification with market development, the unending colonialist assaults on land and culture, and events like the Lenni Lenape's medicine bundle theft (many other examples of which are undoubtedly absent from the historic record), converged at the nexus of religious practice in the sequence of a protracted and still-ongoing process of change to and re-inscription of tradition.[40] Still other predicating conditions include the petitions and invitations for missionaries to open schools that came from the conservative National Council governing body. The sweeping changes that were made to such an important part of the society cannot be singularly attributed to a scapegoat mixed-blood class. Particularly missing from most analyses of Cherokee religious history is consideration of Cherokees' own volition in the changes made, which if incorporated in scholarly perspectives might incline us to look more toward development rather than decline, which is the inevitable, defeatist narrative of Native disappearance authored by a perspective that fixes tradition in stasis.

Availing itself of the evangelistic zeal of the Second Great Awakening, Congress as early as 1792 allocated funds to help solve "the Indian problem" through the civilizing, collaborative efforts of missionaries.[41] During this time they couldn't just march into Indian nations without threat of reprisal, which could still take on a violent aspect.[42] Missionary work in Cherokeeia during the late eighteenth and early nineteenth centuries appeared neither by missionary zealotry nor colonial ambition alone, which would have been interpreted—and responded to—as an act of unauthorized intrusion. Instead, missionaries arrived at the specific requests of the rapidly adapting Cherokee government and of local towns. In their desire for schools the Cherokees collectively deliberated the costs and benefits (those technological, economic, and political must surely have weighed heavily) and elected to invite several missionaries from Moravian, Presbyterian, Congregationalist, and Baptist denominations.[43] The missionaries were allowed to stay at the pleasure of the National Council, as the Moravians discovered when they were nearly expelled for failing to develop the educational program envisioned by the progressive conservatives. The opening of the Presbyterian school seems to have taken some of the heat off the Moravians, allowing them to remain in operation.[44]

The powers converging at this historical moment created a peculiar balance of powers: while the Cherokees were hardly a subjected people, they by necessity deferred to the military and consequently at times the political persuasion of the United States. But at perhaps the greatest moment of religious influence in the country, Cherokee communities had more or less exclusive sovereignty over the spread of Christianity within their borders, even as religious groups held court over much of the government's public policy, and perhaps even more over public opinion. Muddied as this is, what should be clear is that in the early stages of contact with Christianity—when Native invitations and permissions characterized their relations, not evangelical intrusions and prescriptions—traditional Cherokee communities were hardly a passel of feckless, whitewashed dupes.[45]

Despite occasional checks, more than once U.S. military power and colonial policy superseded American public opinion, overwhelmed Cherokee defenses, and disorganized Cherokee social and political structures. Following a series of military defeats and problems with rogue treaty making, dispersed Cherokee towns responded by coalescing into a formal, nationalized political body. Several changes attended this centralization (discussed in greater detail in chapter 4), perhaps the most drastic and far-reaching of which officially codified and sanctioned a shift from matrilineal and matrifocal clan-based social structures towards patrilineal and patriarchal institutions. Theda Perdue has discussed the long-term effects of this shift on Cherokee society generally and women in particular at length in her history, *Cherokee Women: Gender and Culture Change, 1700 to 1835.* Men traditionally acted as leaders in the political world, so finding them continuing in those roles as the nation developed comes as no great surprise. It is worth noting, however, that prior to the shift, not only were chiefs' traditional powers dramatically circumscribed but also the political realm itself actually governed very little in the old world, being confined generally to questions of external relations. Internal matters were by and large administered not by a government or state but by clan or priest leaders.[46] As the national body became entrenched, however, it assumed ever-increasing dominion over internal affairs, and women found themselves at an ever-greater remove from the constricted and constricting center of power.

GENDERED RELIGIOUS DEVELOPMENT

Despite the systematic attempts to redefine power as something held by men, women were not without a voice. They protested formally and separately to the Cherokee National Council and to the U.S. Congress against land cessions, and certainly they continued to influence political policy, albeit in less institutionalized and more nuanced ways than before the ratification of the Cherokee Constitution, which was a milestone in the movement away traditional forms of governance. Perdue contends that while women might have lost political and economic power, as men focused their efforts more on external affairs, women's power within their societies may actually have increased. Confining herself to the period between 1700 and 1835, she contends that "even the 'civilization' program, the most direct assault on Cherokee conceptions of gender, failed to transform the relations between men and women in most Cherokee households."[47] I believe Perdue is correct in her argument that Cherokee women grew stronger internally, not strictly in response to but rather in tandem with political centralization, I would add. After 1835, however, there are still other significant ways (and significant numbers of Cherokee women who became Christian) in which they redefined the scope of their power in progressive-traditional consonance with an alternative cultural understanding of power.

As traditional religious practices and male religious leaders' authority waned, as Cherokee men led the assumption of clan powers by the polity, and as missionaries endeavored to spread Christianity, female leadership flowed into newly imagined religious spheres, primarily emergent Christian communities. While Christian and traditional religions clearly had points of difference—irreconcilable for some—they also shared several principled practices that others found blended easily. In many respects the spiritual leadership roles that women assumed mirrored those they filled in traditional communities. In both traditional and Christian cases, men filled the head positions as "priests," but women administered many of the requisite ceremonial practices, figured prominently in their symbology, and educated children in religious traditions. Most important, I imagine, was their general social leadership in a society long accustomed to matrilineage and matriarchy.[48]

Perhaps the contradictions between Cherokee religion and Christianity arising at this historical juncture seem too distinct, the ruptures too radical to indicate anything but a revolution in cultural continuity. Not every change, however, heralds an utter cultural revolution. Many major developments, such as those involving social, religious, and gender roles, clearly effected immediate and subsequent upheavals, but they were volitionally enacted in order to maintain the greater part of the Cherokee way of life, and when enacted, they often drew upon or refashioned already-familiar principled practices, at least to some of the women in Cherokee country.[49] That most scholars have failed to recognize the persistence of traditional principles and practices following so obvious a shift, however, recommends it as an obvious place to begin exploring the potential strength of cultural perseverance.

The suggestion that Cherokee women became leaders of the religious/spiritual sphere during the politically centralizing period of the colonial encounter recalls Partha Chatterjee's subtle and sophisticated theorization of a similar change in East Indian history when nationalism constituted a similarly gendered sphere for women. This cultural space was defined against the scientific, technological, and political sphere wherein the West had proven its superiority, persuading the postcolonial nation to model itself after the Western world's successful strategies in these areas—this would be, literally, a man's world. Chatterjee's description of the corresponding woman's world can help us think through the complexities of the interactions between politics, gender, and religion. He writes: "The material is the domain of the 'outside,' of the economy and of statecraft. . . . The spiritual, on the other hand, is an 'inner' domain bearing the 'essential' marks of cultural identity. The greater one's success in imitating Western skills in the material domain, therefore, the greater the need to preserve the distinctness of one's spiritual culture . . . but it is not as though this so-called spiritual domain is left unchanged. In fact, here nationalism launches its most powerful, creative, and historically significant project: to fashion a 'modern' national culture that is nevertheless not Western."[50] Forming a distinct culture, an insulated repository of what constitutes the people's exclusivity, requires then the identification and elaboration of difference, separated from both Western influence and the antiquated remnants of traditionalism that do not conform to the freshly imagined national culture. This domain, which would encompass religion, domesticity, and other aspects of culture, was constructed as "an inner domain of sovereignty, far removed from the arena of political contest with the colonial state,"[51] but according to Chatterjee fell into nationalist service in developing internal cohesion.

Chatterjee keenly traces political nationalism's cultural ideological program, but we might also look for the political program of the culturalism operating apart from the nation-state, or at least its political effects. By following the exchanges between the private and the public, we can see women influencing politics dramatically from the sphere ostensibly set aside for them by men. They created a Cherokee Christianity and shaped schools' curriculum, for instance, and also affected the course of external politics in relatively direct ways through their given or withheld support for the state's various enterprises that required their participation.[52] The ramifications of these projects and others still reverberate politically in Cherokee country today, as women-led communities shape institutions and leaders and hold them accountable to the "depoliticized," cultural-spiritual sphere.

In Cherokee history, nationalism was not so able to bring about an entirely new purpose for the spiritual domain or for people who thought of themselves as spiritual as in the East Indian history Chatterjee describes. He celebrates Benedict Anderson's definition of nationhood as existing in the imagination more than in a checklist of attributes, but points out Anderson's myopic focus on the Euro-American nation-state as the standard to which all others are compared.[53] Chatterjee in *The Nation and Its Fragments* finds innovative imaginations at work on questions of community and resistance by looking beyond the normatively constructed center of power to the periphery, but he too examines power primarily of the nation-state. By reimagining power and ways it may be exercised—with the authority of cultural tradition rather than of legitimized coercion, say—we may yet find it at still further remove from the normative national center, out in the decentralized, anarchistic wilds. To be fair, Chatterjee is not here writing a study of local culturalism but of nationalism and its interpolating strategies, one instance of which I will take up in chapters 4 and 5. Here, suffice it to say that power proliferates in all sorts of ways.

Before taking up the (masculine) polity's troubled relationship with culture, I would like to suggest that one of these ways appeared when Cherokee women launched their own creative projects that sought no less than the preservation and/or creation of their own versions of community through strategies alternative to the nation-state but no less political for their religious, social, gendered, and communal emphasis. These projects may at times have worked in conjunction with the nationalist project, but they often overtly and covertly opposed it, or at least certain directions it took. In terms of their flow into leadership roles in the religious sphere, where superintendence was desperately needed, they undertook responsibility for the dynamic administration of religion and tradition not because they were unwittingly indoctrinated with and determined by a masculine, nationalist ideology (neither Cherokee nor American). Neither were they cordoned off into a controllable, apolitical, or powerless zone; they instead willfully enacted an imagined sense of culturally preservative integrity. Though early missionaries' efforts concentrated on converting males, historian William McLoughlin claims that the majority of new Christians were women, including among the Moravians, both pre-removal and climbing to dramatic numbers following removal, when women accounted for two-thirds of mission church members. Furthermore, two-thirds of post-removal converts were full-blood women.[54]

Whatever the official Christian/missionary policy on women's leadership and despite the prominence of several male converts like Elias Boudinot and Jesse Bushyhead, women, too, took on conspicuous and influential roles as teachers and community leaders, and in many ways their centrality to and superintendence of Christian churches persists today, both in sheer number and force. Even the early twentieth-century stomp dance religious societies with their prominent, male-only chief and firekeeper positions, which in some ways inaugurate a remasculinization of Cherokee religious leadership, retain for women significant, regnant roles over the rejuvenated clans, other women's societies, children's education, ceremonial participation, the feeding of participants, and more.[55]

Neither were Cherokee women subject to isolationist forces so strong as Chatterjee identifies at work in India. Cherokees were more willing to consider changes to the scientific/political and religious/cultural spheres and others so long as the bulk of Cherokee sovereignties—political, cultural, religious, economic, and so on—might remain intact and distinguishable as Cherokee. In terms of the religious change orchestrated by Christianizing women, some scholars have argued that traditional Cherokee religion and Christianity were radically incommensurable—and these scholars have admittedly included Western academics, Cherokees (academics and others), Christians, and traditionalists. The two religions share several important dispositions, however, like prayer, fasting, and worship, some of which I will outline in the next chapter. If studied in detail, these would offer strong support to a more robust theorization of religious consonance than I can offer here, but challenges to the possibility of bringing these together coming from such wide and authoritative quarters need looking into.

TRADITIONALISM REVISITED

Among the strongest assertions of Indian/Western difference is Mary Churchill's refutation of Charles Hudson's opposition of purity and pollution as an interpretive concept in Cherokee religion. Churchill sees the binary as borrowed from Western philosophy that does not well translate or describe balance in Cherokee thinking. This view of oppositionality without antagonism is shared by Daniel Heath Justice, and a related critique advanced by Jace Weaver and Eva Garroutte emphasizes the communal over the individualist focus of the Cherokee worldview. None of these theorists argue explicitly against the possibility of religious blending, but each identifies a fundamental point at which they believe Cherokee and mainstream thinking to be farthest apart, a difference with extensive and sometimes exclusive results. Besides their identification of such tensions, they offer on their own terms well-developed descriptions of Cherokee philosophy and nuanced strategies of reading literature in a cultural framework, or at least in particular aspects of one.

Churchill confronts Hudson's examination of ideas of purity and pollution in Hudson's seminal 1976 work, *The Southeastern Indians*, arguing that although he claims it is only one lens among many for looking at Cherokee religious beliefs and practices, it in fact becomes the controlling paradigm of his study. She summarizes his position: "In Hudson's interpretive model, oppositional elements are separated from one another by means of boundaries. While these elements may merely differ from each other, conflict or antagonism can characterize their relationship as well. . . . For Hudson, purity is associated with order and the maintenance of boundaries between different categories, while pollution entails chaos and the mixing of categories or the crossing of categorical boundaries. Beyond these somewhat descriptive understandings of *purity* and *pollution*, however, there are value laden aspects of—and even moral dimensions to—these terms."[56] Not to be obtuse, but the moral dimension, then, favors purity to pollution, which seems reasonable enough. The problem, Churchill argues, is that both concepts have been imported into Cherokee studies beginning with late-eighteenth century protoethnologists like James Adair and William Bartram, with subsequent scholars replicating their Western-derived encoding.[57] Initially acquiescing to Hudson's position, Churchill argues that Cherokees might have understood some concepts as pure or polluted but concludes that Hudson overextends the dichotomy, while using concepts that have their primary referents in Judeo-Christian traditions and are thus not careful enough translations of Cherokee ideas. Of greater concern to her than the inaccuracy of the descriptors, however, is the structure of Hudson's analysis, the pairing in antagonistic opposition.[58]

Drawing on Joseph Epes Brown, Joan Scott, Jacques Derrida, and others, Churchill interrogates how the elements of the binary are constructed, attempting to show in Hudson's case the Western genealogy that informs his understandings of purity and pollution that he then superimposes on his analysis of Cherokee religion. She finds in binary opposition and the related dialecticism two primary limitations: first, they posit an antagonism where none may in fact exist. The theoretically originated tension imparted to the terms of a binary further implies a normatively valued preference for the first, so that in common constructions, such as purity versus pollution, culture/nature, settler/native, separation/border-crossing, and so forth, the former term accrues favor and is positioned to demonstrate its superiority. Second, she levels a deconstructionist critique that identifies the connections and interdependencies between the elements of the binary.[59]

Her hypothesis of the interdependence explores the distinct power belonging to particular categories, power that can be accessed by means of crossing into those spheres. Boundary crossing thus becomes a mediating and harmonizing process that unites rather than opposes the elements. Pointing to the respected and positive power of menstruation and of the Uktena, the mythical serpent-monster, examples Hudson used to demonstrate their "abominableness" because of their categorical ambiguity, Churchill rescues them from their classification as "polluted."[60] From this revaluation of their power, she inductively argues that they "point to the centrality of boundary-crossing and category-blurring to sacred endeavors. Instead of being opposed to the sacred, 'anomalies' were sources of access to it."[61] Cherokee religion, according to her, recognized "the reality that contact with 'abominations and anomalies' was an unavoidable part of life and that for the well-being of the community such contact was necessary and sought after for the spiritual power it could bring."[62] She extrapolates the concept of boundary crossing to interpret other common religious dispositions, such as ceremonial scratching and going to water, in addition to the major annual religious event, the Green Corn ceremony. Scratching, she argues, draws on the usually negatively connoted power of blood in a possible reenactment of menstruation; going to water enacts a crossing from this world to that under us (the source of the waters), and Green Corn marks the threshold of the old and new years, with attendant rejuvenations in forgiveness, the sacred fire, and other relations and symbols.

Though Churchill does not discuss retrograde movement, border crossing cannot go on infinitely in the regular ceremonial system she describes, for there must be a movement back to the more or less discrete spheres in order for the boundary to be crossed at intervals. The act of crossing, however, for her enacts the unifying necessary for the maintenance of balance, the principle she puts at the heart of Cherokee religious traditions. She writes, "In sum, it is balance and synthesis, opposition and unification, as simultaneous complementary processes that Cherokee traditions maintained, not purity, as Hudson's interpretation suggests. . . . While Hudson's model is based on the elimination of crossed boundaries, mine incorporates liminality as an essential positive feature of Cherokee religious traditions."[63] With balance understood as a state of nonantagonistic opposition between equal and complementary forces and synthesis as a moment of border crossing between them, Churchill dismisses purity more or less entirely, supplanting it with the synthesis represented by boundary crossing (which presupposes bounded, oppositional spheres—usually two but occasionally four in sets of two, as with the cardinal directions) as the purposive method or goal of Cherokee religion.

Despite the elegance of her description, Churchill insufficiently details the variety of Cherokee religion or traditionalism. To begin, balance, like the harmony ethic critiqued above, is not only constituted by but is also dependent upon, connected with, and in the service of other principles: it requires equality to work; it is affiliated with all sorts of social, political, religious, and other principles, such as power; and it labors for the maintenance of still more, such as righteousness. Opposition and boundary crossing by themselves cannot make sense of this reticulated complexity. Additionally, not all oppositions are fruitfully synthesized, not all boundaries are usefully crossed, if indeed there is such a thing as negativity—healthfulness does not seek out illness, for instance. Healing doesn't rush to the power of harming: while inoculation can build resistance, a hatchet won't cure a headache. Boundary crossing is not undertaken for its own sake alone, but as a method interwoven with a series of principles and practices whose efficacy and function we would do best to discuss precisely before we discuss them generally.

Churchill's Derridean insight that the components of a binary commonly thought to vie for dominance may in fact be interrelated or interdependent does not, however, seem to keep her theory out of another trap against which Derrida warns. Derrida cautions that the negatively connoted second term may simply be reconstructed and reconstrued as positive in an inversion of the binary that does not transcend limiting dualist thinking. Churchill does not strictly celebrate the "positive implications of 'pollutants,'" but she is much interested in rescuing many negatively connoted practices and in deconstructing ideas of purity in Cherokee religion.[64] Her reinterpretations of going to water, the Green Corn ceremony, menstruation, and others give the appearance of dismantling the purity/pollution dichotomy, but the oppositional categories themselves, however renamed, are more or less retained intact, for without their existence, boundaries between them could not be crossed.

Moreover, the boundary crossing foundational to her theory of Cherokee religion looks much like the mediation that structuralist anthropologist Claude Lévi-Strauss finds temporally uniting binary elements, at least until the irreconcilable binary surfaces again, in the same guise or in another. If we substitute "religion" for "myth," Lévi-Strauss could be summarizing Churchill's argument when he writes, "The purpose of myth is to provide a logical model capable of overcoming a contradiction (an impossible achievement if, as it happens, the contradiction is real)."[65] Shifting the emphasis from opposition toward mediation of opposition as a controlling principle of both individual and social religious reasoning—only a repositioning of a continued structuralist, monist focus still dedicated to describing *the* purpose or *the* method of a people's thinking—does not say enough about the diversity of Cherokees' religious principled practices. It doesn't seem plausible that Cherokees conclusively could not or did not conceive of purity as a pertinent religious concern—it is not the sole province of Christianity, after all—yet Churchill in her attempt to displace purity with balance and boundary crossing dials up as narrow a field of focus as Hudson does.

Early in her argument she acquiesces that purity *may* be a feature of Cherokee religion: "Many American Indians do characterize some of their traditions as purificatory. Even some Cherokees do. . . . I am not arguing that no Native American religious traditions value purification; instead, I am suggesting that a close examination of Cherokee traditions makes such a description of Cherokee sacred ways suspect."[66] But by the time she offers as an example the Keetoowah Society's Seven Clan law, which explicitly states, "Have a white, a *pure* and *cleansed* heart, they say," her suspicion has become radical skepticism aimed at establishing boundary crossing as foundational by disparaging purity as spurious.[67] Describing the practices of sacrifice and touching medicine, Keetoowah elder Benny Smith, too, discusses purity and cleansing in relatively straightforward language: "The fire keepers make the burnt offering, often called feeding the fire. The burnt offering is usually a small game animal or a white chicken; each signifies purity." Besides interpreting symbols of purity, Smith also sees purity as a goal pursued: "After dancing all night, the Keetoowahs use what the white man calls the 'black drink.' The Indians call it medicine. . . . The Keetoowahs drink and wash their hand[s] and faces with the black drink. This is an act of external and internal cleansing to help maintain purity."[68]

Churchill isn't convinced. She writes, "Allusions to purity can nonetheless be found in statements by twentieth-century Cherokees, however. Why would this occur? Surely, Cherokees themselves would employ more accurate terms for discussing their beliefs and traditions, one would think."[69] One would think that given her call for dialogue with and respect for Cherokees' own understandings of their traditions, she would be more inclined to lend credence to their interpretations.[70] Such pronouncements, however, might be seen as lending too-great support to Hudson's position, which she sees as constructed out of Western ways of thinking. She offers this interpretation of the Keetoowahs' true import: "Despite the Christian meanings that are evident in statements by contemporary Cherokees . . . it is important to note the relevance of harmony to these beliefs. The Keetoowah Seven Clan Rule *really* addresses the means to promote and maintain harmony in the community. . . . Relying on the ideas of the harmony ethic and white path, we can understand at least some statements about purity by twentieth-century Cherokees as efforts to live by means of 'balance and synthesis and the non-material nature of reality' that Kilpatrick has identified as foundational to the Cherokee thought world."[71] Churchill translates traditional religious practitioners' wording and dispels their characterizations of purity as a primary religious concern. If purity is significant, it is through its service to social harmony, itself a subset of the primary, controlling principle of balance, and both are achieved through the synthesizing mediation of opposition.

Against Hudson's suggestion of purity and cleansing as central, Churchill proposes her model of balance and boundary crossing in their places, essentially replacing one set of dialectical terms with another, without altering the underlying structuralist synchrony.

This out-of-time essentializing more problematically interprets Cherokee culture through its broad methodology than through its specific focal points. Describing Roland Barthes's shift away from structuralism, Catherine Belsey offers a succinct description of what is troublesome about the sweeping claims of structuralism and other totalizing paradigms. She recounts Barthes's rumination on critical theorists' attempts to see the big picture framed by a single, coherent structure, one that would be necessarily replicated in all the world's small pictures—the macrocosm repeated in the microcosm. Belsey cautions, "Suddenly, the grand claims of structuralism appear absurd. Once you have found the single determining structure, there is nothing to choose between the universe and a bean. The microcosm simply becomes an illustration of the general pattern, another instance of the same—thrilling for the system-builders, but then what? What can further investigation discover? Only endless repetition. The big questions have been answered in advance."[72] By reducing to balance and boundary crossing such diversities as the story of the first people Selu and Kanati, the practice of going to water, the Green Corn ceremony, beliefs about menstruation, the Uktena, death, gender differences, and more—in seeing one pattern in so many things—Churchill doesn't venture far enough into the liminality she wants to celebrate: rather than dismantling the structuralist framework built up around Cherokee religion, she rebuilds it on another site.

Daniel Heath Justice's nationalist perspective on Cherokee literature in his literary history, *Our Fire Survives the Storm,* fills out an alternative complementary dualism using Churchill's structural framework, a theoretical debt he acknowledges. Like Churchill, he rejects a Hegelian dialectical narrative of progress. He stops short, however, of indicting binarism when constructed with a relationship characterized by balance rather than by antagonism, writing, "Whereas the progressivist interpretations of various Cherokee dualisms presume an inevitable eclipse or erasure of one of the pair, a more culturally rooted understanding looks to the *relationship* between them."[73] Accepting Weaver's insistence that community is at the heart of Indian identity, and believing that "Nationhood . . . is the political extension of the social rights and responsibilities of peoplehood," Justice turns his focus to the Cherokee dual political structure that used a standing polity called the white government in times of peace and a red organization during war.[74] From this governmental dualism he extrapolates what he calls a "Beloved Path" and a "Chickamauga consciousness," paired Cherokee cultural and political attitudes that offer him a culturally specific methodology of contextualizing and interpreting Cherokee literary texts.[75] His description is worth quoting at length:

> What I call the red "Chickamauga consciousness," [is] so named for the nationalist resistance movement of the late eighteenth and early nineteenth centuries that was devoted to armed response to U.S. violence and expansion into ancestral territories. Chickamauga consciousness, an extension of the red/war governmental division, is centered in Cherokee intellectual and artistic separatism, in a rhetorical rejection of literary, historical, or philosophical accommodation. Coupled with the Chickamauga consciousness is a white "Beloved Path" reading that places peace and cultural continuity above potentially self-destructive rebellion. Neither exists independently; there is a necessary tension that brings the war and peace perspectives together in constant movement—again, the idea of nationhood as dynamic concept.[76]

Guided by balance and complementarity, this relationship embraces the interdependence Churchill identifies in border crossing, but Justice is not as concerned with the crossing of one element into the other as with the principles embodied by each. That the red and white structures exist in regular, predictable actuality or potentiality sufficiently binds them together.

The dualism in the political arena that Justice identifies differs conceptually from the structural synchrony Churchill theorizes, insofar as Justice sees metaphorical *traces* of the differing attitudes more than a recapitulation of a constant behavioral or eternal system. If I am reading him correctly, he argues, for instance, that we can understand John Ross's rhetoric as nationalistically defiant in the way that Dragging Canoe's resistance asserted Cherokee sovereignty, but not that Ross's writing or policies played out the schema of a red war chief. By precisely situating his readings in historical contexts, Justice demonstrates how people in historical moments may adapt traditional dispositions to address contemporary dilemmas without abandoning the character of those strategies. Such is the "dynamic nationhood" he reiterates throughout *Our Fire Survives the Storm*.[77]

Though I believe his emphasis on agentive, historical flexibility differentiates his argument from the out-of-time, structuralist binarism I find in Churchill's emphasis on balance and mediation (despite Justice's professed debt to this model), his separation of literary political postures into the red/Chickamaugan/defiant and white/Beloved Path/accommodationist spheres strikes me as too similar to the traditionalist/progressive dichotomy. I acknowledge Justice's claim that complementarity rather than antagonism renders the model inherited from Churchill a creation of a wholly different cloth.[78] He may be entirely correct in his claim that "the established body of Cherokee scholarship has generally focused on a limiting dualism that is rooted in Eurowestern progressivist ideas of savagism and civilization. Yet the dualistic structure itself isn't inherently problematic, as various complementary pairings are deeply embedded in Cherokee culture and history, although not inevitably along the progressivist spectrum."[79] Dualism we may have, but to it we are not bound. Justice and Churchill show that their models of a Nativist binarism can offer compelling readings and empowering insights, especially in political structure and gender divisions; for that matter, Lévi-Strauss demonstrates that Western dialecticism can do the same thing. But like any good building contractor, we have many framing options. If we were to look more pluralistically at the traditional political world, for instance, we might find that besides the red and white governments, the political structure extended certain powers and influence to clans, priests, women's councils, towns, and even outsiders (how many is that?), among others. These are not accurately enough described by any given pairing. By theorizing the roles such actors have played, we might discover the ever-widening benefits of pluralism and the ever-expanding options of anarchistic organization.

I gladly embrace Justice's thoughtful development of the Chickamauga spirit of resolve and the Beloved Path dedication to peace, along with the lucid readings they inspire in Cherokees' political and literary representations. Yet these are but two among innumerable postures. While politics are clearly central to the lives of many Cherokees, a point Justice's astute readings of the Cherokee

Constitution, John Ross's rhetoric, and the Treaty of New Echota, among many other texts, firmly establishes, it is worth remembering that when compared with the traditional social power of the clan, that of the polity was markedly lesser for most of the life of the nation-people. The extent and implication of this diffuse political-social dynamic I take up in greater detail in chapters 4 and 5.

As Justice asserts, "Nationhood is, fundamentally, the *political* expression of a people's understanding of themselves as a people."[80] He elects to situate himself as an expressly political reader of Cherokee literature, believing that "the exercise of nationhood continues to be a dominant social ethic among Cherokees. . . . It is in relationship with the tribal nation that the individual Cherokee is defined."[81] As Craig Womack has argued, most existing criticism of American Indian literature has been conspicuously apolitical, with a tendency to ignore contemporary issues, to focus on benign cultural differences, and effectively to write tribal nations out of power. In this regard his and Justice's development of a nationalist criticism represents an important exercise of politically creative intellectual sovereignty. But if indeed the social and political are not fully coextensive, if the latter does at times attempt to assert its dominance over the former, a nationalism not fully disposed to suspect the nation-state of abuse might too readily throw its support behind the polity, which is too often the impediment to peoples' freedom. This, too, is a political criticism, but an anarchistic one that aligns itself more stringently with people in local communities, the primary source of cultural agency, the governors of the government.

It is fair to say that balance, boundary crossing, harmony, righteousness, and purity are among the more salient concepts of Cherokee religion, along with community responsibility (Weaver's *communitism* or Garroutte's *responsibility to reciprocity*). Future scholars will theorize yet more prominent features—but still we have failed to think through "more a way of living with variety than of subduing it," as Wayne Booth eloquently puts it, and have only "sailed the coast" in our attempts to discover the values in variety itself.[82] Not least among these is the combinatory and generative capacity to script infinitely innovative responses that incorporate the conservative, accommodate the new, and open pathways rather than forever stage a fundamentally unchanging balancing act.[83] We can see such agency in the fusions of traditional and Christian dispositions narrated by Catharine Brown in the early nineteenth century to Sequoyah Guess in the late twentieth. Perhaps these connections, too, represent mediations, but they are not everywhere predetermined by binary pairs, nor any one great structuralist script. The new dispositions are instead made up of principles and practices that move through, with, around, over, under each other, creating strategies that navigate an array of possibilities through constantly changing waters.

KT

CHAPTER 2

Gaining Knowledge and Religious Improvisation in Catharine Brown's *Memoir*

At the turn of the eighteenth century, the missionary zeal of the Second Great Awakening had failed to open many roads into Cherokee country. Although Cherokee lands had been drastically reduced by treaty and war over the course of interactions with the British, French, and Americans, the Cherokees nevertheless represented a powerful military and political force impervious to unwelcome overtures from evangelistic missionaries, however enthusiastic.[1] By the close of the nineteenth century, though, missionaries' inroads were well established, and thousands of Cherokees had converted to Christianity. Among the earliest of converts was Catharine Brown, the daughter of a relatively affluent family from an Alabama town and an early attendant of the Brainerd mission school, established in eastern Tennessee in 1817 under the direction of the predominantly Congregationalist American Board of Commissioners of Foreign Missions (ABCFM). On her arrival the missionaries were doubtful that the proud and beautiful Cherokee woman could acclimate to their strict lifestyle, but she soon became a favored student whose enthusiasm led many of her family and other Cherokees to the new religion. Less than two years after her conversion, she was sent to take charge of a school at the town of Creek Path. Only three years later, in 1823, she died of tuberculosis at the approximate age of twenty-three. Her story was widely spread as an exemplum among the Cherokees, earning her an almost saintly reputation. After her death Rufus Anderson, corresponding secretary for the ABCFM, began a biographical article on her, but he found the subject matter compelling enough to warrant a book, which he compiled from Brown's letters, journal, and others' recollections and documents.[2] Her memoir, though heavily edited and assiduously framed by Anderson's ready hand, offer a rare opportunity to consider the progressively traditional strategies imagined early in the imperial encounter, although most critical treatments of Brown have done little but dismiss her and her writing as uncomplicatedly assimilated.

The few critics, such as Theda Perdue, Carolyn Ross Johnston, and Arnold Krupat, who have written about the young Cherokee suggest that her conversion to Christianity and her approximately six years spent with the missionaries at Brainerd eradicated any connections to Cherokee culture. A careful, tribalist reading of her memoir and of the archival documents uncovered by Joel Martin, however, demonstrates the need for a theoretical model of interaction attuned to the complexity of multiple layers of experience, for by placing them within a cultural context, we find that Brown's "Cherokeeness" becomes a more salient feature than previously thought. Martin astutely notes several principled practices that evidence the strength of Brown's cultural ties, including her outdoors worship and her reliance on dreaming as a spiritual hermeneutic. In his historical novel *The Singing Bird: A Cherokee Novel,* which was likely written sometime between 1935 and 1945 and published posthumously, Cherokee author John Oskison dramatizes Brown's life, legacy, and just such habits of hers. Brown's retention of these dispositions taken together with her practice of Christianity substantiate the simultaneous presence of what Martin calls the "religious creativity and spiritual resiliency" of Native peoples in general and Brown in particular.[3]

That the Christian Indian identity she put together from a Cherokee cultural paradigm has led to her critical depiction as assimilated suggests that the descriptors *traditional* and *progressive,* separately and together, may camouflage more options than ordinarily supposed. It is tempting to cast the meeting between American Indian people and "civilizing" missionaries in a Hegelian dialectic, pitting opposite if unequal opponents in a fight to the assimilationist death.[4] Just as most scholars who have written of Brown point to her as a signpost at the outset of the Cherokees' road to civilization, so did the missionaries who were her contemporaries. According to Anderson, Brown was indeed the first Cherokee baptized at the Brainerd mission school, but this fact reveals very little about the confluence of multiple forces that her conversion represents, forces such as intertown tension in Cherokee country, the spiritual revival of the nineteenth century, the erosion of matrilineal power in Cherokee society, the American nationalist land grab, anxiety among Cherokees over white belligerence, the growing threat of removal, and deepening immersion in Euro-American economic structures.[5] The Brainerd school could never have been established had not the National Council and town councils, influenced by earlier Cherokee converts like assistant chief Charles Hicks (later principal chief), invited missionaries to open schools in Cherokee lands.[6]

Perhaps this same complexity has discouraged theoretical discussion of an earlier Cherokee converted by Moravian missionaries, described by the ethnologist James Mooney: "Later on they established missions among the Delawares in Ohio, where their first Cherokee convert was received in 1773, being one who had been captured by the Delawares when a boy and had grown up and married in the tribe."[7] Where to begin the categorizations, and from which oppositions? Is he Cherokee, Lenni Lenape (Delaware), male, Christian, pagan, displaced, adopted, civilized, Indian? Once one dialectic is synthesized, how much of the defeated antithesis persists? Questions of identity, rather than being confronted from a structuralist paradigm by a sequential series of dialectics, are better addressed by admitting the possibilities for multiple, lateral comparisons, which we can begin by disassembling the vocabularies of synthesis. For example, if we work backward from the solutions *adoptee=Cherokee vs. (>?) Delaware* and *convert=Christian vs. Indian,* we could learn something of how interactions with the Delaware altered Cherokee society itself, how Christianity was changed by Indian converts, or how a converted Delaware-Cherokee adoptee fused his particular traditions with Christianity, rather than how one affiliation dominated another, then another and another.

The urge to set up elements in conflict may come readily, for as Wendy Doniger writes in her foreword to a collection of lectures by Claude Lévi-Strauss, the granddaddy of the theoretical binary, "Language itself predisposes us to attempt to understand ourselves and our world by superimposing dialectics, dichotomies, or dualistic grids upon data that may in fact be entirely integrated. And underneath language lies the binary nature of the brain itself. . . . The simplest and most efficient way to process experience seems to be by dividing it in half, and then to divide the halves in half, reformulating every question so that there are only two possible answers to it, yes or no."[8] Lévi-Strauss, who founded structural anthropology on binary theory, applauds another of its wonders: "It is only the present state of scientific thought that gives us the ability to understand what is in this myth [and mythical thinking in general], to which we remained completely blind before the idea of binary operations become familiar to us."[9] He sees in mythical thinking an early manifestation of the structure of all thinking, including the scientific, which with its practical empiricism synthesizes and supersedes the mythic, rendering it knowable for the first time.

The binary model has its utilities, but its flowchart-strict interpretive capacities become clumsy when more than two pertinent elements enter in—a limitation Doniger implicitly admits in passing swiftly over the "data that may in fact be entirely integrated." Further, the "us" to whom both Lévi-Strauss and Doniger refer universalizes a Euro-American, pseudoscientific theory premised upon antagonism. Apart from Fredric Jameson's influential critique of structuralism's synchrony, its out-of-time logic, there are several other analytical troubles with binary thinking: first, its insistence on absolute and exclusive value.[10] If there are tensions between the Cherokee and Lenni Lenape aspects of the man Mooney discusses, a binary limits him to either Cherokee or Lenni Lenape identity, for according to the logic of the dialectic he cannot finally be both, either through mediation, which enacts a temporary bridging, or through synthesis, which is a new creation, an evolutionary hybrid. We cannot know how this man thought of himself, but as Anne McClintock astutely notes, "Race, gender and class are not distinct realms of experience, existing in splendid isolation from each other;

nor can they be simply yoked together. . . . Rather, they come into existence *in and through* relation to each other—if in contradictory and conflictual ways."[11] If I can get metaphorical for just a second, what McClintock says here suggests to me that there are ripples of influence on our ideas of ourselves. We may take a snapshot of a pooling moment that we then title an identity—and that representation may even be faithful for a great long while—but it is no more eternal or complete than it is the moment itself, and we may never see the other currents pushing or pulling our subject into frame. McClintock's emphasis on experiential reticulation is well taken, yet she, too, narrowly defines the spheres of identity in Eurocentric terms, privileging currently acceptable neo-Marxist categories. In the midst of the Second Great Awakening in Cherokee country, religion, age, clan, town, and more swirl in other relevant eddies of experience and belonging.

Second, attempting to work out tensions through a dialectic model can lead to the construction of faulty pairings, such as setting Cherokee identity against gendered or religious identity in an antagonism that does not necessarily exist. Some argue that there are fundamentally opposed precepts of Christian and tribal identity, a position undoubtedly shaped by the many disgraces in the history of Christian and Indian interactions. But significant numbers of Christian Indians like Brown have identified fundamental tenets of traditional religion and Christianity and found them not preclusive but rather supplementary, a relationship ill described by antagonistic dialecticism. Still another Jamesonian problem extends from the first two, in that a binary construction's inability to account for degree of power (and thus perseverance) and its inattention to historical circumstance lends itself to arbitrarily limiting, normative definitions. Initial forces (overcome in a Hegelian dialectic, essentialist in a structuralist binary) become generalized, unchanging components against which all future interactions are measured: the Cherokee in 1800 must be the same Cherokee of 1900, 2000, 2100, with no regard for historical developments. Jameson argues that a binary model conceals its synchronic telling of history. In American Indian literary theory and history, this tendency appears when deviation from the Indian norm is interpreted as cultural deficiency, once again, "not really Indian."[12]

WEBS OF COMMUNITIES

In her 1998 book, *Cherokee Women: Gender and Culture Change, 1700-1835,* historian Theda Perdue mentions Brown in passing and sees in her story no harmony but only conflict between Christian and Indian: "Few women in the Cherokee Nation could equal Catharine Brown or, at least, her memory. Most did not seem to want to. They preferred their traditional religion, which did not distinguish between the physical and spiritual worlds, which emphasized harmony and balance, and which placed the needs of the community above those of any individual. Those Cherokees who converted to Christianity became part of a hierarchical religion that promised little control over the physical world (that is, illness and weather), defined relationships to the natural world and other human beings in terms of dominion and submission, and placed responsibility for salvation, behavior, and success squarely on the individual."[13] Despite Perdue's outstanding work on Cherokee women's perseverance, she does not fully interrogate ways in which Brown might have reconciled apparent contradictions in her life. Discourse dedicated to division gives rise to the trope of "walking in two worlds," an American Indian cliché about as sublime as a greeting card: Indians "walk with one foot in a moccasin and one in a wingtip" or "have a foot in two canoes." These metaphors offer little toward understanding the complexity of identities and the dispositional strategies that they make available. Power comes from multiple sources that work in conjunction, not in isolation. Traditional Cherokee stories, such as those involving powerful supernatural threats, teach a similar lesson in which communities of all sorts must come together to survive. In the story of Untsaiyi, a group of men imprison an evil gambler who wagers for lives; women's collective power defeats Nunyunuwi, the Stone Man; Utlunta, the Spearfinger, would not have been killed without the aid of the animal community—Tsikilili, the chickadee, indicated the monster's vulnerability. These and other traditional stories emphasize survival through the harmonious union of *diverse* communities' powers, a lesson resonant for indigenous anarchistic communities then and now (and which I'll take up in greater detail in the next chapter). In such ways, Catharine Brown drew strength across gendered, religious, and cultural groups and in so doing imparted that strength back to those and other communities struggling with political and social changes.

Packing all these different identities into one person is not always such an easy thing, but it is aided by conscious planning and the unconscious vetting of the habitus. These strategies of coping with change play out in Catherine Brown's memoir, as we see her making a life for herself as a Christian Cherokee and dealing with the competing demands of missionaries near and far, her family, and other Cherokee people engaged in similar interactions, such as female peers or her students. Her active blending of Christian and Cherokee principles and practices evokes the verb-based foundations of the Cherokee language, which prioritizes doing in constructing meaning rather than the "thingness" of a phenomenon. To demonstrate: ᏧᏂᎳᏫᏍᏗ, the word for church, means "where they gather to study"; ᎧᏃᎮᏛ is "Gospel," meaning "spoken outward"; and the word for God, ᎤᏁᏝᏅᏒ, is "Creator," or more literally something like "he provides" or "apportions."[14] Cherokee syntactical structure and the suffixes, prefixes, and affixes of Cherokee verbs, which conjugate for time, direction, texture, duration, number, causality, and animation, among other factors, also emphasize the primacy of process in Cherokee epistemology, in contrast to the noun-based structure of English.[15] From a Cherokee perspective, we might see in Brown's life less a concatenation of discrete events in displacing series and something more like a sophisticated portaging among pathways.

TRADITIONALIST MEDIATION

Perhaps because they see Brown as an Indian who quit to become a Christian, Theda Perdue and Carolyn Ross Johnston are among those who suggest that there are diametrically opposed fundamentals of Indianness and Christianity, at least Christianity as practiced by nineteenth-century missionaries. They are far from alone—some missionaries and many members of Congress also argued that Indian culture and Christianity were mutually exclusive.[16] Thankfully, contemporary Christian approaches, even those as conservative as in the Southern Baptist denomination, have largely abandoned this position and now encourage missionaries to respect indigenous cultures and to develop cooperative models of Christianity and indigenous customs and values.

This paradigm shift depends on a surprising kind of strategic essentialism, wherein indigenous thinkers and others forced evangelists to reexamine missionaries' complicitous roles in the genocide of the Americas and to scrutinize the foundational elements of their doctrine. For Mark Custalow, former national Native American missionary of the North American Mission Board of the Southern Baptist Convention, the immutable doctrine concerns the sufficiency of God's grace for salvation. So long as teachings do not contradict this tenet, the mission board's official line seems to encourage respect for cultural practices such as sweat lodges or other cleansing ceremonies.[17] The evangelical work of early Native Christians, such as Brown, Hicks, Boudinot, and many more, and the leadership roles assumed by American Indians in modern Christian churches demonstrate the changes that may eventually be wrought by cultures in contact. For example, in 2008 the Baptist General Convention of Oklahoma and the national Southern Baptist Convention elected as presidents Emerson Falls, a Sac and Fox-Choctaw; and Johnny Hunt, a Lumbee, respectively.[18] This is worth pausing to consider: the major fundamentalist Christian denomination in America and Oklahoma was headed by self-identifying Christian Indians—white Baptist church leaders looked to them for spiritual guidance and direction, perhaps conscious that their church's history of race relations is less than spotless and that they might not be able to generate among themselves satisfactory answers to ongoing race-related problems. Such changes do not excuse the immorality of imperialism, but they do offer examples of what can come of Indian agency, in contrast to the proliferant narratives of victimization. In fact, the present coming together of Christian and Indian religious beliefs and practices bears a striking resemblance to that accomplished much earlier by Brown and others.

One of the most intriguing convergences in Catharine Brown's case concerns her understanding of Christianity through her Cherokee cultural framework. An account of a dream in which Brown meets a "little boy" was not included by Anderson in her memoir, but it survives in the letters of the ABCFM. Joel Martin reproduces it in *The Land Looks after Us*:

> In my sleep I tho't I was traveling and came to a hill that was almost perpendicular. I was much troubled about it, for I had to go to its top. I knew not how to get up. She said she saw the steps which others had gone and tried to put her feet in their steps, but found she could not ascend in this way, because her feet slipped. Having made several unsuccessful attempts to ascend, she became very weary, but although she succeeded in getting near the top, but felt in great danger of falling. While in this distress in doubt whether to try to go forward or return, she saw a bush just above her of which she tho't, if she could get hold it she could get up, and as she reached out her hand to the bush, she saw a little boy standing at the top, who reached out his hand; She grasped his thumb, and at this moment she was on the top and someone told her it was the Saviour.[19]

This account offers glimpses of textual dimensionality invisible to binary logic, despite the unsettling shift in point of view revealing its overt mediation.

The little boy is likely one of the Yunwi Tsunsdi, whom Mooney describes as " 'Little People,' who live in rock caves on the mountain side. They are little fellows, hardly reaching up to a man's knee. . . . They are great wonder workers. . . . They are helpful and kind-hearted, and often when people have been lost in the mountains, especially children who have strayed away from their parents, the Yûñwí Tsunsdi' have found them and taken care of them."[20] For many Cherokee people, the Yunwi Tsunsdi represent a powerful spiritual force in the world, and Brown may well have believed that an extraordinary being communicated with her through her dream.[21] Dreams were a powerful source of knowledge about matters both uncommon and everyday in Cherokee culture, and, as Martin forcefully argues, through her dream knowledge Brown found guidance through a new path, divergent though dependent upon the steps others had taken before her.[22] This path was not available to Catharine Brown the individual outside of history and community, but was opened by and was the consequence of the spaces created when Euro-American political and religious expansionists encountered Cherokee people who respected their traditional values and adapted to a rapidly changing world.

Just as Cherokee, if less dramatic, is Brown's concern for "her people." For Brown, as for many Cherokees, a fundamental compassion and concern for others extends from an idea of identity intimately connected with community. (And sure, I remember downplaying community earlier—what I wanted to say there, and here, is that community is an important *piece* of identity, but it's not the whole of it, and that communities should be clearly defined.) This priority finds expression in Brown's preoccupation that she, along with other Cherokee converts like her brother David, be prepared "for usefulness among my people" given "their awful situation while out of Christ."[23] She repeats this sentiment in some form a dozen times throughout her brief memoir, reiterating the centrality of service to the Cherokee people she could reach in her moral vision, which did not escape the attention of Anderson and other contributors to the *Memoir*.[24]

In a more comprehensive biographical essay written about a decade later than the sketch in *Cherokee Women*, Perdue revises her assessment of Brown (that few women wanted to equal Brown's Christian devotion) and attends to her melding of the personal and the communal, rightfully foregrounding the value of community: "Unlike Christianity, which concentrated on the salvation of individual souls, Cherokee religion focused on community well-being. Convinced of the correctness of Christianity, Catharine agonized not over her own soul, but over the collective soul of her people. . . . Her baptism seems to have opened the door for other Cherokees. Soon over a hundred adults joined her in Christian fellowship."[25] This concern for the well-being of the community calls to mind Eva Marie Garroutte's responsibility to reciprocity and Jace Weaver's communitism, discussed in the preceding chapter, and the Keetoowah belief in God's law to love one another.[26] At the risk of redundancy, it may be worth reiterating that for all its importance, *community* is not fully coextensive with the entire network of relations and ways of relating in a given world—unless community names the web itself, in which case it still pays more to discuss how its strands tie together.

Several critics have seen a corollary between a decline of women's political power and Christianity's introduction, assuming a doctrinal emphasis on personal conversion and a political complicity with the goals of the U.S. civilization program, which set aside roles for women in the private, domestic sphere and specifically not in the public, political sphere. In an influential 1966 article emerging out of feminism's second wave, Barbara Welter explores nineteenth-century ideas of femininity that coalesce in what she dubs the "the cult of true womanhood," whose attributes "could be divided into four cardinal virtues—piety, purity, submissiveness and domesticity."[27] Perdue joins Welter's concept of true womanhood with her narrative of conflict between white and Christian against Cherokee and traditional. She writes that the missionaries who taught Cherokees to be true women inculcated in the "elite" classes an expectation that Cherokee women "conform to the ideals of the cult of true womanhood, that is, to be sexually pure, submissive to fathers and husbands, concerned primarily with spiritual and domestic matters, and excluded from politics and economic activities outside the home."[28] Like the conflict between whites and Indians more generally, the outcome of this gendered tension appears foregone. Women found that "domesticity brought influence, not power. Similarly, purity and piety seemed almost anachronistic in a culture and age that tended to value the material above the spiritual."[29] While Wilma Dunaway argues that most Cherokee women resisted the imposition of foreign gender roles at least until removal, she too sees in missionary history white culture attempting to steamroll Native culture and sees in the so-called cult of true womanhood a locus for acculturation, albeit among a minority.[30]

Common to such binaristic histories of the heteronomy of gender roles is the tendency to see assimilation or resistance as the only options available, the ossifying tendencies of which I have already discussed. They are further complicated by what Shirley Samuels has called "the double logic of power and powerlessness," which simultaneously affirms the historical separation of women from spheres of power and indicts them for failing to exercise the political power they purportedly did not possess.[31] As Samuels argues, closer examination reveals far greater overlap between the public and the private than theories of discrete spheres allows. Despite the suggestions that a woman like Brown was simply playing out a stock, assimilated (then domesticated) character's role scripted for her by an alien culture, I argue that not only did she speak to the immediate social and political concerns of Cherokee people, but she also offered to the missionaries her own philosophy of being useful.

The piety of true womanhood for her, at least, entailed concrete engagement with major political problems, which offered missionaries chances to put their Hopkinsian theology into practice. Broadly speaking, the theological position named for missionary, writer, and preacher Samuel Hopkins emphasized social harmony, justice and equity, kindness and generosity, and equality, along with a protoracial consciousness.[32] According to American studies scholar Joseph Conforti, unlike facile caricatures of Christianity as individualist and materialist, Hopkins, presumably along with his followers, "was disquieted by the conflict between traditional social values and the behavior of New Englanders in a time of critical change. Like other evangelicals, he inherited a social ethic that stressed corporate obligation, personal restraint, and communal harmony and simplicity. But the economic and demographic expansion of New England during his lifetime promoted acquisitive, egocentric patterns of behavior at odds with those norms."[33] (It seems harmony and community were known and valued outside Native circles.)

Like Hopkins, Brown also urged a humanist usefulness that I would argue extended from an existing indigenist anarchism committed to practicality and cooperation. Joel Martin alludes to Brown's social consciousness when he writes, "Conversion to Christianity often seemed an effective way to gain respectability, recognition from powerful whites, and a good education. Like Catharine Brown, converts were able to use their enhanced access to the dominant culture to better promote the causes of their people."[34] The imminent causes for the Cherokee were rights to life and land, and while it is mostly tacit, in the assembly of the *Memoir* anyway, many missionaries following Brown's lead took her materialist concern on these matters to heart, politically advocating for the Cherokees despite the opposition of their governing authorities.

Leonard Sweet in his history of the female seminary movement argues that for Protestant women "the principal sphere of usefulness was the home," but he clarifies that, theoretically at least, usefulness as a concept was more closely concerned with evangelism, with both linked to the pressing millenarianism of the nineteenth century.[35] Convinced that Christ's Second Coming was imminent, believers felt they needed to make ready the way with all due haste. Sweet writes, "Usefulness, while it included the component of the home and family, was defined primarily in terms of building the kingdom of God on earth."[36] Others echo this explanation of usefulness as proselytizing.[37] Brown, too, seems to share this sense, seen in her connection of "doing good" or "being useful" with her sorrow "for my Cherokee brothers and sisters, when I consider their awful situation while out of Christ."[38] The belief that the end of the world was at hand assuredly lent some immediacy to Brown's conversion efforts, just as it did to the missionaries', many of whom believed their labors uniting the nations under Christ could hasten the longed-for day.

The prospect of deliverance must have been attractive to many Cherokees like Brown, beset as they were with political troubles and plagued by recurrent epidemics of smallpox, measles, and other diseases. During the years of Brown's life, tuberculosis especially imperiled the Cherokees—no fewer than three of the Browns died of it, including Catharine. Elias Boudinot wondered if the "Cherokee Nation is destined to fall by this Instrument of Death."[39] Brown also might well have been motivated by the religious vacuum emerging from the medicine men's loss of spiritual authority, pushing her and other women to become spiritually useful. In addition, the Cherokees' worsening political conditions as they attempted to protect their borders against illegally encroaching white settlers and the United States' attempts to remove them west no doubt added a social dimension to her idea of utility. When Brown's memoir was published in 1824, the year after her death, the Cherokees had only just escaped the second removal crisis of 1819 at the cost of some four million acres—more than a quarter of their remaining land—when they were confronted by still more requests for cessions by President Adams's administration, whose term-long machinations set the stage for the final theft carried out under Jackson.[40] The perennial demands for land, the attacks on persons, the designs on cultural and political cohesion, and the ubiquity of death that Brown directly experienced—such conditions persuaded her father to join the Old Settler emigrants to Arkansas before the Trail of Tears—help contextualize the desperate urgency in her oft-expressed desires that she and her family "do good" and "be useful" to their people.

Conversion to Christianity in this intricate and perilous historical context not only provided a metaphysical satisfaction in working for the sake of others' souls and Christ's earthly kingdom, but it also supplied evidence for a practical political and ethical argument that would testify to the civilizability and civility of the Cherokee. Much as immigration apologists must take pains to prove the obvious, that Mexican people *do* work and Muslim people by and large are *not* suicide bombers, Cherokees felt compelled to counter their stereotypical, "scientific" categorization as savage or barbarian, below and therefore without the rights of civilized people, the force of which sanctioned a trove of oppressive actions. The acceptance of Christianity, the pursuit of education, and the adoption of "civilized," Euro-American ways of life, labor, and society were to warrant against accusations of savagery that denounced Indian interest in the land as an imperfect right of occupancy only. Removing a group of savages could be justified as benevolent protection, but removing a civilized people could only be seen as robbery. While conversion might indeed result from spiritual epiphanies, it also emerges as a strategy by which women both create communities of novel shapes and enter those communities' gendered and social critiques into the political and legal discourses from which state-centric forces were at pains to remove them.

Despite Brown's social focus, Perdue sees in her conversion a disconnect between her need for integration with the community and the community's willingness to extend it: "At the same time that she sought and found community in her new faith, conversion drove a wedge between her and the vast majority of Cherokees. . . . Instead of uniting her people through Christianity, Catharine found herself estranged from many of them because of her faith."[41] Although Perdue in this essay, the last of Perdue's pieces on Brown, suggests that Brown's conversion to Christianity did not effect total erasure of Cherokee culture, her insistence on structuring the juncture of Christianity and Cherokee culture as antagonistic passes over a great deal of the complexity of Brown's and other converts' experiences. A number of Cherokees opposed to increased contact with Euro-Americans generally and the missionary project specifically would no doubt have ostracized her, but many others in fact welcomed her. Anderson records, "Catharine and David were employing themselves diligently at Brainerd. Once, in particular . . . these two young Cherokees, aided by a pious Indian woman of great age, collected a little group of their people, who had come to spend the Sabbath there, and held a religious conference, with prayer and praise, all in the Cherokee language."[42] Not long before her death, Brown spoke to Laura Potter, wife of missionary William, of her work with local Cherokee women: "I have no desire to live in this world, but to do good. But God can carry on his work without me. I hope you will continue the meetings of females. You must not be discouraged. I thought when I should get to the Arkansas, I would form a society among the females, like ours. But I shall never live to get there."[43] Perhaps Brown, in her hope that the meetings of women would carry on, foresaw that the women would soon be in the best position to provide for Cherokees' religious and spiritual needs.

Her transversal of Christian and Cherokee communities through her organization of gendered religious societies set a precedent for female superintendence of religion that would in short time become the dominant pattern in Cherokee society. That pattern in many ways perseveres in Christian Cherokee groups today, where women are the backbone of the communities that provide religious "usefulness" to the greatest number of Cherokees, through spiritual support, material assistance, cultural continuity, and more. Like the majority of women who would follow her in conversion, Brown was also committed to the survivance of *her* people and their ways of life, whether in their eastern homelands or in the West. Though she desperately sought to stay with the missionaries at Brainerd and not to go to the Arkansas territory with her family who joined other Old Settlers out west some two decades before the Trail of Tears, she implicitly belies the assumption—because she has firsthand knowledge to the contrary—that removal was tantamount to death. Though circumstances away from home were difficult and dangerous and countless reasons discouraged leaving, Cherokees if compelled could live—were living—in far-off places and were still Cherokees there.

Perdue's suggestion that Brown's evangelism was a relative failure expects a great deal of a woman who died at twenty-three, in the earliest stages of proselytizing in Cherokee country. Considering the prominence of Christianity among Cherokee people today, Brown's evangelical work could easily be reframed as part of a larger traditionalist circuit, in which she appears more an innovator than an anomaly, especially given her age in a community that generally looks to elders for spiritual guidance. Perdue also normalizes both Cherokee and Christian religion, which for her "stood at odds . . . on fundamental issues. Cherokee religion promoted cosmic balance, not sacred hierarchy, and community welfare, not individual salvation."[44] Cherokee religion was incorporated in the daily lives of individuals and was therefore largely an individual or local experience, guided by certain commonly held tenets.[45] Central among these was, as Perdue and others note, the well-being of the group. But were the missionaries, such as Samuel Worcester, Daniel Butrick, and others with whom Brown lived and studied, indeed preaching sacred hierarchy and abandonment of the community? These men who put their lives on the line to advocate for Cherokee people, Worcester in a Georgia prison cell and Butrick traveling with Cherokee people on the Trail of Tears? Brown certainly did not take from them such a message. She writes, "O may I be enabled to follow the example of my teachers, to live near the Saviour, and to do much good. I wish very much to be a missionary among my people. If I had an education—but perhaps I ought not to think of it. I am not worthy to be a missionary."[46] The good she sought to do, which she saw lived out by the missionaries, was to work as a Cherokee missionary to Cherokees for their sake—and their most pressing needs surrounded the political and social removal crisis, which she and her family would well have understood, several of them already having joined the Old Settlers in Arkansas.

THE POLITICS OF RELIGION

Such political and social concerns are rarely overtly addressed in the letters and diary entries that Anderson assembled in the *Memoir of Catharine Brown*, but they so haunt the collection that in many ways it is itself an expression of political solidarity with Cherokee people and a defense of righteous treatment for them. The rhetorical figure of ellipsis, or the omission of grammatical or conceptual elements, characterizes Brown's anxiety, as in her lamentation, "Frequently do I weep for my Cherokee brothers and sisters, when I consider their awful situation while out of Christ."[47] The conventional consequence of being "out of Christ" or "wander[ing] in darkness," another allusive phase she commonly employs, is of course damnation, but she seldom arrives at such forceful language. She does at one point, however, articulate a fear of "eternal destruction" for her "poor Cherokee brethren and sisters, who do not know the blessed Jesus."[48] Her use of ellipsis, however, leaves open other possibilities of not being Christian. These, I argue, include this-world fallout authorized by the logic that the United States need not recognize the rights to life, limb, or property of "savages"—an appellation coextensive with "heathen" or non-Christian. Being useful thus entailed laboring for the Cherokees' good not just in the next world but also in this one. Her letters not only advocate the political expediency of conversion, but they also reprove the nation afflicting the neophyte Cherokee attempting to grow in the faith, though that chiding is done with great rhetorical subtlety.

Brown levels such a political critique in her reference to Isaac Watts's hymn "The Song of Moses and the Lamb: Or, Babylon Falling" in her closing of a letter to a missionary's wife: "And now, my dear sister, may we both be faithful to our Lord, and do much in the world. And when time with us shall be no more, may we be permitted to meet in that world, where Christians will be collected to sing through eternity the song of Moses and the Lamb."[49] Brown leaves unspoken two of the hymn's stanzas proclaiming the sinfulness of nations and their impending punishment:

> Who dares refuse to fear thy name,
> Or worship at thy throne!
> Thy judgments speak thy holiness
> Thro' all the nations known.
>
> Great Babylon, that rules the earth,
> Drunk with the martyr's blood,
> Her crimes shall speedily awake
> The fury of our God.[50]

While the Cherokee nation, if it dared refuse to proclaim itself Christian would surely suffer God's fury, no less would the United States. Cast in this light, the Americans become persecutors of the faith, whose crimes were with every added convert committed against Christian Indians, now become martyrs. To be sure, by the early nineteenth century it was no longer the Cherokees who were spilling the most blood. Brown thus appropriates Christianity and claims the moral high ground for the Cherokees. Though there is some almost-but-not-quite mimicry in Brown's missionary-taught language, she speaks here not with a difference of deficiency, but rather with a tacit assertion of superiority, saying in effect that those saving souls and laboring for others' social and material needs, and patently not those preying upon others, are the true Christians. In the comparison to Babylon, on the other hand, the Americans invite their own destruction and damnation through their wanton viciousness. Similar rhetorical tactics in which Indians are cast as the long-suffering, righteous meek can be found in many other religious writers such as Elias Boudinot, William Appess, Samson Occom, and more. Such examples provide a deeper historical context for Andrea Smith's provocative theorizations of alliances among contemporary Indian female activists and Christian fundamentalists in her recent *Native Americans and the Christian Right*.[51]

Perhaps Brown was more forthright in her indictments of U.S. policy in other instances not included in the *Memoir*. Anderson might have thought such direct political critique coming from an Indian woman impolitic or inexpedient and so muffled Brown's voice. In his gloss, though, he does articulate in two instances an explicitly polemical position in a harmonious counterpoint to Brown's voice, uncommon to such mediated, double-voiced narratives. In the first case he recalls an eastern lecture series given in 1824 by Catharine's brother, David Brown, who was studying at the Andover seminary: "The addresses, which he delivered in many of our principal towns and cities, on the wrongs and claims and prospects of the American Indians, will not soon be forgotten by those who listened to them."[52] The second, delivered in the closing commentary, urges conversion as the most direct means of righting those wrongs and allaying the troubles besetting not just the Cherokees but Indians in general: "Various unpropitious causes press heavily upon the poor Indians; and it is believed, that nothing will save them from extinction, as a people, but the general prevalence of true religion. All things else will be vain without this. . . . Bring this religion to act strongly upon the Indians. Give them the full enjoyment of Christian ordinances. Then their 'winter will be past, the rain will be over and gone.' Agriculture, art, science, legislation, and literature, the germs of which already appear, will grow in rich luxuriance, and the Indian character will be respected by the nations of the earth."[53] Conversion here is made both a sacred and secular means of salvation, the former undiluted by the latter. That evangelism entails positive political effects is rather indicative of its rightness. Just as striking as this politicization of conservative religion for a progressive cause is that Christianization is urged not as means of unadulterated assimilation but as a strategy by which Indians might retain their sovereignty and distinctness as a people, their "Indian character." Undoubtedly the missionaries would have advocated Euro-American cultural and political ways as nearly universally superior, but they left more room for difference than they are generally given credit for.

One reason for the lack of clear denunciation of U.S. Indian policy in the *Memoir* was surely that that critique was to some extent understood by the audience. Despite its ostensibly apolitical official position, the ABCFM made clear by its actions, interests in Cherokee education and civilization, opposition to removal, and in its general purpose that it would break with government policy and stand with American Indians when it believed that policy contrary to its work or the tribes' best interests. During the removal crisis of 1819, ABCFM representatives even assisted the Cherokees during treaty negotiations in Washington as they fended off expulsion.[54] The ongoing depredations by encroaching white settlers experienced by Cherokees living near the national borders, like Brown and her family, are referenced in the *Memoir.* Anderson recounts her father's motive for moving his family to Arkansas: "The old grey-headed man, with tears in his eyes, said he must go over the Mississippi. The white people would not suffer him to live here. They had stolen his cattle, horses, and hogs, until he had very little left."[55] Brown's willingness to distinguish between the whites at Brainerd and those stealing her family's property and safety is remarkable. In recording the crimes committed by white settlers and the civilized response of Indian converts, Anderson mounts a definite critique of the federal government's failure to protect the Cherokees, as agreed to by treaty, though the criticism is largely implicit.

Because much of their funding came from federal sources, mission boards had to be careful in appearances, but individual missionaries like the Congregationalists Samuel Worcester and Elizur Butler and the Baptists Evan and John Jones often risked a great deal in their support for Cherokee political and social issues. Opposing Jacksonian removal, several ABCFM missionaries together with Evan Jones and two others from the United Brethren signed a joint resolution published in the *Cherokee Phoenix* that proclaimed, "Resolved, that we view the Indian Question, at present so much agitated in the United States, as being not merely of a political, but of a moral nature—inasmuch as it involves the maintenance or the violation of the faith of our country. . . . Resolved, therefore, that we view the removal of this people to the West of the Mississippi as an event to be most earnestly deprecated."[56] Their statement further implicates the political with the religious, the religious with the political. Later in the crisis the ABCFM left the decision to sign Georgia's oath pledging allegiance to the state up to individual missionaries, but intimated that it would financially and legally back any missionary willing to challenge the edict and, by extension, Georgia's jurisdiction over Cherokee territory. Taking up the cause, Worcester and Butler spent more than a year at hard labor in a Georgia prison waiting for the Supreme Court to render its unenforced decision in *Worcester v. Georgia*, which declared the states had no power over semisovereign Indian land, before following the ABCFM's lead and giving up the cause.[57]

Though initially supportive of Jacksonian removal, the Baptist mission board came to side with Evan Jones, who did all he knew how to do in opposition, authoring petitions and anonymous tracts as well as speaking at Cherokee councils, in Cherokee.[58] He went so far as abetting if not leading a vote among his congregation that condemned the fraudulent signing of the New Echota treaty, which authorized the sale of eastern lands and removal, and excluded the signers from fellowship. Of this move, also taken by ABCFM missionary Daniel Butrick, McLoughlin writes, "Nothing marks more clearly the politicization of religion in this crisis. It also indicates how closely missionaries such as Butrick and Jones had come to view politics and Christianity from the Cherokees' perspective."[59] Neither would removal spell the end of missionaries' involvement in Cherokee politics. As an abolitionist Jones would go on to play a role in the organization of the Keetoowah Society, which was simultaneously social, cultural, and political in its factional traditionalism, and in later years his son, John, also a missionary, advocated for the Cherokees as a federal agent and spoke out against allotment.[60]

For Baptist and ABCFM missionaries, pragmatic mission work was most productive in gaining converts when it was consonant with the Cherokees' own goals and methods of attaining them. While it should not need repeating that advocacy for Cherokees' educational, material, political, and cultural goals originated not with missionaries but with Cherokees themselves, nor that the sacrifices made by Cherokee people during the era dwarfed those made by missionaries, the importance of the missionaries' volitional choices cannot be overemphasized. Though some critics have broadly painted the missionaries' goals and methods as oppositional to Cherokee culture—arguing, as Bethany Schneider recently has, "that going to that holy place," in other words, converting to Christianity, "entails the renunciation of culture, language, nation and life itself"—exception upon exception calls that rule into question.[61] Several missionaries' interest in oral traditions, the communal atmosphere of camp meetings and the group labor employed at them, the eventual acceptance of medicine men into Christian fellowship, and the parallels between the Cherokee purification going-to-water ceremony and Christian baptism have all been seen as intersections between Cherokee and Christian pathways that enabled later enduring blendings.[62] Language figures prominently in two other intersections that historian William McLoughlin argues worked most forcefully to make Christianity a viable option for Cherokees: the training and subsequent efforts of Native ministers who preached in Cherokee, and the translation of the Bible into Cherokee.[63]

The Cherokees' desire for and the steps they took to establish schools, discussed in the previous chapter, represent another consonant interest for Cherokees and Christians that also touches on the question of language. Missionary schools in their instructional methods employed Cherokee more often than we might suspect. Given the affinity between language and cultural ways of knowing, the missionaries' indulgence and sometimes their use of the Cherokee language bears closer investigation. While McLoughlin writes of the ABCFM schools, "Their missionaries made little effort to learn Cherokee . . . [and] none of the teachers thought it necessary to employ interpreters or try bilingual education," the translation and publication of the Bible and other material certainly represented an attempt at bilingual education, if not in a classroom setting certainly in wider society.[64] Both Samuel Worcester, who wrote several articles on the language for the *Cherokee Phoenix*, and Daniel Butrick showed great interest in learning Cherokee, even if neither ever mastered it.[65] Worcester in particular was enthralled by the complexity and expressiveness of Cherokee and worked closely with Elias Boudinot on getting the language into print by adapting the syllabary to work more easily with a printing press. In the diary of the Moravian mission, Anna Gambold recounts explaining to a visitor who discouraged the missionaries from bothering to learn Cherokee, "However, we told this dear and well-meaning man that we believed if one heathen of this nation is actually awakened in his heart through the Spirit of God, Who knows enough means and ways to work in the souls of humans, it could happen that such a person might be in a position to express his ideas. The mouth passes these on though they are still foreign, because the heart is full. He accepted this."[66]

As Rufus Anderson notes, Cherokees like Catharine and David Brown and John Arch provided translation services and conducted prayer and study in Cherokee.[67] In light of Anderson's approving (if patronizing) tone discussing the Browns' leadership of "a little group of their people" who were praying and praising "all in the Cherokee language," and David Brown's statement that he would "sometimes preach myself in the sweet language of Tsallakee," it seems likely that Catharine Brown would have taught more than a little in Cherokee when she headed the school at Creek Path.[68] The ABCFM missionaries likely approved of her doing so. The Brainerd mission school's journal contains an entry recommending Catharine Brown for the teaching job at Creek Path that puts it most plainly: "I think it would be well for her to come as she can talk & there will be no good interpreter."[69]

As another exception to the rule of Christian education opposing Cherokee language and traditions, the Baptist preacher Evan Jones's case is even more complicated. McLoughlin writes:

> Although the Joneses were committed to bilingual education, the Cherokee council ruled that its public school system (adopted in 1841), supported by Cherokee funds and taught by Cherokee teachers

> (all mixed-bloods), must be taught in English. Not until after John Ross's death in 1866 were the Joneses able to persuade the council to try their plan. In 1866, the council adopted a series of bilingual textbooks in arithmetic, geography, and history that were to be written by John Jones and published on the Baptist printing press. . . . Unfortunately, the Cherokee Nation lacked the funds to implement this plan fully. It was strongly opposed by the wealthier English-speaking parents who wanted nothing to do with the old language.[70]

Mixed-bloods, it appears, can be held responsible for any evil. Even though John Ross was purportedly the champion of the full-bloods and headed the government that included the National Council, which was controlled by full-bloods as late as 1861, he opposed teaching Cherokee youth how to communicate in their language.[71] Is this a traditionalist value? Meanwhile, representatives of assimilation like Elias Boudinot editorialized in Cherokee, Samuel Worcester disseminated the Sequoyah syllabary, Catharine Brown taught activist usefulness, and Evan Jones preached the Gospel in Cherokee.

ADAPTATION AND EXCLUSION

Ross, however, was plainly more than a simple opponent of Cherokee language, as shown by his use of translators for national addresses, for example. He and the council leaders undoubtedly sought to offer future leaders the best academic preparation they could get, perhaps thinking they could pick up Cherokee after class. My point is not to tarnish traditionalists' reputations but that each of these Cherokee people and Cherokee allies worked as best as they knew how for the people's survivance in complex situations with competing demands. They might have been more or less effective, and in some places destructive, true, and scholarship has a responsibility to analyze and critique what worked better and what worse. But we should understand that this pattern of criticizing mixed-bloods or assimilation advocates for all sorts of ills—really, for being mixed-bloods—like the binaristic opposition of Christian and Indian, says as much about contemporary scholarship's own attitudes as it does about history, culture, or literature. And what it says is that many are prepossessed with circumscribed and defeating notions of what Indians may do for themselves, often pulling up short at changes in education, exploration, worship, or anything that appears to drift too far from a contained and often romanticized idea of the past.

Such a limited historical focus should clue us in that some powerful normalizing forces are at work in describing Cherokee community in the early 1800s. This division of the population marginalizes Christian Cherokees of all degrees of blood. Cherokee converts were an important and growing component of Cherokee society, both in the East and among the Old Settlers in Arkansas. Though Catharine Brown dreaded the prospect of going to Arkansas, concern for the welfare of the Cherokees there motivated her to help organize a women's charitable society that contributed to its mission station, indicating the support she found for her evangelizing.[72] Of Brown's impending move to run the new Cherokee school in Alabama, Anderson writes, "When it was known at Creek-Path, that she was to take charge of the school, the most enthusiastic joy was occasioned among the people. They seemed to feel that the preparations could not be made too soon. Not less than fifty Cherokee men, besides negroes and boys, assembled immediately to build a house, which, in two days, was nearly completed according to their stipulation."[73] Through such steps, Cherokee people reformulated their educational models to work most effectively in their circumstances while retaining the character of local, self-directing, and self-perpetuating (that is, indigenous anarchist) communities.

If there was indeed a "wedge," as Perdue has it, lodged between Brown and the Cherokee communities of her time—local communities in independent charge of their affairs—they seem to have worked around it. Brown, like other missionary educators, would have served at the pleasure of the community; that she stayed at Creek Path for nine months speaks as much of the agency of the indigenist anarchistic collective as of missionary zealotry. Her tenure at the school resembles the community vetting of new knowledge discussed in chapter 1. Having gone out to gain knowledge from the missionaries at the Brainerd school, Brown returns to Cherokee people to demonstrate what she has learned and to offer them the opportunity to accept, reject, or modify the information she offers, as they see fit. A similar process is acted out more locally among Brown and her immediate family members. That Anderson's political agenda results in selective information must be kept in mind, however, for he might exaggerate the response to the school or equivocate the greater enthusiasm for education than for Christianization. Anderson might also have downplayed Brown's continuing ties to community or traditional practices, either by choosing to omit materials such as the story of her dream or by simply not being able to understand what he saw before him.

Besides seeing only what they expected to see, some of the missionaries at Brainerd neglected to question their narrow, culturally determined definitions of what constituted spirituality. Brown retained and practiced more traditional Cherokee spirituality than we have suspected, I believe, such as when she periodically left the mission to pray alone. Anderson records the illustrative narrative of Laura Potter: "In the warm season of the year, the adjacent woods was the place of her retirement. She not unfrequently spent whole days in fasting and prayer. One fine summer's day, she had been absent nearly all the forenoon in the woods, and . . . I felt anxious for her safety. . . . She returned, expressing much concern that she had caused me so much anxiety, and added, that she was sorry she had not told me of her intention to pass that day in the mountain."[74] Describing the preferred sites for Keetoowahs' deliberative meetings, modern Keetoowah leader Benny Smith affirms the traditionalist propensity to go to "high mountains seeking revelation from heaven . . . usually in the woods and preferably on a mountain. The main requisite was for it to be a still, quiet place away from interrupting activities."[75] Joel Martin, too, argues that Brown seems to have shared this traditionalist proclivity to worship in the mountains.[76]

In her later, more thorough piece on Brown, Perdue does see Brown's retention of Cherokee tradition in her reclusion in nature and her uncommon and frequent fasting. Perdue writes, "Even in her biography, written primarily to convince potential contributors of the efficacy of Indian missions, evidence emerges that calls into question the missionaries' success in the complete eradication of Native culture. . . . There are no clear examples of apostasy. Instead, we have ambiguous practices that probably represent a blending of

Cherokee and Christian beliefs."[77] Ross Johnston concurs: "Although she was a Christian convert, she also continued traditional Cherokee practices such as fasting, and she participated in women's prayer groups, often in the forests and mountains. Brown and her parents continued to enlist the help of traditional healers. Thus, she may have retained more of her Cherokee beliefs and been less acculturated than the missionaries' account claimed."[78] These are but a few of the traditionalist dispositions that we can see that Brown enacted; many more are likely invisible to us from such a historical remove. Though there may be a threshold beyond which adaptation becomes not blending but assimilation, given such examples of retained traditional practices, it is not clear that Brown crossed it, whose past or present authority established it, nor what quality it would measure.

Like the missionaries, contemporary scholars may see only what is familiar to them. In the anthology *Native American Autobiography*, Arnold Krupat writes of Catharine Brown, "We will not learn of Cherokee lifeways in the early nineteenth century from Catharine Brown. But hers, too, is a Native American life, one that needs to be taken into account in any generalizations we would make about Native people in the Americas."[79] The implicit assumption here is that Brown's Christian conversion renders her not-Cherokee, although she can still be "Native American" in some vague way. What besides Cherokee lifeways do Brown's inexhaustible concern for community, especially women, her outdoors worship, her fasting, her interpretation of Christian precepts through Cherokee cultural symbols, and her worship in the Cherokee language teach us? Craig Womack offers an alternative way of thinking about religious change: "When an Indian converts to Christianity, not all of him gets converted, no matter how thorough his newfound convictions."[80] That part remaining—which for some might well be the entire web of principled practices, in addition to new additions—is best understood from a cultural perspective as familiar as possible with tribal epistemologies and prepared to see in educational dispositions such as gaining knowledge programs of development instead of displacement.

Brown drew power from dispositions of many communities to which she belonged, including her family, Christian friends, Cherokee traditionalists, educators, women, and more, many of them in difficult contention. In her conversion, her teaching at the girls' school at

Creek Path, and throughout her brief life, Brown assembled a complicated identity, but it was not solely assembled from her individual labor. Communal (and nonstatist, by the way) agency is central to this interaction: the school at Creek Path would not have existed had the people of the town not built it and had the surrounding communities not elected to invite the missionaries to Cherokee country. The missionaries, too, served at the pleasure of the communities.[81] Clearly, if Brown hoped to keep her post, she needed to attend carefully to the expectations of the Cherokee families with students at the school and to those of the Cherokee political leaders. The administrators of the Brainerd school no doubt had expectations of Brown and the school occasionally at odds with those of the community, and the expectations of the Cherokee girls and mothers must have contrasted sharply at times with those of the white women at Brainerd—that Cherokees and missionaries sometimes crossed paths does not mean, however, that they were unable to find common ground.[82]

Gender, race, and religion move in conjunction in Brown's dream of evangelizing to Cherokee women living west of the Mississippi, if she were bound to go there. For her, a community of women—Cherokee, Christian, Women—was of abiding importance as a source of much-needed spiritual and physical strength in desperate and dangerous times for Cherokee people, during which their traditional religion was for a multitude of reasons providing less support to increasingly fewer people. This erosion was not total, however, insofar as traditional principles and practices directly and indirectly continued to inform politics, attitudes toward community, gender roles, and Christianity itself.

Stories of the first woman, Selu, reinforce the traditional centrality of women's power. Selu is the Corn Mother, without whose gift of corn, the Cherokee would not be.[83] As Perdue notes, Cherokee women played important, powerful roles in traditional communities, which were both matrilineal and matrilocal, and women also participated in governance and warfare. They were responsible for a great deal of labor and retained control of property and children during marriage and in the event of divorce, which they could initiate; men not wishing to be divorced had little recourse. Women also retained control over sexual and reproductive matters.[84] In short, Cherokee women were well accustomed to power over affairs we might now understand as political and outside of female social jurisdiction. They formed strong communal ties among themselves in extended kinship and political networks, often stronger than those they formed with men. As their example demonstrates, a multitude of sociopolitical powers can well be administered in forms alternative to the nation-state, and they thus offer another powerful example of indigenous anarchistic organization in action. Catharine Brown's religious and educational work with Cherokee girls and her dream of continuing that work issue from her immersion in dispositions connected to Cherokee gender. Christianity offered her a means of strengthening Cherokee communities, especially the women, to whom she was closer than to the men, and of helping them in their efforts to maintain their fellowship, powers, lands, and identities.

ᏅᎩ

CHAPTER 3

GATHERING STRENGTH IN SEQUOYAH GUESS'S *KHOLVN*

Like Catharine Brown with her connections among traditionalists, Christians, women, locals, expatriates, and more, an array of affiliations also characterizes the work of self-publishing author Sequoyah Guess. The authorial description in his novel *Kholvn* offers a succinct, pertinent biography: "Sequoyah Guess is a full blood Keetoowah/ Cherokee and a Traditional Storyteller. He has served as Chairman for the Historical Preservation Committee and senior Cultural Site Investigator for the United Keetoowah Band of Cherokee Indians in Oklahoma. He still serves as a consultant to the Historical Preservation Office of the UKB. He's a member of the Seven Clans of the Fire Cultural Camp committee and the infamous Turtle Island Liars Club. *Kholvn* is his first novel. He also produced, directed and wrote the script for the made-for-video movie version of this book in 1993–1994. It was the first movie to ever be produced entirely by Native Americans."[1] While he might not have a lucrative book contract, Guess is certainly possessed of a great deal of cultural capital. He is frequently called upon by both the Cherokee Nation and the United Keetoowah Band of Cherokee Indians (the UKB, of which he is a citizen) to tell stories at national events; by local universities to lecture on Cherokee traditions; by film festivals, museums, and so forth. He has been nominated as a Living Treasure by the Cherokee

Nation and the affiliated museum, not least for the artistic and cultural services he has rendered, including his instruction in the Cherokee language, his seven novels, a practical Cherokee language book, and a collection of traditional stories passed on to him by his grandmother.[2] Also a sixth-generation descendent of Sequoyah, he is, in common parlance, a traditionalist.

His first novel, *Kholvn*, published in 1992, is named for the monstrosity of Cherokee tradition, the ravenmocker, a cannibalistic witch who prolongs its own life by shortening those of its victims. The narrative begins with its ordinary-people protagonists scattered across the United States. The major characters are Cody Clearwater, a Cherokee Baptist preacher living in New Mexico with Navajo people; Ira Jammer, a Cherokee tribal policeman working in South Dakota with Lakota folks; Morgan Booker, a white woman and former love interest of Clearwater in Tennessee; and Summer Moccasin, a young Keetoowah traditionalist together with her grandfather George Autumn of Cherokee-country Oklahoma. The characters' names carry their own culturally dense symbology. For instance, the preacher Clearwater needs just that for his baptizing, and Summer Moccasin walks the White Path. After all have dreams or visions prompting them to return to their fictional hometown of Herald in northeastern Oklahoma, they assemble and are confronted with Henry Longbush. In the backstory, Longbush is a medicine man unhinged by the arson-caused deaths of his wife and children. Though he has lost his sanity, he has gained the powers of the ravenmocker. Blaming the people of Herald for his family's deaths, he is rapidly consuming townsfolks' livers, the means by which he steals their remaining days, and it falls to the collected heroes to defeat the evil that even other witches fear.

To help illustrate the deficiencies of reckoning identity according to the tired traditionalist/progressive or full-blood/mixed-blood dichotomies, this chapter follows up Brown's *Memoir* with Guess's modern fiction works that narrate traditionally progressive Cherokee dispositions, especially those related to worship, and that defy binaristic logic. Like Brown's *Memoir*, *Kholvn*'s representations of the complexities of Cherokee life demonstrate that the varieties of identity-related principled practices cannot accurately or usefully be described with such narrow options. Some of the parallel practices in the *Memoir* and *Kholvn* include praying and smoking, dreaming and listening for the Holy Spirit, and going to water and baptizing. We'd also have trouble splitting similarly harmonious principles of worship, love, charity, faith, and righteousness into easy "white" or "Indian" columns. All of these are in addition to cultural principles and practices like the communal vetting affiliated with gaining knowledge, political and material inflections of usefulness, and the mediation of meaning through the Cherokee language. Assembled together, these several principled practices (though a paltry sample in comparison to the multitude contained within the habitus) operating among several different Cherokee communities begin to suggest that the very diversity of dispositions is itself a strength, and one that well serves cooperative groups imagining ways of handling problems not related to the nation-state. Though it is not overtly discussed in either *Kholvn* or the *Memoir*, a pluralism of effective problem-solving tactics emerges as a traditional metastrategy of long and privileged standing. Some of these component tactics may promote change, while others reject it; some may recall traditions long unused or nearly forgotten; still others might improve both traditional and progressive ways of thinking by fusing what is best in each. Such is Brown's and Guess's religiously minded pluralist pragmatism.

KEETOOWAHS AND CHRISTIANS

Some historical circumstances that set up Guess's writing include the revival of traditionalist practices and beliefs that attended the rejuvenation of the stomp dance and Keetoowah Society in Cherokee country near the turn of the twentieth century. As an organization characterized in its various historical moments by voluntary affiliation and confederation (with other stomp dance societies, for example), consensus-based decision making, veneration for tradition, opposition to the state, respect for in-group and out-group diversity, participatory operation, and agrarian practices, among other dispositions, Keetoowah societies exemplify the indigenous anarchism I have been playing up in *Progressive Traditions*. According to oral history, the Keetoowah Society dates back to the earliest of times in the eastern homelands, with the word *Keetoowah* sometimes used synonymously to refer to Cherokee people. Mooney writes, "A strong band of comradeship, if not a regular society organization, appears to have existed among the warriors and leading men of the various settlements of the Kituhwa district from a remote period."[3] Leading up to the Civil War, the abolitionist missionaries Evan and John Jones played some role in helping reorganize the society, which then was composed primarily of conservative full-bloods, to whatever extent those descriptors can describe, who opposed too-rapid acculturation, especially manifested in slavery and alliance with the Confederacy.

The Society seems to have waned somewhat in the years following the Civil War, but in the 1890s, Cherokee traditionalists found great cause for concern as they were confronted with the federal government's allotment policy, and they again reformulated the Keetoowah Society as a cultural, political, and religious collective brought together not least to oppose the U.S. state-sponsored breakup of the tribe's government and lands. To confront America's ongoing "Indian problem"—a euphemism that referred to Indians' lack of opportunity, lack of representation, lack of resources, and America's lack of Indian-owned land—many paternalistic sympathizers such as the Friends of the Indian resurrected the Jeffersonian assimilation policy with a vengeance and lobbied for the termination of tribal governments, the breaking up of reservations, the dissolution of common title to lands and their dispersal in individual allotments, with surplus lands going to white settlers. The Dawes Act, the legislation authorizing such measures, passed Congress in 1887, and the Dawes Commission arrived in Cherokee country in 1894 to begin negotiating for what threatened to be the end of tribal life. Although many Oklahoma tribes fended off the Dawes Act measures for several years, the Curtis Act of 1898 effectively spelled the end of Indian Territory and national tribal autonomy until the Indian Reorganization Act of 1934.

According to Robert Thomas in his 1953 history of the Keetoowah Society, Cherokee traditionalists to some extent blamed themselves for the negative changes heading their way, believing they had failed to uphold God's laws. They therefore took steps to bring themselves and their followers religiously and culturally back into favor by recovering "what the Ketoowahs had lost."[4] They set about this project according to established dispositions of gaining knowledge and community vetting, discussed in earlier chapters. Thomas describes several instances in which changes were not implemented until a committee of elders came to a collective consensus about the meaning of an individual's vision or idea and an agreement that it accorded with what the group understood to be distinctively Cherokee ways of thinking, doing, and being.

As early as 1889, several traditionalists including Bluford Sixkiller, Ned Bullfrog, "Old Man" Chewey, and George Benge, together with Redbird Smith, met as a body to reconsider the purpose of the Keetoowah Society. They reasserted that it was primarily religious, perhaps in an attempt to distance the organization from political troubles that had plagued it in the past. Despite their efforts, politics would continue to beleaguer the organization, and sometime around 1898 a split over how best to confront allotment would splinter it into the Keetoowah Society, the political forerunner of the UKB; and the Nighthawk Keetoowah Society, the religious stomp dance worshippers.[5] For his prominent leadership role, Redbird Smith is so closely associated with the Nighthawk revitalization movement that many historians have given it his name, but as Thomas has emphasized, several people before Smith's time played a role in bringing about the conditions under which his work prospered. Not all of them were even Cherokee. Redbird Smith's father, Pig Smith, prepared his son for superintending Cherokee traditions by sending him to live and study with a man known as Creek Sam, who Thomas reports was part Cherokee but primarily identified as a Natchez Indian. The Natchez in general and Creek Sam in particular were recognized as keepers of the southeastern Indians' cultural traditions. Smith and the other committee members also drew on the Creeks' knowledge of old stomp dance customs and beliefs, both their own and the Cherokees'.[6]

This scenario invites a cosmopolitanist interpretation of the hybridity of identities, even those held up as the most traditional or removed from out-group contamination. Given the fact that Cherokees were never *not* interacting with non-Cherokee people, the idea of unadulterated cultural purity is fictional or at least rhetorical. This goes not just for the Keetoowah Society but also for Cherokee society as far back as it can be traced in both the historical records of the Western written and the Cherokee oral traditions. Ancient migration stories that have Cherokees arriving from the south and east as well as the north, the linguistic connection of Cherokee and Iroquois languages, the commerce with other peoples, the occasional adoption of other individuals and sometimes entire tribes, and more all testify to the fluidity and dynamism of culture, even from its imagined inception.[7] But there *are* pragmatic, observable differences among peoples, and those by and large durable distinctions matter more to peoples' ideas of themselves than the comparatively fewer and more discrete moments of cross-cultural interaction. That Cherokee, Iroquois, Natchez, Creek, American, and British peoples interacted with and influenced each other does not render them identical in their hybridity—why else would they continue to differentiate and call themselves Cherokee, Iroquois, and so forth? Principled practices like gaining knowledge and community vetting demonstrate the habitus tempering and utilizing the effects of external interaction, and also governing change proposed from within.

Above all, theories of hybridity can be prone to an all-or-nothing concept of mixing—a paradoxical idea of homogeneous heterogeneity wherein "we're all mixed." This stance, though it attempts to complicate us-them binaries, yet reinforces a dialectic, suggesting that between purity and adulteration only the latter is possible. But such one-size-fits-all generalizations desperately require attention to the options attending cultural interaction, where communities and individuals may select, reject, alter, preserve, and innovate in all sorts of discrete and special combinations. The failure to discuss agency together with hybridity veils a deterministic sleight of hand that portrays assimilation or mixing as natural and inevitable—not too far a cry from an apologia for colonialism—and out of the hands of its proponents, resisters, or more interestingly, those imagining innovative ways of fulfilling yet-unrealized human potential. That said, while any course may be pursued volitionally, it is doubtless still subject to both the vagaries of force and to unconscious mediation through the habitus, which even though it may have diminished in overt theorization of tradition nevertheless also replicates its own historical dispositions and structuring conditions.

One attempt that the Nighthawk Keetoowah Society revitalization made at regulating religious change was in its constitution's early codified exclusion of Christian worshippers, a practice certainly at odds with the disposition of inclusiveness. The section read: "We shall not have two kinds of religion, only Keetoowah religion, which we worship God, and we shall all be loyal to that. If any person shall join any other religious denomination, he shall forfeit his membership to our Keetoowah Society." A member's application was also to indicate that "he is not a member of any religious denomination. After his acceptance, the secretary shall write his name, if he has any children or just a wife; he shall enroll them giving their age, their clan, showing they were not members of any other religious denomination."[8] Finding this exclusion untenable for whatever reason, perhaps because of the increasing number of Christian converts desiring admittance and already covertly practicing both the Keetoowah and Cherokee religions, or due to the prominence of the Baptist church among Cherokee people, the Society elected to admit Christians to membership. They amended the constitution with a remarkable piece of theological fusion, worth quoting at some length:

> *Concerning the Adoption of Christ, September 16, 1934, Buffalo Town*
> Today, Keetoowah Society of the several towns, seven clan council assembled, hereby amend its constitution so that from now on it shall be this way: thereas, since we find Jesus Christ was born here on earth, the son of God, He shall be accepted by the Keetoowahs. But he shall not be accepted completely according to the Bible. But whereas John the Baptist, has said when he was baptizing some of his followers, "It's true I'm going to baptize you with water now. There's one coming after me who is mightier than I am. I'm not even worthy to bear his shoes. When he comes, he will baptize you with the Holy Ghost and the FIRE." We see furthermore, when Christ came, when he went into Solomon's temple, he found the money exchangers there inside the temple and he drove them out. They had several kinds of animals and birds there for sale, to be used for sacrifice in the fire. He told them, "This is not for to make money. It's for the Lord's work." Also he told them, "I didn't come here to destroy the law. I come here to fulfill it." Therefore, we, the Indians (Keetoowahs) have the FIRE, and the Holy Ghost was given us, and we can see that the taking in of our new members and the escorting of them around the FIRE seven times represents the FIRE Baptism. (Since Christ baptized by fire, he was therefore essentially a Keetoowah, and so he should be accepted in Keetoowah religion.)[9]

There are several relevant religious improvisations in this astonishing passage, which again demonstrates the importance of community vetting, and in this case theorization, of cultural change. To begin, there are some particular religious meanings attached to the prominently featured elements of fire and water that deserve some explanation. Of fire Charles Hudson writes, "The most important Cherokee spirit was the Sun, who was thought to be an old woman. They called her 'grandparent.' She was the source of all warmth and light. Sacred fire was her representative on earth."[10] Note the female gendering of the principal deity—perhaps such a minute difference makes no difference. Or perhaps the personification of the ultimate source of creation as female is not so minute. Mooney does not draw as direct a link between the sun and the fire, but he certainly links the two as the most powerful of deities, together with water. He writes, "The sun is called Une′′lanû′hĭ, 'the apportioner.' . . . Missionaries have naturally, but incorrectly, assumed this apportioner of all things to be the suppositional 'Great Spirit' of the Cherokees, and hence the word is used in the Bible translation as synonymous with God. . . . The sun is invoked chiefly by the ball-player, while the hunter prays to the fire; but every important ceremony—whether connected with medicine, love, hunting, or the ball play—contains a prayer to the 'Long Person,' the formulistic name for water, or, more strictly speaking, for the river."[11] Whether the missionaries and their translators misunderstood or deliberately appropriated the Cherokees' closest deific parallel seems more of an open question than Mooney allows. The invocation of the elemental deities in the Keetoowah constitutional amendment retranslates the adoption of Christianity back into a primarily Cherokee religious vocabulary (even in English), so that the Cherokee-inflected, plain-language summaries of the Gospel message are put into the service of a Cherokee material discourse.

While the elements of Christianity discussed in the amendment may be familiar to Western audiences, their abruptness and seemingly arbitrary sequence (Jesus is God's son, his arrival was foretold by John the Baptist, Christ will baptize with fire, the cleansing of the temple, the fulfillment of the law, the operation of the Holy Ghost) on closer examination reveal a skillful and subtle statement on the possibility and potential of mixing Christian and Keetoowah religions, along with an application of Christianity to immediate Cherokee concerns to illustrate the utility of that combination. The argument leads off by finding Jesus "here on earth," that is, not aloof or abstract but interested in and connected to human interests. Recounting his coming through reference to the prophecy of John the Baptist, the authors of the amendment offer Cherokee readers a relatable figure. The religious Cherokees would likely have witnessed some prophesying at the ceremonial grounds, and John's baptizing in its resemblance to the going-to-water purification ceremony would also have been familiar. If they knew more of biblical teaching, as many undoubtedly did, some might also have found John's bare subsistence on locusts and wild honey while living in the wilderness resonant with their own lives, meager in comparison to more affluent Cherokees and whites. John's preaching of repentance and his rebuke of the Pharisees' legalism and the Sadducees' politicism might too have seemed apropos to the challenges they faced years earlier in resisting allotment, which more than a few Cherokees advocated, if only as an unstoppable expediency. Besides the connection between Jesus and fire that helps to establish his deity, the subsequent baptism by fire brought by Christ represents an eschatological judgment that must have seemed long overdue—and it is the idea of judgment that reveals the passage's hidden logic. For the Cherokees drawing closer to the Creator by walking the White Path, which included the Keetoowah fire baptism, judgment would bring justification; for others, unpurified, something less desirable.[12]

And who are these forsaken? The amendment (again, dated 1934) jumps from discussion of fire baptism to the story of Jesus's expulsion of money changers and sellers of sacrificial animals in the temple, whose commerce exploited those who came to leave offerings and desecrated the place of worship. Their simony closely resembles a problem the Nighthawk Keetoowah faced in the years after allotment culminated in statehood in 1907. Keetoowah elder Benny Smith describes the trouble that arose some time after the Nighthawk split: "The Keetoowahs have been approached a number of times to give up the old cultural ways of worship. Some members, seeing the possibilities of great financial gain, attempted to convert the ceremonials into a paying attraction."[13] By showing Christianity's antimaterialist philosophy established by Jesus's willingness to confront the financially powerful hypocrites, the amendment affirms the nonfungibility of things sacred, which included ceremonies, traditions, and undoubtedly for many, land. The indignation over what the Nighthawk Keetoowahs saw as unlawful and wrongful theft of their lands—their farms, their worship grounds, their schools, their graveyards, barely sixty years after the Trail of Tears, when the nation vowed it would protect and secure the Cherokees' rights—also registered those whites and complicit Cherokees into the roll of the den of thieves who would one day be called to account.

In order to dissolve the cultural and communal attachments that discouraged the individualism that American society claimed to reward, however, the appropriation of Indian lands was again given the appearance of lawfulness and benevolence. The amendment's next segue, to Jesus's assurance that he came not to destroy but to fulfill the law by returning it to its principles rather than its forms, such as the Pharisees manipulated, again speaks to the concerns of Keetoowah people. They felt that the Curtis Act's dissolution of the tribal government without its consent ran contrary to the spirit of the law, if not to its letter. Moreover, well after the allotment of land in severalty, unscrupulous whites were "legally" divesting Cherokees of their holdings by all sorts of devices. Jesus's confirmation of the value of the old law could easily be understood as an acceptance on principle that Indian traditions and laws need not pass away but could instead even provide full complemence, as Crosslin Smith has it, to Christianity and the imperialist nation that styled itself as Christian.

The amendment's assertion that the Keetoowah people are possessed of the fire and the Holy Ghost also claims for them a proper and superior understanding of the spirit of the law. The ambivalence of the phrase "But he shall not be accepted completely according to the Bible," however, betrays a lingering anxiety over the fusion of the Cherokee and Christian religions. Though the amendment asks for no theological contributions from Christianity, enough members were apparently not getting all they needed at home spiritually to prompt the authorization of Christian membership. While the very act of revisiting the constitution implicitly admits the need for modification or supplementation, the amendment provides only for a limited degree of change. But it calls for change from more than one quarter. The indictment of Pharisaic duplicity in the modern era and the appropriative claim to the Holy Ghost as sacred fire go beyond limiting alteration of Keetoowah society to proposing a reciprocal complementarity. That the biblical script cannot be "completely" accepted means Christianity itself stands in need of a supplemental interpretation, an interpretation more complete and better because more aware of the spirit of the law than others that penetrate no deeper than the outward forms. The amendment's intriguing last sentence establishing the Keetoowahness of Christ through the practice of baptism by fire—Cherokee by doing—admits no Keetoowah inferiority to Christianity but instead declares the religion equally as fit to sit in judgment as Jesus. The Keetoowah theorization of religious innovation offers this righteous discernment to Christianity in exchange for the right to admit and retain Christian members.

DISPOSITIONAL DIVERSITY IN *KHOLVN*

The recognition of incompleteness and the occasional acknowledgement of different cultures' discretely held, preferable understandings inform the deliberate pluralism that itself performs a central dispositional strategy for Cherokee culture's maintenance and development. This pluralism as practice is at work in Guess's *Kholvn,* the Keetoowah constitutional amendment, Brown's *Memoir,* and in many indigenous anarchistic communities that need diversity to sustain them. Such "outsourcing" might again recall Partha Chatterjee's identification of how nationalism keeps separate the masculine technological/material and feminine spiritual/cultural worlds, but besides the historical remasculinization of religious leadership seen in the Nighthawk revival, there prevails in Cherokee history a greater conservative tendency toward less severe cultural isolation. While certain beliefs or practices might be inviolable, all that might be considered religious or cultural is not and has not been off-limits, but rather in charge of its own perpetuation and development. Throughout religious, cultural, economic, technological, and other spheres, Cherokees kept up what traditionally worked and supplemented it with select beliefs and practices that worked better, all the while engaged in internal development with internally generated purposes and methods. Long affiliated with stomp dance societies, Guess is undoubtedly familiar with their traditional means of handling change, and his texts often incorporate the theme of pluralism within and without cultural groups as a means of resolving conflict.

In *Kholvn*, disparate groups' coming together against common problems, recognizing their strengths and weaknesses, and admitting their commonality in their mutual worship of a single God emerge as recurrent elements of a moderated pluralism. Almost exactly midway through the novel, Baptist preacher Cody Clearwater and Nighthawk Keetoowah George Autumn, the most forceful spiritual personalities in the narrative, meet for the first time, dramatizing an intra-Cherokee cultural convergence of religious outlooks long in tension. Autumn's granddaughter Summer Moccasin facilitates the meeting of the four major protagonist groups, in a pivotal passage that deserves a lengthy quotation:

> "We were all meant to be here," Summer said and turned to her Grandfather as he spoke again.
>
> "Yowa, our Father in Heaven, has brought each of us to this point," the young woman said.
>
> Cody held up a hand.
>
> "Hold on a second," he said. "Hisvnoyis?"
>
> The old man nodded.
>
> "Jantas Jisa jistawidido gesv?" Cody said asking if the old man knew he was a follower of Jesus.
>
> "Agwantada," George said telling the younger man that he did know all about him. "Hatljadohvsgi. Advsqu. Ejula Edoda Galvdihe gininvsido. Yowa jiyoseho, nihihv Jisa hiyoseho. Asesgina, ejula Edoda enoseho. Uwasvda uwanda doust doyu gesv. Yowa yi-ga. Ale Jisa yiga. Asesgina nigada egidoda."
>
> Summer translated for the rest what the two men had said.
>
> "Are you Nighthawk?
>
> "Do you know that I follow Jesus?"
>
> "Yes, I know you are a preacher. I am also a preacher. We've both been sent by the Creator. I call Him Yowa. You call Him Jesus but we both call Him Father. Only He knows which is truly right. Whether it is Yowa or Jesus. But He's the Father of us all."
>
> "I know the Nighthawks love our Father in Heaven. We Christians do too," Cody said. "I know that both our people believe in the Spirit of God, that He lives in His children. But I also know that the

Nighthawks don't believe in Jesus, the Son of God. Maybe someday they will."

George Autumn smiled and said in Cherokee, "Perhaps. But don't the Christians say their God is three in one?"

"Maybe you're closer than most folks think," Cody said returning the older man's smile.

"Maybe closer than Christians," Summer said.[14]

The Nighthawk theological position on the acceptance of Christ remains murky in this passage (and throughout *Kholvn*), and despite Clearwater's affirmation that they acknowledge God and the Holy Spirit—and his two-out-of-three-ain't-bad optimism—Autumn suggests that acceptance of one is sufficient and that the mystery of the Trinity, which has escaped many Christians' full understanding, recommends an intellectual and spiritual humility, and a greater measure of tolerance for others' divergent beliefs. It may also be the case that the society or grounds to which Guess belongs has not codified its relationship to Christianity the way the Keetoowah Society did in the constitutional amendment, or that the society's relationship to Christianity continues to develop.

Moccasin's closing jab, like the Keetoowah constitution's claiming of the Holy Ghost, presumably with the insights it imparts, goes one step further in proposing the possibility of Nighthawk spiritual superiority. Perhaps her reaction voices Guess's distaste for the judgmental and racialist attitudes of some Christians toward the stomp dance, the experience of which he describes in an interview with Cherokee literary scholar Chris Teuton: "It was up to us, which way we wanted to go, the way of Christianity or the old ways. I really never had a preference all my life. I'd go to church with them [his parents], and sometimes I'd go to a stomp dance. And there are a lot of people like that now. In this day, they'll go to both. But the thing was the Christian communities looked down on the stomp dance. There's not so much of that now, but there's still a little bit of it. But the stomp dance people never had a bad word to say about Christianity, which was always kind of funny to me. . . . It doesn't matter to me which one I go to. They're both places of worship, and I know who I'm worshipping. Being acquainted with both worlds, I was able to translate it into *Kholvn*."[15] The translation to which Guess refers turns up in several ways. Autumn and Clearwater's dialogue contains the most Cherokee language of any passage in the novel. That Guess narrates their exchange first in Cherokee and subsequently translates it more or less verbatim into English announces language itself as an important marker of cultural identity and as a middle ground. While Clearwater speaks Cherokee, which is important to his characterization as a Christian Indian, all the other Cherokee protagonists but Autumn do so haltingly if at all, and the two of them thus fulfill important cooperative roles as linguistic as well as cultural authorities and mediators. Guess himself linguistically translates in multiple ways, both through the narrator and in his choice of writing in transliterated Cherokee instead of the Sequoyan syllabary, opening the Cherokee passages to audiences who cannot read Cherokee. On one hand, Guess is thus able achieve one of his "underlying goals" of helping "people to be learning something without really realizing they're learning something. . . . I put in words or traditions or history hoping that it will stay with the reader, whatever it is that they pick up."[16]

On the other, he does something quite extraordinary despite its obviousness: he composes fiction in Cherokee. This is no small thing, to offer Cherokee passages of creative writing, however brief, to Cherokee-reading audiences, helping to inaugurate a people's literature in their language. Though Cherokee readers are perhaps the primary intended audience of such sections, Guess is quick to let other readers in on the story with democratic accessibility. In my experience, most contemporary Cherokee speakers are similarly accommodating to nonspeakers, offering quick summaries, explanations, and vocabulary lessons as they carry on conversations. They by and large want to teach the language and want others, Cherokee and non-Cherokee, to learn it if they are willing. Their amicability, like Guess's linguistic openness, stands at odds with the stereotypical view of full-bloods or traditionalists as standoffish and private.

Guess draws on language differences for humor in the novel, as well. Much of it comes from linguistic tricks with a bathetic Cherokee/English language creolization or with the difficulties nonspeakers can have with Cherokee. For instance, when the characters first learn about the ravenmocker from Eric and Tom Trueblood's father: "'He said he had a dream about a ball of fire but he called it a . . . ,'

[Eric] thought a second. 'A Colon.' Cody shook his head and laughed. 'Colon?' Tom asked. 'That's some kinda mark when you're writing, ain't it?' 'It's got something to do with your insides,' Ira offered. . . . 'What's a Colon?' Eeya asked. 'Actually, it's Kholvn,' Cody corrected giving the word [its] proper pronunciation. 'Legend stuff. A story to scare kids with when they won't go to bed or come in after dark.' "[17] Such linguistic false friends provide endless opportunities for laughing instead of worrying about differences.

Sharing Clearwater's skepticism of oral traditions, most of the Cherokee characters except Autumn, Moccasin, and Longbush are at some distance from both the Cherokee language and Keetoowah traditions. Though he identifies himself as a Baptist preacher, in the story itself, Clearwater functions more as an intermediary than as an exhorter, and in fact his doubts about Christianity rival the conflict with Longbush's black magic for thematic centrality. Guess has said Clearwater's seeking paralleled his own: "Cody was modeled after me and at the time I was kind of battling which way of life was right, the old ways or Christianity. I finally realized, like Cody did, that it's not about Christianity or the old ways; it's not whether Keetoowah beliefs are right or whether the Christian world was right. It's faith. Faith in what we believe, that's the ultimate reality, that's the ultimate truth."[18] When at the end of *Kholvn* the assembled protagonists struggle to defeat the original demon-ravenmocker, Nicotani, Clearwater has an epiphany: " 'It's not about the differences between the Nighthawk Keetoowah religion and the Christian religion,' Cody said. . . . 'It's not about religion at all. . . .' Behind the preacher, the prayers of the three drifted up. Ira and Morgan spoke English while Summer chanted ancient Keetoowah words in a soft, lilting tone. Around them a soft, pure white light began to radiate. 'It's all about faith,' Cody said. 'Faith in the Creator! In Yihowa! In Jesus! In God!!' "[19]

Revisiting the question raised in the meeting between Autumn and Clearwater of how to address God, this section similarly names many names, apparently verifying the medicine man's claim that only God himself has knowledge of which is proper, but also suggesting that many may work. This admission of weakness through the limits of language, the boundaries of the knowable, is a paradoxical strength of a pluralistic approach to knowledge, insofar as it is loath to close the door on new interpretations or applications of traditions, practices, or beliefs, not seeing in them a once-and-for-all "answer" to what they might mean. The faith that Clearwater through Guess translates here admittedly has monist dimensions to it. I do not mean in translating "their" statements in *Kholvn* to assert that they are "really" saying something else, or that faith is less important than the text makes it, but the text itself does certainly do other things—and communicating the idea of a faith available to disparate communities is not least among them.

WHITE PATH PLURALISM

Kholvn represents the theme of a uniting faith through the symbolism of the White Path, discussed in chapter 1, which is represented as a white cross connecting people from the four quarters of the Earth. In the novel, the main sets of protagonists converge on Cherokee country (which Cherokees have traditionally understood as occupying the movable center of the universe) from each of the four directions. The novel does not mention the White Path by name, but the imagery it evokes leaves little doubt as to the cultural allusion invoked by the description of George Autumn's vision calling him to help against the kholvn:

> In the last vision, he saw the people. They were coming from the four points of the compass. And that, he thought, was as it should be.
>
> Two, probably a man and his wife, came from the north. They were Indians. The man was Tsalagi. The woman was Ayvwiya, what kind, he wasn't sure. Perhaps Lakota. The man hid behind a shield which was both good and bad. If a person was hidden by a shield he was safe but that person wasn't able to see.
>
> A woman, filled with tears, came from the east. She was bringing a friend. This was strange. They were both Aniyonega. White folk. The woman would overflow with the tears she so desperately held back.
>
> From the west came a sad man. He was tired beyond his years. At his side was his son. . . . Though the sad man was drained of strength, he was a man of the Father In Heaven and knew where he could receive more. He came reluctantly. The man of the Father was Tsalagi. His son was half.
>
> The old man saw himself coming from the south. He was hurrying, trying to meet the others before something happened.[20]

Keetoowah leader Crosslin Smith further explains that early oral histories held that "you must have medicine from the east, and you must have medicine from the west, then you must have medicine from the north, and you must have medicine from the south," in order to maintain the laws governing the proper loving and connected relationships among various peoples and with the Creator. Smith represents this system with four colors of people (red, white, black, and yellow) positioned in a circle quartered by a white cross, symbolizing the "white righteous road," "the first cross of extreme deep religious meaning" tying people together that they might remember each other.[21] According to Mooney, each direction is associated with specific symbolic meaning: the east with power or war, the south with peace, the west with death, and the north with defeat.[22] The colors Mooney has corresponding to the directions, however—blue to north, white to south, red to east, and black to west—are separate from the colors corresponding to peoples in Smith's formulation, and so the other powers connected with the directions may differ from Keetoowah ideas as well.

Through his characters' spatial affiliations, Guess demonstrates that other symbolic associations are possible in the traditional framework and that the ethnological account of Cherokee cosmology is neither definitive nor exhaustive. Autumn's traditionalism matches up conventionally with southern peaceful associations, but the police officer Ira Jammer's northern connection is less clear. Jammer does experience loss through the death of his Lakota wife Angela (called Eeya, or "Pumpkin" in Cherokee), but her dying may not be especially telling—Guess has stated that he decided which characters would die by pulling their names out of a can.[23] Jammer's character is the most empiricist in the novel, perhaps associating him with a secularism that like his badge, "shields" him from problems too esoteric. The sorrow connected with the white woman Morgan Booker coming from the east also expands on the customary interpretation of war or power as a positive site of aggressive assertiveness. Having fled her hometown after a romantic falling-apart with Clearwater and the death of her parents, Booker's sadness is the product of a lack of meaningful connections with other people, particularly with Clearwater. The strangeness that Autumn feels extends from the linkage of the east with "white folk" who have come not to conquer but to ally and perhaps unite more intimately with the Cherokee. Clearwater, too, complicates the pat joining of the west with death. He is plagued less by death itself than by doubt, about whether he serves a benevolent God, whether he is worthy of loving or being loved, and other problems. Death, Clearwater's stand-in for the problem of evil, may dwell in the west, but so does the preacher, led there by God's calling and possessed of strengths that will be important to others.

In the symbolic structure of the White Path, each component requires the others, not only in a binary pairing, but in a reticulated plurality. In the penultimate battle in a graveyard, the united group defeats Longbush by sculpting a representation of the White Path cross. Searching for a way to defeat the ravenmocker, "Summer walked to a wreath of lilies. A wooden cross was suspended with wire in the middle of the circle. She studied it carefully. There was something . . . Summer tore the cross from the wreath and threw it on the ground then proceeded to stomp [dance?] on it. Morgan noticed the Nighthawk Keetoowah girl desecrating the religious object and screamed for her to stop. . . . 'I'm not after the cross,' Summer said holding it up. 'I want the wood. . . . Cedar!! . . . Help me,' she cried. . . . 'I need three more.' "[24] The heroes position the planks at corners, using the pieces of the Christian cross to shape a physically and metaphorically larger one, and in short (spoiler alert), they trick Longbush into impaling himself with them.

In his defeat, sacred medicinal properties of the cedar in Cherokee traditions converge with the Christian symbolism of the lily as Jesus, and the cross of Christ merges with the cross of the White Path.[25] Summer Moccasin's declaration that she needs "three more" refers not so much to her need for three more cedar planks as to the need for the integration of the powers represented by the crosses. Morgan Booker, however, does not aid the others in dismantling and reconstructing the crosses (also in wreaths, that is, encompassed in a natural circle) and only "watche[s] broodingly," perhaps suggesting that the brunt of the work of coming to the table in religious understanding is borne by Indians.[26] She is at least present during the conflict and does later join the others against the demon ravenmocker. The elements of the entire structure are thus united, not one element coupled with a second, but each to every other: Cherokee and white,

Christian and Keetoowah, sacred and secular, full-blood and mixed-blood, pragmatic and idealist, aggressive and peaceful, progressive and traditional—each is connected not just to a dichotomous counterpart but to every part of the whole.

Like the White Path symbolism, Guess encodes other traditional principled practices in *Kholvn* without parading their Indianness; some he intentionally obscures. Like the language, many traditions are in the public domain in a sense, but others are kept more private. Guess warns his readers at the outset, "I have deliberately omitted songs from the Keetoowah Nighthawk religion in keeping respect for the 'old ways.' But their teachings, I believe, are held intact within the words of this book along with the teachings of Christianity."[27] He also admits to self-censoring his work in his interview with Teuton, claiming, "It's a fine line on what I want to expound upon and something that I just want to mention and not go into much detail about. And, of course, it's mostly when I'm talking about the medicine or some beliefs that I have to watch how much I do let go of. It's kind of fun sometimes, trying to see how far I can go without really actually letting the cat out of the bag."[28] Much of the reticence about certain beliefs and practices assuredly comes from the spotty history between traditionalists and academic-types—first ethnologists, then anthropologists, now literary critics—who often had little regard for their subjects' privacy or anything but their own agendas, failings I hope to avoid, needless to say.

Despite his elisions, several of Guess's references to traditional dispositions, like purification ceremonies and dream interpretation, are apparent to those literate in Cherokee culture. Alluding to a going-to-water ceremony, for instance, Guess cursorily writes, "George and Summer attended the medicine council where they walked through the cleansing cedar smoke and were taken to a nearby stream where they were prayed over as they washed the evil away."[29] He explains this section further to Teuton: "What I do when I'm writing is, like in *Kholvn*, I went back through and read it, and I had to delete quite a bit of stuff. For example, the good medicine man and his granddaughter go to water, and I describe the ceremony. Later on, I thought, 'That's not good. I better take that out.' And so I kind of edited it down to where it said they went to water and splashed, and that's all I kept on that."[30] The lack of detail on the actual practices or prayers involved in going to water helps maintain the ceremony's integrity to the extent that while some readers or researchers might recognize some splashing for the religious ceremony it represents, they could not hope to replicate it substantively, discouraging cultural appropriation. As Teuton observes in his questioning, Guess's refusal to clearly represent such cultural practices leaves out many readers or at least keeps them from as full an appreciation of his novels as they might have.[31] His choice of an audience narrowed by expectations of familiarity with the subject matter and even the limited availability of the books themselves to some degree parallel the progressive traditionalism of the narrative, enacting a conservatism that manages community change through community involvement. Changes are brought about through conversations with cultural others, but the discourse is partially restricted to others involved with the communities through organic connections.

Guess references a tighter version of community vetting in several places in *Kholvn*, such as when George and Summer consult with group of Keetoowah leaders: "They talked with the Council of Elders of the Stomp Grounds they attended. The old man and his granddaughter told the group of [fighting the ravenmocker] the night before and the fact that George didn't think the work was over. He told them of the vision that wasn't complete yet. The Council agreed with them. Before the two left, the Council sang a prayer of protection over them and those who would soon work with them. And when they finished, the Elders felt that victory was at hand."[32] This scenario closely follows the method of solving problems described by Benny Smith in chapter 1 and also testifies to anthropologist Robert Thomas's observation that "vision seeking among the Cherokees . . . is controlled and channeled by the group."[33] The scene dramatizes an instance of consensus-based decision making such as anarchism aspires to in concrete cultural detail. While we do not learn whether the council elders experienced a vision like Autumn's, every member of the novel's major collective—the progressive, conservative, moderate, Keetoowah, Cherokee, Christian, and agnostic Indians and non-Indians assembled to fight the cannibal—was visited by a dream that imparted some sense of the trouble to come and the roles they would together play in confronting it. These kinds of supernatural goings-on may be conventional in horror or fantastical genres, but in the case of *Kholvn* they take on an apparent culturally traditional dimension even as they happen to Cherokees and non-Cherokees alike.

Cody Clearwater's calling is intriguing in light of what we have so far seen of dreams in Cherokee literature. In his dream, "He stood on a high bluff beside someone. There was no need to turn to see who it was. He could feel the love and peace radiating from the person. Below them at the bottom of the bluff, a picturesque, whitewashed, slat-board church building stood."[34] The parallels with Catharine Brown's dream are striking—the personal contact with an unnamed deity, presumably Jesus; the ascendance on a high bluff; and the experience of God in nature. In terms of genre, *Kholvn* and the *Memoir* could hardly compare, and even in these pointed passages the similarities between the two are not so close as to suggest that Guess was borrowing from or even referencing Brown—but that makes the cultural continuities across almost two hundred years that much more surprising. Other traditional principles and practices connected to names, clans, oral histories, land, and more that appear throughout *Kholvn* and Guess's other works beg further looking into.

Again like Brown, Guess is concerned with the spiritual and cultural well-being of Cherokee people, and *Kholvn* foregrounds contemporary social and material problems. Chief among the issues Guess takes up are problems stemming from American racism, such as economic disadvantage, unemployment, and anxiety over mixed-race romantic relationships. Other social concerns include problems like substance abuse and discrimination based on blood quantum, that while preconditioned by American racism might be alleviated by Cherokees' own agency by pushing back against the U.S. and Native nations' established identity boundaries. This social consciousness that subtly figures throughout the novel helps explain the apparent non sequitur Clearwater proposes in the denouement. More or less out of the blue, Clearwater announces that he intends to take the lessons he has learned fighting the ravenmocker with group support to the political arena. The passage reads, "'You know?' Cody said thoughtfully. 'The Cherokees have always been divided by something or other. They've never been truly at peace with one another. But I found out that if we would only try to get along . . . we can do it. And that's what I'm gonna tell the councils . . [.] on both sides. We CAN get along. I[n] fact, we must get along if we're gonna survive.' "[35] The councils he refers to here are not those of the elders at the stomp grounds, but the Cherokee Nation's and United Keetoowah Band's political councils (monsters for a sequel?), which he looks to engage with a participatory pitch that rejects the antagonistic posturing of national figureheads in favor of an ethic of democratic, populist—that is, indigenist anarchist—cooperative confederation. Laudable as his spirit is, these bodies have been at odds over policy, land, resources, power, control, and so on, for as long as anyone can remember.

These conflicts continue today, with the Cherokee Nation claiming authority over lands the UKB claims and at multiple turns opposing the UKB's efforts to exercise sovereignty by moving land into trust, administering housing funds, and claiming jurisdiction. The official position from the Cherokee Nation has asserted the UKB government is little more than an upstart that has no claims to jurisdiction, treaty rights, or successor status to the Cherokee Nation's claims on the United States, although the Cherokee heritage of UKB members is undisputed.[36] The rhetoric against the UKB's right of self-governance, however, appears increasingly anxious over Keetoowah claims to land within its borders and the confusion that would result from an *imperium in imperio*, or a state within a state. The Bureau of Indian Affairs has moved toward support of the UKB on this question, but whether it wins or loses, the Cherokee Nation's unironic application of the same logic that opposed Cherokee nationhood in the East in the early nineteenth century is surely a failure of some sort.[37] For its part, the UKB has attempted to establish its legitimate governance on a platform of superior cultural authenticity by making disingenuous historical claims to an uninterrupted history of Keetoowah leadership steeped in traditionalism and bloodedness from the time before European contact and by simultaneously challenging the legal and cultural legitimacy of the Cherokee Nation.[38] Several times the two sovereignties have—again, without apparent irony—looked to federal courts to settle questions over who is entitled to what rights of independence.

Once more standing in for Guess, Clearwater refers to divisions that hinder Cherokee unity and that have direct effects on the daily lives of Cherokee citizens. For Guess, "getting along" or being "at peace" with each other does not mean wiping out the differences among Cherokees, for even the four survivors of the encounter with the kholvn after their victory "went their own separate ways to collect themselves and see which way their lives would go," embracing the temporariness of their collective.[39] Clearwater does not advocate a single way of believing or a single set of practices in helping Cherokees survive as a coherent people. There is not even mention of a single government. The focus is on working for survivance, not just by looking past difference to commonality, but rather by marshaling the resources represented in difference. Guess, like Brown and other women and men who took up leadership roles in religious communities, extends recognition and respect for others' power. He does not look to drain it off nor erase it—although this respect has not always been Cherokee people's strategy, as the next chapters will show.

In indigenous anarchism (or even indigenous nations), there must be space for difference, and there must be room for differing, that is, practices of diverging, disagreeing, and dissenting. While the "councils on both sides" have become skilled at disagreeing with each other, the opportunities even for discussion have narrowed considerably within the tribes, as the political leaders take ever-stronger measures to fortify their positions. The UKB, for instance, recently disallowed dual tribal citizenship, excluding many citizens from scholarships, hardship assistance, and other aid for which they would otherwise have been eligible. Again with distinct social consciousness, Guess early in *Kholvn* presents an analogous state of affairs when people traded authority for security but wound up with coercion and fear. The prologue relates the oral history of the anikutani, the mythical caste of priests whose tyrannical rule became so egregious that the Cherokees in their most anarchist moment rose against and executed them. Imagining a lone survivor of the massacre, Guess invents the origin of the kholvn.

At the novel's outset, this early story of revolution is what Clearwater hears from his grandfather: "It was a horrible and bloody lesson that needed to be passed down. And maybe, if the Complete People were lucky, they would never have to learn it again."[40] This story and the story that remains to be told, of how the councils might resolve, accommodate, or perhaps even capitalize on their differences, bookend the novel's cultural and religious messages. A similar political and social engagement characterizes much of Cherokee literature, from Catharine Brown to Elias Boudinot to Sequoyah Guess. Encouraging the Cherokee and UKB councils with a message of peace may not seem revolutionary or dangerous, but if a culture gives itself over to centralized control, to a for-or-against politics, alternative ways of doing, being, and believing can invite remarkable overreaction from the state—disavowal, disenfranchisement, and worse. As the next section on the traditional dispositions of dissent demonstrates, there are indeed bloody lessons to be learned.

Part Two

ᏧᏦᏂᏃᏍᏛᎪᎢ

We Argue

ᏅᏍᎩ

CHAPTER 4

Deliberation in Town and Country

If the traditional Cherokee social milieu was anchored in the clan, the political was anchored in the town, of which there were around forty at the turn of the nineteenth century, down from more than sixty in the eighteenth. In many principles and practices, Cherokee towns exemplify how I am conceiving a traditional model of indigenous anarchism. Towns ruled themselves through a decentralized system of governance that mingled power structures political, religious, and social, which ensured a far-ranging diversity of opinion on public questions. A prevailing principle of egalitarianism encouraged widespread participation from a town's people at internal town councils and in intertown, protonational meetings. A remarkable feature of Cherokee political philosophy was its pointed lack of enforcement mechanisms at the local and national levels, features now considered requisite not just for the polity's operation but for its very definition. In the absence of coercive governmental bodies and even legitimating principles of institutionalized coercion, leaders coordinated consensus through the exercise of persuasion, good judgment, respect for others' autonomy, and representative solicitation.

The United States' perennial demands for land cessions and its habit of treating with unauthorized representatives challenged these methods of achieving harmony and seemed to require a more deliberate and consolidated political apparatus to be headed by those acculturatively skilled. Prominent leaders like John Ross and Elias Boudinot emerged in the removal crises of the early nineteenth century to preserve the nation, if not in the towns then at least in the country. Set against the backdrop of the traditional political world, Cherokee stories of permutation, progress, and perseverance unmask the contradictions, complexities, and continuations of the habitus's infinite generative capacity. Typical histories describe these nationalist developments as attacks on full-bloods, traditions, and their defenders, like Ross, orchestrated by a ruling class made up of men like Boudinot, who are accounted as constituting a mixed-blood, wealthy, and assimilationist elite. Although this dialectic has long been accepted, this chapter will try to prove it inadequate to the task of fully narrating Cherokee history. I will attempt this first by uncovering early indigenist anarchist traditions of constituent representation and building consensus so that we can see how even after the troubling shift toward centralized governance, "assimilationists" often enacted traditional dispositions, and vice versa. This chapter will also present biographies of John Ross and Elias Boudinot that detail the personal paradoxes that superficial splits into mixed-blood/assimilationist and full-blood/traditionalist cannot account for. I'll close with a brief history of the removal crisis to set up the next chapter's reading of the two figures' rhetoric that competed over the direction of the nascent nation.

Nationalization, whether praised or attacked, is synonymous with neither traditionalism nor assimilation. As a widespread effort to retain independent control over society and land, it required input and consent from many quarters of the Cherokee social and political spectrums. Although not everyone equally participated in the nation's formation nor shared in the powers the state accumulated, we can no more write off nationalization as the product of a smoky room conclave than declare it the fulfillment of a traditionalist's vision. It was rather a necessary adaptation to historical circumstances attended by both successes and failures as it drew from, improved on, and betrayed traditions. Making the most of its successes will likely once again require across-the-board support, given the challenges of redistributing power from a center long accustomed to monopolizing it. More stigmatizing division is unlikely to help.

PLACE AND POLITICS

The precontact centers of Cherokee social, political, and religious life, towns were autonomous population centers that shared a council house and ceremonial grounds and were linked by kinship, language, and other indices of self-identification. The average town of some three hundred people and three hundred acres also shared food, land, and community resources.[1] In cultivating common fields and orchards, towns were guided by *gadugi*, a principle and practice of economic and labor cooperation that required input from all able members of the group. Raymond Fogelson and Paul Kutsche note the linguistic similarity between *gadugi* and the word for town, *skadugi*, suggesting etymologically the relationships between the philosophies and practices of being and working together in a place.[2] While this chapter focuses primarily on the political practices of indigenous anarchism, *gadugi* names one practice more economic, an area that urgently needs looking into. The drop in the number of towns in the early 1800s reflects the shift from the tribalist agrarian economy toward the market economy of the fur trade that accompanied the Cherokees' increasing reliance on trade goods, together with their adoption of Euro-American agricultural principles. These entailed several changes to crop diversification, gendered labor practices, and more, but most importantly in terms of settlement demographics, emphasized individual over communal labor.

The United States' Indian civilization program also promoted individual land ownership. When Cherokees participated in civilizing efforts that brought plows, spinning wheels, looms, and missionaries, they abandoned urban centers for more isolated family farms. As important as the towns were, by no means did all Cherokees live in them, before or after the movement toward more nuclear arrangements. In her demographic study, Betty Anderson Smith finds evidence for a healthy number of Cherokee people who lived outside of towns. She suggests that many of the 160 geographic names she finds in the eighteenth-century historical record likely denote "semipermanent hamlets" that "were probably smaller villages occupied for a while, then abandoned as natural resources were depleted."[3] I pause on this rural diversity to point out that even as I attempt to unsettle the nationalist emphasis on central government by shifting focus to the more politically dispersed town structure, the histories of significant parts of the Cherokee remain untold. Rural Cherokees likely had their own ways of doing things, and living apart from major population centers, modes of individualism may well have already figured in them.

For town and country folk alike, no single chief represented the whole of the people. During times of peace, executive positions for each town were filled by a "white" chief who oversaw internal matters, organized agricultural labor, and administered the town council; during times of war a "red" chief took over leadership. Some evidence indicates that red chiefs acted as representatives in towns' international commerce, although white chiefs were also involved in external negotiations. Both in times of peace and war, the chiefs led by example and persuasion, having next to no coercive powers. The general form of executive leadership persisted through settlements' dispersal well into the nineteenth century. A council of medicine men or priests advised both red and white chiefs, in addition to the rest of the populace, on the religious implications of problems big and small. Even after being deposed in precontact history for overstepping the authority granted them by the people, their input was still considered requisite on policy and conduct both public and private.[4] In addition to the priests, deputy chiefs, and assistants, town chiefs were aided in their offices by two male advisory councils made up of clan representatives and of elders called Beloved Men. These in turn were advised by female councils and female heads of the clans, who generally did not publicly speak during council meetings but advised privately, both before meetings and during private caucuses while town councils were in session.[5] This structure ensured that the interests of diverse groups were represented.

A woman who had earned renown in war was known as *Ghighau* or Beloved Woman. As heads of female councils, such women could affect public policy, and at times even determine it, such as when deciding the fate of prisoners, whose release or punishment could lead to serious international ramifications. Historian Theda Perdue implies that women's councils may not have been standing bodies but also suggests that women may have regularly caucused during town councils. Whatever the duration of the women's councils, it seems clear that they were readily convened and carried significant weight. My focus on the town council, where most women were not allowed a voice, might suggest that women exercised little political power, but theorists of Cherokee traditionalism like Perdue, Rennard Strickland, and Laura Donaldson assure us this was not at all the case. They demonstrate that a great many institutions generally assumed to be the domain of the state in fact came under the purview of the social clan structure, and the seven clans in the Cherokee matrilineal system came under the leadership of the clan women. The administration of justice in the case of homicide, for instance, was invested in clans through application of the retaliatory "blood law," which required the life of the killer or a stand-in from his clan.[6]

The clan figured prominently in the shape of the traditional polity through its ubiquitous presence throughout the habitus. Although Duane Champagne argues that a high degree of structural differentiation among social, religious, and political systems in Cherokee society facilitated rapid political centralization, particularly at the national intertown level, he also explores the degree of integration of these spheres both nationally and locally, identifying limited ways through which clan and religious structures facilitated a national political identity.[7] Strickland argues further for the clan's importance: "The clan was, without doubt, the major institution exercising legal powers," over, for instance, marriage, property, inheritance, religious ceremonial duties, murder, sexuality, parenting, witchcraft, and other internal domains, as distinct from political powers concerned with external affairs.[8] It has to be admitted that while political structures were noncoercive, the same cannot be said of social structures, which had a host of punitive measures to combat deviancy at their disposal. Whether they differed in kind or substance from those administered by a state, I cannot say, but it seems plausible that punishments handled by family members would be tempered with greater compassion and concern for social welfare. Although clans were not given discrete positions in town or national council meetings, they did have a representative voice in both, given the influential role of the clan elders' council, in addition to their pervasive powers in internal affairs. For most of the eighteenth century, national councils rarely met, but the presence of members from each clan in all towns large enough to have a council house and ceremonial grounds united Cherokees in a protonational social structure.[9]

Further contributing to Cherokee social coherence, religious ceremonies provided opportunities for towns to interact under formal circumstances and lent a widespread spiritual dimension to political processes, going beyond the priests' influence on political leaders. Fred Gearing points out the strategy of scheduling national councils to correspond with major harvesting, planting, and other ceremonies to foster a sense of communal well-being and reciprocal relationships.[10] Not only were medicine men or priests invested with permanent advisory roles to the chiefs, but they also presided over ceremonies and acted as the principal interpreters and keepers of the sacred laws governing belief and behavior. All this they did in a culture for which spirituality was warp and woof, informing perhaps every conceivable practice from hunting to farming to marriage. In essence, medicine men represented and maintained the cultural repository.[11] A practice as common as making a hunting bow, for instance, requires adherence to spiritually and scientifically informed methods, such as knowing when the tree should be harvested and which sides should be used or discarded based on directional energies. We can only speculate on the vast religious considerations of international politics. Although Champagne argues that medicine men primarily exercised power locally because of the limited scope of national consolidation, their influence was indeed considerable given their importance to social life and to the town leadership. Champagne recounts one instance in which a priest's counsel weighed enough to prevent a group of Cherokees from joining their insistent British allies in a war party because his divination from a crystal told him the time wasn't right for military action.[12]

Neither priest, chief, nor clan elder levied much coercive power, especially in regard to political action, but despite the absence of institutionalized cohesive power, Cherokee towns nevertheless maintained affiliations among themselves, practiced a distinctive tribal identity, and leveraged a national political presence. Those connections persevered not on the basis of negative threats coming out of a central authority, or even from potential ostracizing by other towns, but on a reciprocal respect for autonomy in harmonious relations. This indigenous-anarchist ethical precept, which also guided interpersonal relationships—rooted in religion, incorporated in the clan, branching throughout the milieu—was the foundational principle organizing the nonbinding, confederated form of Cherokee governance.[13] Under such rule, towns' decisions and actions were independent of other towns', and while they could and did unite for particular purposes, during times of war, for instance, partnerships were temporary and end-based, dissolving when the crises that brought them together were resolved. Refusal to join with another town brought no reprisal, and similarly, individuals could not be compelled to enter into agreements to which they did not consent.[14] Intrinsic recognition of and respect for the autonomy of towns and individuals to associate and disassociate freely were encoded in the practices of coalition.

For the sake of harmonious relations among autonomous agents, delegated leaders worked with principled practices that ensured their representations corresponded with their constituencies' desires. In the event leaders did not act in accordance with consensus opinion, they could be deposed, but such measures were generally kept unnecessary through the chief mechanism for arriving at consensus, one integral to indigenous anarchism: repeated and regular consultation with the elective communities.[15] This habitual returning to represented bodies—to check in, to inform, for approval, for veto—kept them informed and regulated against misrepresentation. Gearing describes the series of deliberation, negotiation, and reporting through which consensus evolved: "Each clan attempted to reach a corporate opinion. The older men from the seven clans (the beloved men) then joined the village priestly officials and became for the moment the body of elders. They talked over the sentiments of their various clans. Then these beloved men talked again with their own representative clans, reporting opinions of the other clans, then gathered again as elders, and so on. Probably both sets of discussions included public speeches; a general council probably gave the outward appearance of a New England town meeting, with un-New England-like caucuses going on intermittently. Councils continued in this loose manner for days or, with interruptions, for weeks."[16] This "caucusing" recalls the communal vetting associated with the practice of gaining knowledge discussed in the book's first part. It survives in traditional communities in the shape of committees called to offer guidance on matters of debate, and it helped shape the Keetoowah Society's revival of the stomp dance in the early 1900s.[17] This communicative cycle ensured leaders' accountability and the politic body's active participation. As a disposition of the political habitus it was both essential to and representative of the practices generating and perpetuating the consensus-based model of anarchistic local rule.

Most researchers have tended to emphasize the negative or injunctive aspects of Cherokee dispositions. The harmony ethic, for instance, has been described by its discouragement of open conflict, but we should also remember its positive injunction to give of resources generously. Similarly, we might reimagine the general sense of harmony not as a stasis we should avoid upsetting but as an ongoing practice itself—as "harmonizing"—that requires constant adjustment and fine-tuning. Most critics have similarly seen the sharp curtailment of leadership abilities, even in times of war, as a negative lack of coercive power or executive weakness.[18] I understand the absence of centralized power rather as a positive power, but one retained by the people, through which they themselves formed the true executive branch. Harmonizing into consensus required work, not aloofness. In any event, it was not the same thing as unanimity but rather meant that a compromise everyone could live with had been reached until a better solution could be worked out.

Missing from discussions of consensus and the harmony ethic is the sense of these as ongoing, dynamic processes that had to be actively forged and reforged in time, which as Gearing points out might take weeks. Other researchers reiterate the great deal of time required in consensus decision making.[19] A prevailing egalitarianism mandated that all males could speak during council meetings, not only those elected to leadership roles, meaning the expressions of diverse viewpoints were many. Gearing does note that there were social checks in place, especially during the caucusing, which dissuaded people from undue quibbling and unhelpful or inappropriate input.[20] The harmony ethic discouraged overt aggression and individualistic grandstanding, but that hardly means there was no disagreement, only that it required tactful and respectful expression—deliberations where there is no disagreement do not take weeks to resolve.[21]

Principled practices like caucusing that attended consensus governance in the traditional Cherokee world no doubt helped prolong such occasions, but they also facilitated their operation insofar as they reinforced the importance of communal, harmonious agreement to the entirety of the culture. Other practices included caucusing according to clan, age, and gender, and religious practices like preaching, dancing, praying, smoking, fasting, and more.[22] All helped orient political deliberations in a deep cultural context in which decisions were made not by virtue of power invested in leaders more or less independent of community review, but by leaders' persuasion of others to join in assent and action. Individuals might accumulate influence and authority in several symbolic or cultural currencies, such as family position, age, history of success in hunting, war, or diplomacy, or they might be possessed of special charisma or acuity. Proficiency in arbitration and skill at rhetoric were particularly valued for their nonconfrontational means of resolving competing interests and cultivating Cherokee civics.[23]

Consensus was by no means easily built, and when it could not be reached, three options surface in the historical record: no decision at all would be made, those recalcitrant in their dissension could withdraw or abstain from the debate with the understanding that the towns they represented would not be bound by the conclusion, or in extreme cases, dissenters might mount a revolutionary opposition. The second was the usual means of amicably allowing others to forge as complete a consensus as they were able. But as Albert Wahrhaftig explains, for all the importance of harmony to the Cherokee habitus, it was subordinate to "the more compelling ideal of rightly identifying the people's path. Those who are certain that they are right must live according to that knowledge, accepting the consequent exacerbation of disharmony and alienation from others."[24] The last option, for matters in which even withdrawal could not be countenanced, might proceed in several ways, two of which seem to recur: removal not just from a particular decision but in greater or lesser degrees from the body politic, or outright insurrection against the established order. Neither took place as a matter of course, but there are several instances of such dramatic rupture in Cherokee history, including the Chickamauga revolt over land cessions, the Old Settlers' removal to Arkansas to escape white depredation, the legendary uprising against the priests, and White Path's rebellion against too much and too swift acculturation.

By the 1820s, circumstances had led Cherokee culture away from consensus-based rule and toward increasing political and governmental centralization. It was this shift that occasioned White Path's revolt against the ratification of the Cherokee Constitution in 1828. As the demand for Indian lands mounted in the American Southeast, the Cherokees circled their wagons, as it were, to protect against the unscrupulous U.S. practices of treating with autonomous Cherokee groups or towns, attempting to bind the entire tribe to cessions made without their input and punishing all tribal members for the disruptive or aggressive actions of a few. Beginning in the early 1800s, the primary protectionist strategy by which Cherokees aimed to maintain control over lands, coalesce the cultural body, and increase the material economy was through consolidating towns' political powers into a streamlined, central state apparatus that would function as the sole representative body authorized to negotiate on the towns'—now the nation's—behalf.[25]

The development away from the indigenous anarchist model toward a bureaucratic state was swift, from the establishment in the late 1700s of a tribal council modeled on town councils. Often called the National Council, it continued to be dominated by locally minded conservatives. Later came a standing legislative body, the National Committee, in 1817 and a judiciary in 1821. At the same time, what coercive authority there was moved from social to political structures with the uninterrupted inclusion of wartime leaders in the regular government and the creation of a police force in 1808. In 1820 the nation was divided into districts for the purpose of electing leaders to the national government, a shift away from more local election by more numerous towns. The culmination of these measures was the ratification of the Constitution in 1828, in which the Cherokees declared themselves politically on a par with the other nations of the world. Though modeled more or less on the U.S. Constitution, that of the Cherokees differed in several points, such as its explicit assertion of divine authority and the communal ownership of land.[26] Not entirely an unprecedented invention, the Cherokee Constitution mostly codified some structural changes already obtaining in practice, such as the growing political and coercive powers of the administrative bodies and the chiefs (the principal and deputy chief offices had consolidated and supplanted those of the red and white chiefs), whose authority was formerly more symbolically influential than imperiously commanding.

All this movement from an equilateral periphery to a central authority constricted the diversity of heard viewpoints, and putting power in the hands of fewer elected officials not only divested town councils of local control, it also gradually vacated the processes and opportunities whereby town members communicated with their leaders. In the interest of efficiency, the slow and deliberative consensus-based model of decision making formerly practiced within and among the Cherokee town confederation gave way to a swifter, more decisive organization based on majority rule. This central government became the product and producer of a nationalist consciousness that insisted on the subordination of local concerns to those of the larger body, effectively stifling public discourse in its promotion of acquiescence to the greater good, as defined by a concentrating, power-holding cadre. Combined with other changes, such as the decline of medicine men's authority, centralization facilitated the separation of the political complex from those religious and social, disempowering and quieting contributions from priests and women, whose spheres formerly provided the foundations of political power.[27] In the political realm at least, opportunities to express alternative positions and to exercise consensus-based practices managing and incorporating dissent were eroded or lost as the state's leaders assumed greater powers over both internal and external affairs.

FULL-BLOODS AND MIXED-BLOODS

Scholars of Cherokee history have charted the changes to traditional political, social, and economic structures with greater nuance than I can reproduce in this summary, but less careful are their sketches of who created and controlled the state. When not seen as an inevitable but inadequate reaction to the irresistible force of American imperialism, the Cherokee state, if not the formation of the nation entirely, is often understood as an artificiality engineered by meddling Europeans. In the former, slightly more empowering light, the tendency is to lionize traditionalists who pursued the only tragic strategy that offered any promise and to villainize progressives who subsequently appropriated the state and turned it to their own acquisitive, individualist ends. The latter approach skips tribal agency entirely and jumps straight to the perceived opportunism. As history tells it, intermarriage with white traders set the stage for the cooptation of the state by a new class in Cherokee society, that of the elite mixed-blood.

Although I am skeptical about how well "mixed-blood" describes a homogeneous group of profiteers and am positive that "full-blood" when describing better than three-quarters of the population tells us next to nothing at all, I'm not arguing that there was no such thing as traditionalists and no such thing as mixed-bloods, assimilationists, or elites. I am, however, against conflating such simply defined groups with a stock set of beliefs and actions that purportedly determined the course of Cherokee history. Bearing in mind all that is not told about people by describing them as mixed-blood, three dramatic changes set the stage for the ascension of what is called the progressive, mixed-blood class in Cherokee society: Cherokee economics increasingly came to depend on trade with the United States, negotiations with the U.S. government required fluency in English and familiarity with white customs, and the affluence and influence of intermarried white traders effected changes that shifted the material balance of power to mixed-blood inheritors through changes to laws administering property and descent. Cherokees found codification of patrilineal inheritance among the nation's earliest statutes, written into an 1808 law that also established a central police force, perhaps not uncoincidentally.[28] Mixed-blood families were generally wealthier, more likely to attend white missionary schools, proportionately in control of more property, and more often slaveholding than their full-blood counterparts.[29] According to a demographic study of the census of 1835, just fewer than 23 percent of Cherokees were mixed-bloods, and slightly more than 30 percent of families had at least one mixed-blood member.[30]

While the language of blood had come to infiltrate Cherokee discourse before and during the removal era, what terms like "mixed-blood" and "full-blood" meant during this historic period is no less ambiguous than what they can mean now, as they refer frequently in metaphorical ways to beliefs, dispositions, practices, and even things like geographical residence as much as to racial lineage. During the removal crisis, the correlation between advocacy of removal and mixed-bloodedness was not so firmly established as it has become, nor was the opposition of both to traditionalism and full-bloodedness. In fact, American proponents of Indian removal early on had the idea that it was the landed mixed-bloods who most stood in their way. As it turns out, plenty of Cherokee mixed-bloods opposed removal, and more full-bloods than we imagine favored leaving. This is in addition to the couple of thousand Old Settlers, many of whom are often accounted among the most traditional members of the tribe, who had already departed for the Arkansas territory in the early 1800s. Discussing this frequent dichotomization of Cherokee identity, anthropologist Circe Sturm cautions, "The Cherokee population was, and continues to be, far more complex than such a neat division between wealthy mixed-bloods and poor full-bloods allows. This reductivist tendency has shaped too much of the debate about Cherokee identity. Running throughout much of the scholarly literature is an assumption that the racial ancestry of Cherokees correlates not just with their class standing but with certain social values. Full-bloods are often understood as cultural conservatives, as bearers of 'tradition,' whereas mixed-bloods are expected to be oriented toward progress and change."[31] The tendency Sturm identifies is as unfortunately pervasive in history and literary criticism as it is in anthropology. Even critics who are conscious of the contradictions that figures like Boudinot and Ross present and who are skeptical of these categories too often find themselves tangled up in the shorthand vocabulary, unwittingly replicating the binarism that keeps us from thinking through the culture-perpetuating strategies of individuals and groups coming from any background.

Writing against prevailing nationalist approaches in American Indian scholarship, Mark Rifkin mounts a vigorous critique of Native nation-states in his 2009 *Manifesting America*, a project I'm certainly sympathetic to, but one I find misdirected by its reliance on Cherokee history as assimilationist mimicry without enough attention to the origins of the state proceeding from within the culture, for better or worse. The assumption of modular replication of U.S. state structure prevents his critique from investigating the role that the Cherokee people as a whole played (and play) in its construction and from weeding the positive and the negative when it comes to modern developments. He argues that tribal nations are collective identities that in the final tally were engineered by the U.S. federal government as a means of consolidating its own power and creating a cohesive national narrative. In order to agree with its account of itself as committed to justice and liberty, the United States required at least the appearance of general and formal Native consent to federal Indian policies, from treaty-negotiated land cessions, to removal, and finally to consolidation in an amalgamated America. The real trick for Rifkin comes as the United States generates not only political organizations for its Indian adversaries, "producing subjectivities for involuntarily interiorized peoples that are designed to testify to their non-coerced acceptance of their place in national life," but also as it inspires the nationalist attitudes undergirding them.[32] Engendered as these are not by Native peoples' volition but by American ideological operations, Rifkin is concerned with "how native peoples' ability 'to tell their own stories' about their processes of decision making, diplomacy, land tenure, and resource use has been managed by the settler-state in ways that work to legitimize the expansion of U.S. jurisdiction."[33]

According to Rifkin, the most important subjectivity invented by U.S. influences for Cherokee people was that of an elite class "ideologically committed to centralized authority and the privatization of land use, wealth, and kinship, developing a legal code and bureaucracy that rendered subaltern the forms of town-based consensus and clan identification that traditionally had defined and shaped Cherokee life."[34] I don't dispute that control of the Cherokee state, like perhaps all states, wound up in the hands of a select few and that many of them could be characterized in these terms. I do question whether there is any practical difference between this elite class as Rifkin describes it and the mixed-blood class invoked by earlier historians like Grace Woodward, William McLoughlin, and Theda Perdue to tell a tidy history, without the crossovers and complications that we are beginning to explore. I'd like to consider the attributes Rifkin names in turn. The Cherokee Constitution leads off with the assertion that land is to be held in common, not privatized, encoding a powerful indigenist anarchist precept. Rifkin may be referring to smaller family farms that replaced communally tended fields, but that shift was hardly restricted to elites in the early nineteenth century; it was in fact the norm. The commitment to wealth he identifies surely depends on how wealth is defined, and it seems clear enough that the majority of Cherokee people were in favor of acquiring goods like rifles, cloth, and farming implements, if not of storing up capital. Elites, of course, hardly had a lock on commitment to kinship. Neither was a legal code a departure for Cherokee people, as Rennard Strickland scrupulously documents in his *Fire and the Spirits,* in which he traces the development of Cherokee government from its traditional laws and structures, seeing much continuance where Rifkin sees only imitation. Above all, the creation of the government even in bureaucratic shape cannot be attributed solely to this elite class. The National Council was made up predominantly of people commonly thought traditional, and they—like the nation-people as a whole—consented to the centralization of governance. Again, I'm not arguing that kinship, wealth, governance, and so forth were at their heart the same for all people. There were important differences in mode and degree on these matters—important enough that splitting them into two categories, the elite and all the rest, doesn't tell us enough about the tensions and concessions in the complicated forces that developed the nation nor about the peculiarly Cherokee inflection given to the Cherokee state.[35]

Too, it's worth wondering if this ruling class was as homogeneous as it has been made out. What Rifkin says of the concept of Manifest Destiny, that "it largely appears as a monolith, an integrated totality rather than a shifting matrix," could as well be said of elites, traditionalists, and the many modes of resisting imperialism.[36] The Treaty of New Echota agreed to Cherokee removal to Indian Territory, and as a precursor to the Trail of Tears left an indelible mark of assimilationist and elitist status on the minority faction signers. Even more than the plantation owners or those who helped shape the Constitution, these men have come to epitomize the mixed-blood elite as a self-interested, protocapitalist cadre. Setting aside the one to two thousand Cherokees who came to affiliate with the treaty party and looking just at the twenty signers of this document, what we once thought clear starts to get muddy. Though many accounted among the elite like John and Major Ridge were slaveholders, Boudinot urged abolition, and at least six signers owned no slaves. Though many were low-blood-quantum mixed-bloods like William Rogers and Andrew Ross (John Ross's brother), others like Boudinot were of relatively high Cherokee blood quantum, and still others, like Major Ridge, Cae-te-hee, and Tah-yeske, were full-bloods. Many like John Gunter and George Chambers held more than a hundred acres of land, while others like Jesse Half-breed and Archilla Smith held fifteen or twenty, much closer to the average farm size of fourteen acres in 1835.[37] At least six of the initial twenty signers held fewer than thirty-five acres. Several of these family names—Ridge, Boudinot, Rogers, Starr, Adair—are well known to scholars of Cherokee history, not least because the family stories survive in the written record. But what do we know of Cae-te-hee, Tah-yeske, or Half-breed besides the little revealed in the census records of 1835?[38] Unidentifiable in the census (at least by me), what do we know at all of men like Tu gah-e-ske or Tesa-ta-esky? When historical accounts deign to mention them at all, they say only that they were not major players, which reveals more about what we generally value and expect of the historical narratives of exemplary individuals than the full narratives themselves. Ignorant of so many basic details, how can we claim to know anything of these other subalterns' motivations, ties to tradition, or ideological allegiances? The more we learn about these exceptions, the more we may need to unlearn about the histories and theories that have looked them over.

Rifkin makes a persuasive case for where Cherokee nationalism might have gone wrong when he writes, "National discourse becomes the vehicle for a class-inflected translation that asserts Cherokee autonomy from the United States but increasingly defines it through capitalist political-economy, constructing forms of national subjectivity that work to delegitimize longstanding popular systems of decision making, alliance, and conflict resolution."[39] While blaming capitalism and Cherokees' emulation of its governance structures falls short of a more robust critique of the larger problem of power consolidated in the hands of a few, a problem shared by many political economies, his questioning the extent to which early nationalizing steps were meant to "license a centralization of power and policy *among* the Cherokee," as opposed to external, political dealings with the United States, mounts a forceful anarchist-indigenist challenge.[40] Nevertheless, if the bulk of Cherokee people consented to nationalization at a time when they stood in a much more empowered, distanced position to U.S. hegemony than we generally mean in speaking of ideological interpellation in Althusser's sense (for example, through educational or religious institutions), then responsibility for the creation and development of the Cherokee state belongs with the whole of the body politic, and Cherokees as a whole shared, and share, in its successes and failures. Authorization of statism and the practices supporting it cut across the imagined divide between nobly doomed traditionalists and Machiavellian mixed-bloods, wealthy elites, or whatever the Othered group of Cherokees is called.

The argument that the Cherokee Nation adopted a collective subjectivity created for it by the United States is complicated by the fact that many powerful figures in the United States stridently opposed Cherokee "presumptions" to nationhood. For instance, Supreme Court Justice William Johnson in his separate opinion in *Cherokee Nation v. Georgia*, the case that declared Indian tribes are not entitled to the rights of foreign nations, expresses his anxiety that if the Cherokees were to be considered a state or admitted to the "family of nations," savagery would in effect supplant civilization. He writes, "Where is the rule to stop? Must every petty kraal of Indians, designating themselves a tribe or nation, and having a few hundred acres of land to hunt on exclusively, be recognized as a state? We should indeed force into the family of nations, a very numerous and very heterogeneous progeny."[41] As Priscilla Wald keenly observes, "His use of the word 'kraal,' an Afrikaner term for an enclosed village or the animal pen within the village (like the English 'corral'), shows just how loath Johnson was to claim human kinship with indigenes."[42] Much less inclined was he to admit political parity. With the Cherokees historically excluded from nationhood by the United States on one hand and, as Rifkin sets up the matter on the other hand, with them beguiled into taking on a national shape that serves U.S. purposes of treating for land, it looks as if they were damned if they did and damned if they didn't.

Identifying equal and opposite reactions, or more precisely, the limits of resistance, has become one of the most powerful strategies of the critical theory enterprise, and that it sometimes casts successes in a dim light is hardly reason enough to abandon it. Neither should we dismiss successes out of hand, however, and in the case of Cherokee nationalism, its opposition to the United States in external matters counts as a success even if it wasn't successful, hard as that is for an idealist anarchist like me to admit. The Cherokee state's assumption and expansion of coercive power in internal affairs, however, I mark down as an unnecessary and damaging departure from traditional principles and practices. If I read him right, Rikfin and I are together on this. As Partha Chatterjee and Craig Womack demonstrate in the cases of East Indian and Creek Indian nationalization, the rubric of the nation offered plenty of wiggle room for cultural specificity and innovation.[43] This flexibility means not only that land might be held in common, for instance, but also that the coercive powers of the state might have been much more sharply limited than they were in the United States or, indeed, than they came to be in the Cherokee Nation. The form of the nation-state was neither given nor inevitable then, nor is it now—just as Cherokees in the past chose what powers to invest in the state, so we could choose today what powers to curtail.

But movement along this anarchistic front would require widespread participation of Cherokee people that would be undermined by reductive criticism and history that ostracizes "the elite," together with all evils to which they've been linked, like wealth, mixed-bloodedness, Christianity, and private property.[44] We can only too easily see that these and other characteristics of "the elite" (through layers of ideological interpellation and internalization mostly other than those Rifkin identifies) have been derided as suspect and "not the Indian way" by some Cherokee and other Indian communities. One of the most pernicious sites of this kind of estrangement of dispositions and subjectivities is in education. Although traditional socialization inextricably involved education, implicating its formal modes in collaboration with the cultural enemy has led innumerable Indian people to reject pursuing college degrees and even high school diplomas. Part of the reason we consistently rank at the bottom of educational achievement owes to our accepting a view of traditionalism as incompatible with learning, despite the many historical examples of Cherokee communities soliciting schools, venerating Sequoyah's genius, and supporting public education. This dangerous and deceptive line of thinking that alienates the wealthy, the mixed-bloods, the Christians, and the educated from "true" Cherokees abets the deplorable economic conditions of many Indian people, the social divisions that foment not simple disunity or dissent but vitriol, and the atrophy of the spirit of exploration.

Although the customary characterization of the mixed-blood elite class as ideologically assimilated hardly tells us all we need to know about it or the individuals making it up, to this community, popularly imagined in this way, belonged John Ross and Elias Boudinot.

JOHN ROSS, ELIAS BOUDINOT, AND THE NATION AGAINST REMOVAL

John Ross (known in Cherokee as Cooweescoowee) was born in 1790 in Cherokee country to a Scotland-born father and a mixed-blood mother; by most accounts he was about one-eighth Cherokee and was raised in a comparatively nontraditional household, although his contact with other Cherokees was likely frequent and substantive. His father was a merchant who employed a private tutor for his children's education and later sent Ross to the Presbyterian mission school established by Gideon Blackburn in 1803 and still later sent him to other educational institutions. Although Ross was exposed to Christianity early and often, he did not embrace it until late, adopting Methodism in 1829.[45] After leaving school, he entered into business trading, an occupation in which he met with lifelong success, and into land development and speculation, becoming one of the five most affluent Cherokees of his day. He soldiered from 1813 to 1814, when he fought with a Cherokee cavalry detachment alongside General Andrew Jackson against the Creeks at the Battle at Horseshoe Bend. In 1813, he married his first wife Quatie (also known as Elizabeth Brown Henley), a Cherokee woman about whom little is published besides that she was purportedly a full-blood who helped establish Ross's credentials with the nation's conservatives.[46]

In later years Ross would speak no Cherokee, at least not for any of his public addresses. While the historical record is unclear about how much Cherokee he spoke, it seems likely that he at least had some rudimentary conversational skills given his immersion in the Cherokee world. Critics like Boudinot, however, did not miss the opportunity to upbraid him for his lack of facility.[47] Some five years after Quatie died on the Trail of Tears, Ross married Mary Stapler, a white Quaker woman from Delaware. Until her death twenty years later in 1865, she faced with him the desperate violence of factionalism following removal, enjoyed with him the prosperity of the rebuilt Cherokee Nation, and endured with him the ravages wrought by the Civil War. Following a long sickness, Ross died in 1866 in Washington, D.C., in semi-exile as he tried to negotiate a treaty that would ensure the Cherokees' continuity as a united nation while facing postwar division and renewed U.S. attacks on land and sovereignty—challenges that recurred throughout his political career.[48]

Following his military service and despite conspicuous shortages in cultural and symbolic capital, such as his limited command of Cherokee and his remote genealogy, Ross rose to unparalleled prominence as a statesman, beginning with his apprenticeship under the primary chief Pathkiller and assistant chief Charles Hicks. He served with distinction on several prominent negotiating delegations and as president of the National Committee. After the deaths of Pathkiller and Hicks in 1827, Hicks's son served a brief term as chief, but at the next election in 1828, the General Council elected Ross to the office of principal chief, a position he would hold until his death.[49] The intervening years were perhaps the most trying the Cherokee people had ever faced as they attempted to stave off the United States' relentless demands for the Cherokee Nation's final relinquishment of its remaining lands in the East and for its displacement west to Indian Territory. The bitter stories of their resistance and ultimate removal on the Trail of Tears and of the factionalism that plagued the nation from the years before removal and on past the Civil War have come to define Cherokee history for many. Ross's stewardship during these dark and dangerous times testifies to his devotion and capable leadership. He is often accounted the leader of the "full-blood majority" despite his manifest affiliations with the "prosperous minority mixed-blood faction." Some historical scholarship in the late twentieth century has revisited the extent to which Ross represented full-blood sentiments, in effect moving him from one side of the dichotomy to the other, but has more or less maintained the dialectic scheme or left the dichotomy intact.

Bernd Peyer, for instance, argues that full-blood/mixed-blood or the traditionalist/progressive dichotomies inadequately describe the range of social interaction, calling both categories "artificial," but he essentially substitutes the United States for the traditionalists in continued dialectical opposition to an undeconstructed mixed-blood class. He fits Ross smoothly into this category with his claim that "the only marked difference between Boudinot and Ross, other than Boudinot's having signed a treaty without the required sanction of the Cherokee government, was the precise point in time at which he changed his mind about removal. Three years after the Treaty Party's 'capitulation,' John Ross also concluded a removal agreement with the U.S. government even though the majority of the Cherokees were undoubtedly still against it (not to mention his earlier proposals, which had also been made without a public referendum)."[50] While Ross was indeed more prone to progressivism than most critics have allowed, to stop at Peyer's conclusion that the historical period just prior to and including removal "can be characterized as a losing race between Cherokee acculturative survival strategies and the insatiable land greed of an expanding and increasingly aggressive American nation" discourages consideration of the culturally conservative impetus for and continued role in "survival strategies" of various casts.[51] In emphasizing the U.S. lust for land, his analysis well avoids the guilty transference of greed to progressives, but it almost entirely ignores the traditionally preservative purposes to which acculturative strategies were put, effectively proclaiming the a priori triumph of the mixed-blood over the traditionalist and preemptively announcing the winner of the next contest between the United States and the progressive Indian.

For many scholars, Elias Boudinot has personified the dispositions of mixed-bloodedness and progressivism just as Ross has those of full-bloodedness and traditionalism, despite the irony that Boudinot had substantially more Cherokee blood than Ross, as did other prominent, progressive leaders like Boudinot's younger brother Stand Watie, paternal uncle Major Ridge, and cousin John Ridge. About 1804 Boudinot was born Gallegina (Buck) to Oowatie (later David Watie), who was likely either full-blooded or three-quarters

Cherokee, and Susannah Reese, whom historian and genealogist Emmet Starr records as half Cherokee and half Welsh, making Boudinot around three-quarters or five-eighths Cherokee.[52] I note Boudinot's blood quantum only because I have nowhere else seen it computed, although much has been made of Ross's exceptional "overcoming" his dearth of Indian blood. Perhaps pointing out the Watie and Ridge families' high blood percentage would undermine the vilifying association between mixed-bloodedness and assimilation. In other respects, Ross and Boudinot were uncannily similar. Like Ross, Boudinot was raised in a progressive household, in his case in the town of Oothcaloga, a community that practiced individualist rather than communal agricultural principles. He too was educated by a private tutor and in Cherokee missionary schools; the one he attended was established by Moravians at Spring Place, Georgia, in 1801. Boudinot arrived at the school in 1811 and stayed until 1818, when he left Cherokee country to continue his education and training to become a missionary at the Foreign Mission School in Cornwall, Connecticut, run by the American Board of Commissioners for Foreign Missions. John Ridge would join him there the next year. On the way to Cornwall, Gallegina, as he was still known, met the aging Elias Boudinot, president of the American Bible Society and Revolutionary War-era statesman, and the two were mutually impressed. Gallegina took on the elder Boudinot as a benefactor and thenceforth adopted his name. Educational opportunities besides those offered by missionaries were few and far between, and to be sure, many Cherokees like Ross abided their proselytizing for the educational benefits. Boudinot, on the other hand, was a devout Christian wholly dedicated to the cause of converting Cherokee people, having himself converted in 1820.[53]

Also like Ross, Boudinot married a white woman, but with considerably greater opposition than Ross encountered. It was at Cornwall that Boudinot met, fell in love with, and in 1826 ultimately married Harriet Ruggles Gold, the white daughter of a school official, replaying John Ridge's controversial interracial marriage to Sarah Bird Northrup in 1824. The vitriolic reaction by the ostensibly progressive northeasterners—which brought Gold's own brother to the town square to burn her and Boudinot's pictures in effigy—revealed to Boudinot the sharply circumscribed degrees to which Indians would be welcome in white society. They could convert to Christianity, educate themselves, and attend the country's finest institutions (Boudinot aspired to study at Andover, then Yale, but was prevented by illness). In short, they could *mimic* anything whites did so long as they understood that their imitations, born in deficient difference, remained marked by an ineradicable and insurmountable imperfection. In Homi Bhabha's terms, they could become "almost the same, but not quite" (or "almost the same, but not white"). As such, they needed to remain conscious of their difference to dissuade hubristic expectations of equality.[54] Despite the death threats, denouncements from pulpits, editorial invectives, and public condemnation in all shapes of vehement disapproval, Boudinot and Gold were married, four years after Boudinot left Cornwall. She joined him in Cherokee country where they worked closely with missionaries on their civilizing and educational endeavors. Still dedicated to the civilization and Christianization of the Cherokees, Boudinot appears to have been utterly persuaded, however, that Indians and whites would never be able to live together equally in American society and thus turned his efforts to the development of the Cherokee Nation.[55]

In its attempts to strengthen national solidarity and to resist U.S. demands for land cessions, the Cherokee Nation looked for public venues to communicate with its citizens and to make its case to foreign allies. Recognizing Boudinot's literary and rhetorical talents, in 1826 the government set him to work on a speaking tour across the Northeast to raise money for the establishment of a national academy and a newspaper. With uncommon acumen, the government foresaw not only the cohesive, nationalistic force a newspaper would inspire, compensating for the proliferating fragmentation of other social and religious structures, but also its persuasive potential in offering sympathetic audiences alternative accounts of the depredations they faced in resisting the expansion of American empire. The hoped-for school would have to wait, but the speech Boudinot delivered, "An Address to the Whites," reprinted as a pamphlet, earned enough to buy a printing press, and a paper was established with the National Council's authorization. Beginning with its first issue in 1828, the *Cherokee Phoenix* printed news, editorials, laws, and some cultural and religious material in both Cherokee and English, taking advantage of Sequoyah's prodigious invention around 1821 of a syllabary for the Cherokee language. With the assistance of missionary Samuel Worcester, Boudinot drafted numerous editorials, selected content exchanged with other newspapers, corrected proofs, managed the business end, and translated material like the Bible, newly passed and pre-existing laws, and religious tracts, to be published in the *Phoenix* and separately. For a salary of $300 per year, he served as editor of the *Phoenix* from its founding until 1832, when he found himself at odds with John Ross over the question of the editor's liberty in discussing the removal question in the nationally owned forum.[56]

Demand for Indian land was hardly new in the early nineteenth century, but Jeffersonian civilization programs had checked the militancy of early years. Many Cherokees cooperated with the government agents and missionaries, who urged adoption and development of white models of religion, agriculture, education, economy, political structure, and more. Later, in the pages of the *Phoenix*, in speeches, anywhere it might be persuasive, Cherokees pointed to their advancement in civilization according to the measures set before them as a means not just of countering false descriptions of their continued savagery—a tactic trotted out to demonstrate Indians' inability to understand the principles of cultivation and property and to establish their consequently inferior claims to land—but also to demand consistency and follow-through in federal policy.[57] Andrew Jackson, elected to the presidency in 1828, promoted acquiring Indians' remaining eastern lands through their removal well beyond the Mississippi. His removal policy aggressively pursued land cessions through means both above and below board, couched in the benevolent language of facilitating Indian civilization by moving it away from the pernicious influences of unscrupulous whites who could not be controlled by the federal government. Georgia eagerly assented to his plans, emboldened to pursue the acquisition of Cherokee lands under the terms of an 1802 compact with the federal government in which the state relinquished its claim to western lands in return for the federal promise to extinguish Indian claims within its borders as soon as it could be peaceably accomplished. The discovery of gold in Cherokee country only provided added incentive for the state to make "peaceably" a relative term.[58]

The means it found maintained at least the appearance of legitimacy under the rule of law, a guise important to the United States' imagination of itself as a nation of justice and order. Heedless of Cherokees' protests, Jackson's administration exacerbated their troubles in pushing for the passage of the Indian Removal Act of 1830, which authorized the federal government to negotiate treaties providing for final land cessions and removal. Jackson also withheld the annuity payments from previous land cessions that constituted the Cherokees' major operational funding and withdrew the federal troops charged with maintaining order and protecting Cherokee boundaries against intrusion. Attempting effectively to abolish the Cherokee government, in 1829 Georgia proclaimed the annexation of Cherokee country and the extension of its laws throughout the Cherokee Nation, disallowing, for instance, Cherokees mining their gold, contracts between Indians and whites not witnessed by two whites, any action that might dissuade others from removing, the assembly of Cherokee councils or courts, and the testimony of Indians against whites in Georgia's courts. This last especially pernicious disenfranchisement essentially urged Georgians to rob and intimidate with impunity; historians record instances of attempted rape and even murder that went unpunished by the state judiciary branch in its collusion with the Georgia governor. The Georgia Guard militia that ostensibly replaced federal troops to protect Cherokees and their interests more often aided and abetted their harassment, such as when it twice arrested Boudinot on charges of libel.[59]

Despite their difficulties, the Cherokees through advocacy in the *Phoenix* and elsewhere found allies, many of them federalists opposed to Jacksonian politics and sometimes also to his removal policy. Some like prominent missionary and editorialist Jeremiah Evarts advised the Cherokee Nation—acting as a foreign nation—to bring a test case to the U.S. Supreme Court in order to challenge Georgia's presumption of jurisdiction over Indian lands. One case looked like it might fit the bill in contesting Georgia's jurisdiction. George Tassel (or Corn Tassel), a Cherokee citizen, was accused of killing Cornelius Dougherty, another Cherokee citizen, in a drunken desire that he share the same grave with his childhood friend, or possibly in a dispute over a woman. He was arrested and scheduled for execution by Georgia authorities over his objections that he be tried in a Cherokee court.[60] Before Tassel's potentially potent appeal to the Supreme Court could get into full swing, however, Georgia ignored the Supreme Court's order to appear and carried out his hanging.[61] The Cherokee Nation moved on its own in the case *Cherokee Nation v. Georgia* (1831), in which the federalist chief justice John Marshall ruled that Indian nations are not foreign in the constitutional sense but rather "domestic dependent nations" in a state of pupilage or wardship to the U.S. government and so had no standing in the suit as it was brought.

Marshall's ambiguous phrasing then as now left some room for the exercise and recognition of Indian sovereignty, and he himself suggested the court would revisit the question if the matter of jurisdiction were more firmly established. The opportunity arose when the missionary Samuel Worcester and others were arrested for refusing to take an oath of allegiance to Georgia and its laws. In *Worcester v. Georgia* (1832) the Marshall court ruled that Georgia had indeed overstepped its bounds and that its extension of state law over Indian land was unconstitutional and illegal in its encroachment on federal jurisdiction. In ordering the release of Worcester, the court was ordering Georgia to desist its usurpation, but as the case made evident, the judicial branch had no means of effecting compliance with its rulings if faced with a recalcitrant executive or legislative branch. Recognizing the judiciary's powerlessness, untroubled by the revelation that the system of checks and balances rested upon a sandy foundation of good-faith compliance, and unfazed by any compunction to execute a directive contrary to his policies, Jackson, in a probably apocryphal remark, said, "John Marshall has rendered his decision; now let him enforce it."[62]

Elias Boudinot, John Ridge, Major Ridge, and others had long been at the forefront of the struggle against removal, but after it became clear that the United States had no intention of testing Georgia's resolve for the sake of protecting the Cherokees, these former opponents of removal settled on a new course. They began to contemplate the merits of taking the nation away from the Georgia Guard, away from the thieves of their property, their dignity, their lives—but also away from the ancestral homes of their families, away from the mutually constitutive land where they had been since time immemorial. Once Boudinot began to question the tenability of resistance to removal in the pages of the *Phoenix,* he found himself at odds with John Ross, and he resigned his editorship in mid-1832—more on this in the next chapter. Three years after leaving the *Phoenix,* as conditions degenerated and Ross met with increasing stubbornness in Washington against any accommodation for continued Cherokee presence in the East, Boudinot was convinced that removal was the only course that offered any chance of Cherokee survival, in an all too literal sense. He joined the Ridges and some twenty others in signing the New Echota treaty against the manifest wishes of the overwhelming majority of the people, ceding all remaining claims in exchange for $5 million and land in what would become Oklahoma.[63] All signed in full awareness that, in doing so without approval of the National Council, they were more or less subject to lawful, summary execution at the hands of any Cherokee citizen who found it expedient. Major Ridge himself had not only helped pass the law forbidding unauthorized land cessions, but he had also served as co-executioner in the killing of Doublehead, a chief who ceded land without approval in 1807.[64]

Although Ross mounted a persuasive campaign to discredit the fraudulent treaty—publishing pamphlets detailing its spurious origin, marshaling support from the likes of Ralph Waldo Emerson and John Quincy Adams, and gathering some fifteen thousand signers of a petition protesting its ratification—the Senate did ratify it and then-president Martin Van Buren signed it into law in 1835. Ross kept up the campaign for the next three years, but in 1838 federal troops began rounding up Cherokees and moving them at bayonet point into stockades. Perhaps these were the "kraals" Justice Johnson had in mind in *Cherokee Nation v. Georgia.* Removal commenced shortly thereafter, and some four thousand, about a quarter of the tribe, died on the Trail of Tears. Boudinot and the Ridges died not there but shortly after their arrival in Indian Territory, all killed on the same day in 1839.[65] Major Ridge was shot while riding along a trail; John Ridge was dragged from his bed and stabbed multiple times in front of his wife and son. Some men saying a friend needed medicine approached Boudinot while he was constructing his new home, and as he went off to help, they attacked him with knives and hatchets and crushed his skull.

These were the circumstances, these the stakes, these the lives—of my own farming people, leaving their twenty-five acres in corn in the old Hickory Log District for Goingsnake District, a thousand miles away—that mattered in the rhetoric of removal. As I turn now to the literature, I bear them in mind.

ᏈᏝᏢ

CHAPTER 5

The Removal Rhetoric of Elias Boudinot and John Ross

In language commonly thought "assimilationist," both John Ross and Elias Boudinot championed the civilization programs the United States proffered as a means of resolving its Indian troubles, but far from evidencing their acceptance of whites' representations of Indianism, to modify Edward Said's phrase, they tellingly advocated civilization programs not just to Cherokees but also to the United States itself. As they questioned the consistency of the United States' policies of civilization and removal, they insisted that the "civilizers" follow through on their promises to provide the protection and educational opportunities guaranteed by treaties as a matter of general humanitarian concern. When they advocated civilization to Cherokee audiences, however, it was not as an end in itself nor in anticipation of the demise of Cherokee culture, but rather as a secondary means of achieving the primary goal of ensuring the survival of the Cherokee nation as a distinct cultural-political entity. Even when Boudinot concluded that independence could not be achieved in the East and began to consider removal, it was only as a means toward this larger goal. I do not choose up sides in this chapter or attempt to prove that the treaty party members were traitors or patriots, or that Ross was a tyrant or savior. Instead, I look into the contradictions and crossovers between progressivism and conservatism in their writings, speeches, and policies surrounding civilization, removal, and the very act of speaking for the nation. On this last point, I look behind conventional opposition to the changes made to the habitus that restricted the former indigenist anarchist practices of political dissent and exacerbated the factionalism and violence that plagued the nation for decades afterwards. While U.S. colonialism is the primary culprit in this silencing, the Cherokees' own actions and reactions, and their exercise of control over their discursive worlds, matters too. With the understanding that just because an act is volitional, it isn't necessarily justified or even effective, this reorientation toward epistemic continuity and rupture suggests that although political centralization aspired to defend the nation's physical and cultural boundaries, its attendant strategies for establishing hegemony ran counter to the irrepressible dispositions of deliberation and dissent. As a means of rejuvenating Cherokee anarchism's cultural and political traditions and of moving toward progressively inclusive and representative governance, there is no better way to start bringing Cherokee people together than by relearning how to hear them differing.

CIVILIZING THE SAVAGES

Much of Boudinot's writing and rhetoric prior to his pro-removal shift proclaimed the progress the Cherokees had made toward civilization, against competing and pervasive arguments that alleged the savagery of Indians in general and/or Cherokees in particular. In "An Address to the Whites," a speech he gave in Philadelphia in 1826 to raise money for a printing press and a national school, he states, "It cannot be doubted that the nation is improving, rapidly improving in all those particulars which must finally constitute the inhabitants an industrious and intelligent people. It is a matter of surprise to me . . . that the Cherokees have advanced so far and so rapidly in civilization. But there are yet powerful obstacles. . . . The prejudices in regard to them in the general community are strong and lasting."[1] Such prejudices cropped up in debates over whether Indians had the ability to progress into civilization at all, an argument Boudinot counters with concrete evidence, statistics, and specific examples. He imagines that unfair discrimination can be countered with a basic education campaign: "The time has arrived when speculations and conjectures as to the practicability of civilizing the Indians must forever cease. . . . It needs only that the world should know what we have done in the few last years, to foresee what yet we may do with the assistance of our white brethren."[2] The discourse of savagery, like that of Orientalism, was accruing institutional authority and was emanating from religious, scientific, political, and other sectors, and its representations from privileged positions were marshaled as proof that removal was in the best interests of both the savage and civilized.[3] Despite his qualified acceptance of the general developmental paradigm, Boudinot's denial of the belief that Indians were incapable of civilization or progress is no small thing, nor is his turning the tables on his white audience, alleging that prejudice on its part—not incapacity on the Indians'—most stood in the way of progress for both. The realization of that progress would require effort on both sides.

Boudinot returns over and over to themes of progress and civilization, often as distinct from Cherokee traditions, expressing hopes that superstition and savage institutions might soon be eradicated. He uses language we now find shockingly sad, but it was perhaps then calculated to curry favor and excite white audiences to sympathetic activism. For instance, having recorded a description of clan structure and its administration of the blood law of homicide revenge, he writes, "Our readers will say, 'those were savage laws indeed.' They were, and the Cherokees were then to be pitied. . . . But we can now say with pleasure, that they are all repealed, and are remembered only as vestiges of ignorance and barbarism."[4] For Boudinot, ignorance and barbarism are opposed by Christianization and civilization, whose implements—but not whose administration—he solicits from white benefactors. Boudinot's striking antitraditionalist sentiments seemingly leave little room for doubt about his attitudes, but they are called into question by a closer examination of what progress in civilization, apparently the converse of traditionalism, consists in his rhetoric.

In several instances, he in fact calls for the development and retention of already existing institutions, such as the rule of law, and not for the eradication of traditional superstructures in, for instance, governance, worship, industry, or culture. Failing to understand in

Boudinot's rhetoric the narrow construction of "civilization" and the breadth of traditional practices and beliefs set aside from the civilizing enterprise, many of his critics have understood his advocacy of progress as a personal cultural inadequacy. They see it as a failure manifested in a rejection and repudiation of all facets of distinctly Cherokee culture, further inferring a reciprocal rejection on the part of Cherokee communities. Theda Perdue, for instance, writes:

> The Cherokee Nation was composed primarily of traditionalists who clung to the culture Boudinot dedicated his life to eradicating. . . . Boudinot, in seeking to create a homogeneous "civilized" nation, was going against the widespread tendency among Cherokees to accept divergent lifestyles and customs as long as they did not jeopardize the community. And because he was part of a very small minority which tried almost to compel people to undergo a cultural transformation, other Cherokees probably viewed him with some suspicion. . . . Elias Boudinot was a tragic figure not just because he made a serious error in judgment or because he paid the ultimate price but because he could not accept his people, his heritage, or himself. He was the product of colonization, and his thoughts and deeds may well tell us as much about our own culture as about nineteenth-century Cherokees.[5]

Perdue turns the limitations of binarism to her advantage here, on one hand clearing away as internalized colonialism the contradictions and ambiguities Boudinot presents to these generalizations of progressivism (which are only too representative of critical material on Boudinot), and on the other suspending traditionalism in time, withholding from it the means or interest in adaptation, however dire or promising the circumstances. Traditionalists may only "cling" to a disappearing past, hoping against hope to save a static version of traditional culture from the forces opposing it. Perdue does not everywhere cast tradition as so starkly opposed to change. Her work on Cherokee women, for instance, champions Cherokee agency and dynamism, but her methodology and her conclusions in this instance paint tradition as overly suspicious of change. Even as Boudinot's life and work can tell us something of the effects of colonialism, as Perdue suggests, her assumptions of and for a certain audience may indeed "tell us more about *our* own culture" than *we* might wish to know: that Indians, "their" history and "their" agency are for "us" to tell, for "us" to read, and for elucidating "our" interests. This is another suspicious "product of colonization": to have our (without scare quotes now) intellectuals, our histories, our capacity to shape our own lives, stripped away and defined by their connections to the original, the only real, "us." An emic assessment of Boudinot's work must admit his failure to imagine a future for many Cherokee dispositions, but it can also allow us to look beyond this fatalism to see other ideas of his—ideas shared by many traditionalists—as early steps in ongoing efforts to strengthen Cherokee people.

Against Perdue's claim that "throughout his life, Boudinot maintained that the preservation of his people depended solely upon abandonment of their own traditions, culture, and history," I argue that Cherokee traditions, culture, and history were conveyed in his ideas of civilization and progress, though they were by turns overt, tacit, defiant, untheorized, or unconscious.[6] Further, they are enacted in the expression of the ideas. They are enunciatively performed forces themselves, not pieces of flotsam tragically clung to against their eventual, inevitable sinking. I am not claiming Boudinot was everywhere attempting calculated rhetorical subversion or that he was not influenced by or even essentially "on board" with mainstream ideas of civilization and progress. But, insofar as his speeches and *Phoenix* editorials were largely directed toward white audiences, that he would use terms calculated to find favor with them is not surprising.[7] I also wonder how clear a sense we have of how he and other early nineteenth-century Cherokee people understood progress and civilization, developed as they were by Cherokees and for Cherokee purposes, all during a relatively early point in white relations, and thus at a not-too-distant remove from the traditional habitus. Boudinot's notions of these contested programs retain more of tradition and communal agency than we have been able to see.

Most criticism conveniently opposes Ross to Boudinot on the matter of tradition. Maureen Konkle, for instance, points to Ross's cooperation with John Howard Payne on his early ethnography and concludes, "It appears that Ross understood traditional knowledge as *history* and, unlike Ridge and Boudinot, believed that it should not be rejected but rather written down and accounted for, and celebrated."[8] Such sympathies notwithstanding, Ross too found occasion to invoke the language of civilization while repudiating tradition, writing to President James Monroe,

> Father. The ignorant and wretched condition of your red children makes them in some degree inferior to their white brethren. . . . Your magnanimous and benevolent exertions have not been in vain, as respects the Cherokees, education, agriculture, manufacture, and the mechanic arts have been introduced among them, and are now progressing. . . . The liberal encouragement given by the nation for general improvement, cannot fail to accomplish their complete civilization. True, there are many who have been raised under the native habits of their ancestors . . . but under the present aspect of improvement, they will not fail to encourage their children to adopt the prevailing habits of industry and civilizations; therefore as the old stubbles disappear, the new sprouts will flourish under cultivation.[9]

Ross celebrates progress as enthusiastically as Boudinot and just as troublingly parrots the language of savagery and inevitable demise that accompanied white claims to superiority. The agricultural metaphor invoking the passing of the old to make way for the new lends a sense of naturalness to the process, which is applauded by the emphasis on improvement. As with Boudinot, Ross here also speaks to his audience in its own language, calculating that an entreaty that has to be translated will hardly make it more persuasive to this audience.

A year later he would write to President John Quincy Adams in a yet more strident tone: "For the sake of civilization and preservation of existence, we would willingly see the habits and customs of the aboriginal man extinguished, the sooner this takes place, the great stumbling block, *prejudice,* will be removed."[10] Like Boudinot, Ross ricochets the rhetoric of moral inferiority back at those firing the first shot, indicting whites' uncivilized bias as the primary impediment to Cherokee progress, not any deficiency of the Cherokees' in ability or effort. Contrasting the two, Perdue claims, "John Ross was personally as highly acculturated as Boudinot, but Ross represented traditionalists and did so without exerting any pressure on them to change their beliefs or their way of life."[11] Yet Ross, as president of the National Council and then principal chief, aided in the passage of laws altering inheritance, political centralization, and encouragement of civilization, all of which exerts just such pressure for change. The "extinguishing" of tradition through civilization for which Ross seems to be calling, like Boudinot's relegation of it to mere "vestiges" is not, however, unequivocal, for it is subordinated to the "preservation of existence." Though Ross and Boudinot do not say as much, I argue that the eradication of tradition that they seem to advocate should not be understood as the desirable erasure of *all* traditions, but as the alteration or perhaps abandonment of certain untenable or sacrificial practices or principles—or possibly just the appearance of such "progress" for rhetorical purposes—in order that the greater number of other traditional practices might be preserved.

Like Ross, Boudinot adopted the rhetoric and programs of civilization and progress precisely to further a culturally and politically preservative goal, using the most effective defense available. As Ross put it, "The Cherokees, under any circumstances, have no weapon to use but argument."[12] Ostensibly borrowing from what Perdue calls the "basic European creed," Boudinot emphasized several features Cherokees should adopt to become like "'civilized' peoples [who] had farms, republican governments, Christian churches, and systems of writings," as opposed to "'Savages' [who] hunted for a living, relied on frequently brutal customs for their law, worshiped nature or idols, and lacked a written language."[13] In "An Address to the Whites" he details "those particulars which must finally constitute the inhabitants an industrious and intelligent people," in which the Cherokees are progressing and that best "act as a powerful argument in favor of Indian improvement: First. The invention of letters. Second. The translation of the New Testament into Cherokee. And third. The organization of a Government."[14] To these he later adds success in education and industry. He would brandish evidence of that progress in his editorials up to 1832, proclaiming in representative language, *"The common Indian among the Cherokees is not declining, but rising."*[15] Boudinot's writings were practical, not philosophical, and he offers few elaborations on his ideas of "improvement," "civilization," and the like, but statements such as these offer some glimpses into his brand of progress through the affiliations and practices he links to it.

The first evidence he offers of Cherokees' capacity for becoming civilized, "the invention of letters," is fundamentally about their educability and desire for education, the point of which is, again, the preservation of the Cherokees as a distinct cultural and political body. As was true for much of the United States, religious institutions offered the Cherokee the only practical option for education, and in Boudinot's speech both religion and education are linked to writing—distinctively Cherokee writing. After lauding the achievement of Sequoyah (whom he refers to by his English name), Boudinot makes the three-way connection explicit: "The translation of the New Testament, together with Guest's mode of writing, has swept away that barrier which has long existed, and opened a spacious channel for the instruction of adult Cherokees."[16] The barrier of illiteracy stands in the way primarily of evangelism for Boudinot, but the passage's ambiguity also suggests the attenuated opportunities for discourse, which are broadened by writing as a conduit for national communication. This interpretation is strengthened when we recall the purpose of his talk was to raise money for a national newspaper. In 1832 when Ross wrote to Sequoyah, then living with western emigrants, to present him with a congratulatory medal for his invention of the syllabary, he too identifies the similar "untraditional" connections among the Cherokee language and white religion and education: "The present generation have already experienced the great benefits of your incomparable system. The old & the youth find no difficulty in learning to read & write in their native language and to correspond with their distant friends with the same facility as the whites do. Types have been made and a printing press established in this nation. The scriptures have been translated & printed in Cherokee; and whilst posterity continues to be benefited by the discovery, your name will exist in grateful remembrance. It will also serve as an index for the aboriginal tribes, or nations, similarly to advance in science and respectability."[17] Ross demonstrates the value writing has in Christian evangelism and in learning, but in also pointing to its cohesive force—its capacity to bring together in words those separated by geography, age, or religion—he puts writing, "advance" in education, and religion in the service of "nationing," the political movement that makes nations of tribes. Though cognizant of internal differences among Cherokee people in terms of age and geographical residence, Ross understands the differences as ancillary to a unified national consciousness, and he particularly values the roles of education and writing in its service.

Encouraging education as a means of developing a specifically Cherokee civilization appears throughout the rhetoric of this period. In a May 1828 editorial tallying the projected high costs of removal to the United States, Boudinot suggests the funds might be better spent on schooling and hopes that Cherokee learning will continue in the native tongue: "With this money let their [*sic*] be a college founded, where every advantage of instruction may be enjoyed. Let books, tracts, &c. be published in Cherokee and English, and distributed throughout the Nation and every possible effort be made to civilize us, let us at the same time be protected in our rights."[18] Two important dispositions are revealed here: first, as languages in no small part structure and generate the knowledge that inheres in cultures, with marked differences among them, the propagation of the Cherokee language as a component in formal education and in connecting communities in national discourse via the newspaper and other printed material marks a material commitment to upholding profound cultural distinctiveness and independence along the road to civilization. Boudinot's work in translating religious texts with their abstractions, the poetry of hymns with their rhythms and aesthetics, or simply Cherokee's basic classificatory verbs that conjugate for texture, shape, flexibility, and so on, or the ten pronominal prefixes, would have no doubt made him keenly aware that some things can only be said—can only be thought—in Cherokee, with its singular denotations and connotations. Such complexity would surely have inspired in this man made of words a desire for that knowledge and way of knowing to be retained. Though he urges Cherokees to learn English, I have nowhere found that advocacy tied to an attack on the Cherokee language. At Brainerd and at Cornwall, the missionaries' interest in learning native languages to aid their evangelism no doubt helped Boudinot see the advantages of bilingualism. To be sure, not all missionaries were so (counter) progressive, and some marked native languages for eradication, cognizant of the languages' cohesive and "atavistic" influence, an influence Boudinot turned to preservative advantage.[19] Several missionaries, such as Samuel Worcester, Evan Jones, and John Jones, however, made it a point to learn Cherokee.

Second, the closing conjunctive phrase of this excerpt, "let . . . every effort be made to civilize us, let us at the same time be protected in our rights," reminds his readers of their freely accepted responsibilities both to offer access to civilization and education (and, as it turns out, cultural nationalism) and to protect the Cherokees' rights to their land and sovereignty. The U.S. government had pledged itself to do both in Jefferson's civilization programs and since its first treaties with their oft-repeated promise that, by allying with and placing themselves under the United States' "protection," the Cherokees were guaranteed their security. But what precisely were the rights Boudinot wanted preserved? Like the terms "progress" and "civilization," he frequently leaves them undefined, perhaps because he imagines them as self-evident truths, or perhaps because he prefers to allow his readers to hang on to their unproblematic understandings and to allow the cultural resistance in his to go unspoken.

He does offer some clues about rights as he sees them in a January 1829 editorial:

> The causes which have operated to exterminate the Indian tribes that are produced as instances of the certain doom of the whole Aboriginal family appear plain to us. . . . They were precisely such causes as are now attempted by the state of Georgia—by infringing on their rights—by disorganizing them, and circumscribing their limits. While he possesses a national character, there is hope for the Indian. But take his rights away, divest him of the last spark of national pride, and introduce him to a new order of things, invest him with oppressive laws, grievous to be borne, he droops like the fading flower before noon day sun. . . . There is hope for the Cherokees as long as they continue in their present situation, but disorganize them, either by removing them beyond the Mississippi, or by imposing on them "heavy burdens," you cut a vital string in their national existence.[20]

Rights, then, are political and national in character as the legitimating principles of self-government—of sovereignty, as we now call it. In his language of organization, he stakes for the Cherokee Nation an equal claim to those rights America asserted in the Declaration of Independence to form a government, "*organizing* its powers in such form, as to them shall seem most likely to effect their safety and happiness," and, implicitly, for the nation to protect itself from foreign infringement and oppressions like those perpetrated by Georgia. With his emphasis on "oppressive laws," he again recalls Jefferson's objections to external British rule: "In every stage of these oppressions we have petitioned for redress in the most humble terms: our repeated petitions have been answered only by repeated injury. . . . We have warned ['our British brethren'] from time to time of attempts by their legislature to extend an unwarrantable jurisdiction over us." By likening Georgia's jurisdictional extension to tyranny, Boudinot draws a political parallel between the Cherokee and the American revolutionaries, claiming for the Cherokees the same rights of liberty. His allusion to "heavy burdens" suggests Matthew 23:4, where Christ says of the Pharisees, "For they bind heavy burdens and grievous to be borne, and lay them on men's shoulders; but they themselves will not move them with one of their fingers," which draws an unflattering religious parallel between the Georgians and the Pharisees, who opposed Roman rule and passed onerous laws by which they themselves would not be bound. Asserting the Cherokees' right to a "national existence," to maintain their own geographic and conceptual limits, Boudinot declares independence for the Cherokee Nation on historical, philosophic, and religious grounds so that its people might deliberate and determine their own course, free of unjust and immoral discrimination.

Traditionalists had taken similar steps in the past, not just in times preceding European contact, but in their insistence on the very civilization programs that later critics have used as evidence of acquiescence to colonialism. Several instances testify to the Cherokees' volitional control over education in the nation, from their near expulsion of missionaries who had failed in their promises to provide instruction, to the community-built schools at Creek Path, to historian William McLoughlin's general sense that "missionary schools tended to be founded in response to local requests for them rather than according to any prearranged plan."[21] The National Council's desire for schools brought it at one point in 1819 to delegate John Ross and others to look into plans "to establish an endowment to support schools by selling a tract of its [the nation's] land that would fetch a good price."[22] They were successful in having the project included in the treaty they signed in February of 1819, allowing for the sale of twelve square miles to establish a school fund.[23] As late as 1833, Ross pressured Lewis Cass, Jackson's secretary of war, to learn "what disposition has been made of the lands reserved under the treaty of 1819 for the purpose of raising a school fund for our nation, and if sold, to state the amount of the proceeds and also the application made of the same."[24] Such a transaction points up the deficiency of characterizations of traditionalism as opposed to or incapable of understanding Christianity, education, or the principles of marketable real estate. For many, the integrity of the nation depended not solely on past principled practices of worship, industry, place, and others, but also on its people and their capacity to exercise agency in a dramatically changed and changing world, one that demanded the benefits of education and adaptability.

The nation's leaders directed Boudinot to work for the same ends. One object of his 1826 fund-raising tour was the establishment of a national secondary academy, the benefits of which he thought so evident that he saw no need to "spend one moment in arguments, in favour of such an institution; need I speak one word of the utility, of the necessity, of an institution of learning."[25] He would, though, write of the project and its proposed funding via real estate profits in a later editorial, arguing, "The Cherokees as a nation have had sufficient time to learn and appreciate the advantages of knowledge: for what else distinguishes them from their brethren? . . . It becomes every citizen then, particularly every ruler, as a guardian of the nation's welfare, to do his utmost endeavor to forward education. . . . It is this which will preserve us from the common burial place of Indians—oblivion, in which many tribes are forgotten, & to which many would suppose us to be hastening."[26] Here, as in Ross's letter to Sequoyah quoted above celebrating the syllabary as "an index for the aboriginal tribes," Boudinot's language suggests an exceptionalist attitude, and while both were Cherokee chauvinists, they situate progress in education as a matter of context rather than of essential predilection. More important than education itself, though, are "the advantages of knowledge," principal among them that the "nation's welfare" may be better guarded and "preserve[d]." If somewhat haughtily, they held up their efforts as methods other tribes might emulate to similarly protect their cultures. According to Boudinot's reasoning, education is not a means by which civilization supplants traditionalist culture but a means of defending its independent character and physically preserving Indian lives; education emerges as the primary strategy by which politicians can uphold their protective duties to the people. For him and other Cherokees, securing access to education was a paramount responsibility of the political arm.

The commitment to education was so much the product of collective political agency that it was written into the sixth article of the Cherokee Constitution of 1827, which was ratified by the conservative National Council. The article reads, "Religion, morality and knowledge being necessary to good government, the preservation of liberty and the happiness of mankind, schools and the means of education shall forever be encouraged in this Nation."[27] In words absent from the U.S. Constitution but present in that of Massachusetts, this article establishes with remarkable clarity the benefits the Cherokee Nation identified in education's interrelationship not just with religion but also with the polity, in its cultivation of an informed, critically thinking population that through the aid of educational institutions established by the government would ultimately improve government itself, "knowledge being necessary to good government." An educated people further works toward "the happiness of mankind" and "the preservation of liberty": goals carefully constructed in parallel phrases that indicate their equal footing with and relevance to the practices of political sovereignty, through the people's principled and informed governance of the government. McLoughlin argues that this clause was controversial among those opposed to change too drastic and swift, noting its careful wording that equivocates how positively the Nation saw the connection between religion and education. The wording, and, of course, the article's very inclusion nonetheless endorse education, undoubtedly anticipating the Cherokees' own administration of their schools.[28]

CIVILIZING THE CIVILIZED

Although not citizens of the United States, the Cherokees' treaties bound the nations together and provided the foundation for their political relations, and appeals to the history and the structure of those negotiations between sovereign equals became staples of Cherokee anti-removal rhetoric. Ross regularly invoked treaty history in his memorials to Congress, his speeches, and throughout his writing.[29] Boudinot, too, criticized U.S. failures in its Indian policies by frequent reference to treaties. In his anti removal editorials, he made the United States' upholding of its treaty obligations an express measure of the nation's constitutional legitimacy, its consistency in its Indian policy, and its morality according to its own professed standards of civilized and Christian conduct. As historian Angela Pulley Hudson summarizes, "He accused the US government of supreme hypocrisy by illustrating the ways in which the measures taken by state and federal officials were wholly opposite to both the spirit and letter of the US Constitution."[30] In the same 1829 editorial in which Boudinot discusses the right of organizing a sovereign government over and against Georgia's attempt to impose its othering laws, he writes, "The United States must either defend us in our rights, or leave us to our foe. In the former case, the General Government will redeem her pledge solemnly given in treaties.—In the latter, she will violate her promise of protection, and we cannot, in future, depend, consistently, upon any guarantee made by her to us, either here or beyond the Mississippi."[31] His call for the federal government to uphold its treaties by claiming the jurisdiction delineated in the U.S. Constitution intersected with the escalating conflict over the powers of the federal government and those of the states, effectively challenging the United States to demonstrate its commitment to constitutional precepts, not just for the Cherokees' sake but to prove that its national presence was not empty posture.

In an 1831 editorial, Boudinot observes the challenge to federal power posed by South Carolina's threat to nullify protective tariffs: "The conduct of the Georgia Legislature is indeed surprising—one day they discountenance the proceedings of the nullifiers of South Carolina—at another, they even out-do the people of South Carolina, and authorize their Governor to hoist the flag of rebellion against the United States! If such proceedings are sanctioned by the majority of the people of the U. States, the Union is but a tottering fabric, which will soon fall and crumble into atoms."[32] His reference to the United States as a "fabric," a contrivance of human hands, denaturalizes the nation as a permanent given and reminds his readers of the need for maintenance against its degeneration, which would require consistency in policy and philosophy. If the United States were to prove unable to carry out the promises made in treaties as *"the supreme law of the land"* (which Boudinot in a later piece quoted from the U.S. Constitution's sixth article), then citizens, states, tribes, and foreign governments likewise could not "depend consistently" on its other guarantees, past, present, or future.[33]

His critique of consistency accrues meaning throughout his editorials. When some members of Congress opposed to the Indian Removal Act amended it with a declaration of the inviolability of preceding treaties, he bristles with irony at the empty display of support: "We confess our ignorance, our utter ignorance, of the views of the majority of the members of Congress, so far as they have been developed, on the rights of the Indians, and the relation in which they stand to the United States, on the score of treaties; nor can we discern the consistency of contending for the unconstitutionality of these treaties, and yet at the same time, declaring that *they shall not be violated.*"[34] He skewers the rational inconsistency of declaring that treaties must be upheld while in the very same act Congress authorizes their abrogation. His rhetoric simultaneously treats consistency as a foundational logical principle and as a defining quality of substance. That is, he interrogates what things consist of—things like treaties and constitutionality. He asks that the United States behave consistently in both substance and method: it should unambiguously declare what treaties are and how they will be treated. To help the United States out of its apparent confusion, he suggests that it simply look to its own definition of treaties as the "supreme law of the land," and appends the Cherokee understanding that they are "solemn instruments," imposing "sacred obligations," entered into freely and supported by the rule of law, which ought to be theoretically consistent in its noncontradiction and its durability.[35] Consistency thus also becomes a matter of temporality. Boudinot argues that if the United States fails to act with predictable regularity toward states' challenges to federal power, as he claims it has not in its condemnation of South Carolina and its indulgence of Georgia, it will not long exist as a nation but will *"soon* fall and crumble into atoms." He prophecies that if the United States will not uphold its treaties and bind states to comply with federal law, the failure to support and exercise the legitimating authority of the Constitution would undermine the United States' moral and structural integrity, and its abrogation of its promises to its peer nations and to itself will jeopardize its ability to long endure, certainly in its self-proclaimed guise as a moral, Christian nation.

Boudinot regularly remonstrates with his audience to reverse the United States' oppressive, coercive, and disingenuous course on the basis of its incompatibility with the Christian precepts upon which the nation was ostensibly founded and operated, and by which it justified its right of expansion. In a particularly philippic letter sent in to the *Phoenix* while he was on another fund-raising tour, he writes,

> To take our lands by force is a serious matter—it is fraught with considerations full of interest to the people of Georgia themselves and to the whole Union. . . . It would be robbery to all intent and purposes. And would the General Government look on with indifference and see its solemn pledges trampled in the dust? "There is a Lion in the way" whether the Government of the United States interferes or not—The integrity of the Union is at stake. As respects the Cherokees . . . they reside on the land which God gave them—they are surrounded with guarantees which this Republic has voluntarily made for their protection and which once formed a sufficient security against oppression. If those guarantees must now be violated with impunity for purposes altogether selfish, the sin will not be at our door, but at the door of our *oppressor* and our faithless *Guardian*.[36]

If his biblical metaphors and references are untraditional, the purposes to which he turns them—the protection of tribal lands, criticism of harmful policy, assertion of inherent sovereignty—are pointedly conservative. Boudinot here invokes Proverbs 26:13 ("The slothful man saith, 'There is a lion in the way, a lion is in the streets' ") in a dual critique that charges the United States with a sluggard's indolence for its failure to intervene in the rampaging, criminal, and sinful "robbery" of Cherokee land. Adding to the verse's customary reading as a commentary on spiritual laziness, he identifies Georgia with the lion, charging it with a predatory rapaciousness that violates not just Cherokee rights, but also the United States' volitional treaty agreements, and even the will of God inasmuch as it was he who established the Cherokee in their homelands.

While Ross does not seem to have been as devout as Boudinot, his rhetoric calling the United States to account on the basis of its own religious precepts is transposable with Boudinot's. He closes an early letter to Congress, "Whilst the Cherokees are peacefully endeavoring to enjoy the blessings of civilization and Christianity, on the soil of their rightful inheritance; and whilst the exertions and labors of various religious societies of these United States are successfully engaged in promulgating to them the w[o]rd of *truth* and *life,* from the *sacred volume* of *holy writ,* and under the patronage of the General Government—*they* are *threatened* with *removal* or *extinction.*"[37] Ross's rhythmic parallelism reveals the inverted, bitter irony of the United States' false patronage, which urged the Cherokees to accept treaties' promises of civilization—the *"truth"* secreting *"removal"*—that they might come to greater security—the *"life"* begetting *"extinction."* That ironic critique also extends to the hypocrisy of promulgators of the faith who, like Boudinot's slothful man/nation, ignore their own culpability in the nation's duplicity.

Protesting the New Echota treaty late in the anti-removal campaign, Ross would level the same comparative strategy in his pamphlet "Letter from John Ross . . . to a Gentleman of Philadelphia": "The first of your ancestors who visited as strangers the land of the Indian, professed to be apostles of Christ, and to be attracted by a desire to extend the blessings of his religion to the ignorant native. Thousands among you still proclaim the same noble and generous interest in our welfare; but will the untutored savage believe the white man's professions, when he feels that by his practices he has become an outcast and an exile? Can he repose with confidence in the declarations of philanthropy and universal charity, when he sees the professors of the religion which he is invited to embrace, the foremost in acts of oppression and of outrage?"[38] Thematic inversion characterizes Ross's movement back and forth between appearance and reality: the acumen displayed by the savage, the native become alien, the benevolence unmasked as rapacity. He syntactically replays his anxiety over the perfidy of the "civilizers," religious or civic, demonstrating his full awareness that just because whites might have said something, it wasn't necessarily so, no matter how sacrosanct their vocabularies. Both he and Boudinot raise the Cherokees' embrace of Christianity as a bulwark against U.S. aggression by demonstrating the hypocrisy of one Christian people assaulting another, particularly after declaring that the Indians' conversion would unite them as allies. Such careful use of irony should also alert us to the possibility that he and Boudinot, too, understand that motives may be prudently hidden by invoking particular discourses that lend rhetorical authority—discourses like, perhaps, those of civilization and savagery.

Boudinot and Ross accuse the United States and Georgia of gross failure to meet their own standards, Boudinot charging that "the intruders . . . have acted more like savages towards the Cherokees, than the Cherokees towards them."[39] Though Boudinot here refers specifically to illegal settlers on Cherokee lands, it seems clear in another editorial that he finds the same hypocrisy in the Georgia legislature's "extension of tyrannical and unchristian laws, which threatens to blast all our rising hopes and expectations."[40] William Apess, a Methodist itinerant minister and author who was a contemporary of Boudinot, similarly offers white readers a look at themselves through a literary mirror framed by the discourses of Christianity and civilization. Writing of Apess, Jace Weaver celebrates his reflective analysis, subversion, and resistant stance in his writings, claiming, "The rest of Apess's work [besides his autobiography] must be viewed as resistance literature, affirming Indian cultural and political identity over against the dominant culture."[41] Though it seems to me (and to Weaver himself, confining his focus to Boudinot's editorials) that this analysis could apply as well to Boudinot's passionate entreaties, invectives against white depredation, and his demands for justice and recognition of the Cherokee Nation in the East, Weaver concurs with Perdue in his final evaluation. He writes that "in his pursuit of 'civilization' for the Cherokee, it says much about his views of community that Elias Boudinot could not, over the course of his lifetime, ever envision any positive alternative other than assimilation or Removal," a summary judgment I find untenable read against the editorials.[42] Between 1826 and 1832 Boudinot staunchly opposed removal. Too, many facets commonly thought part of civilization (like education, worship, and trade) were often already present in some shape in traditional society, or they might be transformed into Cherokee ways of doing things. Cherokee intellectuals were in fact participating in their historical moment in the shaping of civilization and the social and political principled practices that made it up. They did this work for Cherokees, for other

Indian peoples, and for nonnatives, and they lent to it a distinctly Cherokee perspective. Boudinot and Ross intended that their questioning of the legal and moral consistency of U.S. policy would make the Cherokees' problem one of general relevance to "the whole Union," not only as a way to solicit compassion for the Cherokee exclusively, but as a way to argue for the principles of Christianity, humanism, justice, and lawfulness for everyone.[43]

CIVILIZED VS. CIVILIZED: CHEROKEE NATION V. GEORGIA

Boudinot's recapitulations of the United States' official and unofficial narratives of itself, together with his warnings that it would "soon fall and crumble" if it did not act in accordance with them, were meant to spur his readers into activism on the Cherokees' behalf, but they may instead have occasioned a defensive reaction to what Priscilla Wald calls a recognition of the Cherokees' uncanny and threatening reprise of the United States' own founding, revolutionary moment. Elaborating on the consonances between the United States and the Cherokee Constitutions, which also echo throughout Boudinot's editorials, Wald argues that the very similarity between the Cherokees' declaration of nationhood principled on its claim to the rights of a civilized people and that of the United States as a nation born of rhetorically articulated rebellion was more alarming than ingratiating. The Cherokee announcement of its national arrival destabilized the United States' nationalist and exceptionalist autonarrative, which legitimated its formation on North American soil on the basis of natural rights endowed to some (those civilized, for which we may read "white") and not others (savages, or "not white"). She writes of the Cherokees' ratification of their Constitution: "Outrage stemmed from anxieties that were exacerbated by the profound threat of Cherokee separatism to the collective identity. The Cherokee Nation's becoming like but not of the United States political entity, mirroring without acceding to its conditions, seemed to jeopardize the terms of a United States national identity."[44] She sees that the danger to the United States arises from "those ways in which, as Homi Bhabha suggests, 'mimicry is at once resemblance and menace,'" insofar as "Cherokee sovereignty would validate a permanent

Cherokee presence on lands considered by Georgia to belong to the state. Such a presence would challenge the integrity of the state and of the Union," most acutely in the powers it imagined it had to declare its borders and police its interior.[45] If Cherokees did not come under Georgia's jurisdiction yet fell within its boundaries, they would embody the revolutionary anxiety over an *imperium in imperio,* a state within a state, inhabiting an uncontrolled and uncontrollable gap in state power that the Union could not abide.

Wald is most closely concerned with the lacuna the Cherokees' suit in *Cherokee Nation v. Georgia* exposed in the constitutional definitions of personhood, claiming, "In effect, the Cherokee bid for recognition by the United States as a foreign nation was a bid for full personhood within those bounds."[46] I believe Wald's argument glides too easily from what might more rightly be understood as citizenship rather than personhood, a slippage that dodges the question of what guarantees of rights the U.S. Constitution makes to noncitizens. Nevertheless, Cherokees to be sure were negotiating for a limited extension of federal power over the state of Georgia on their behalf, a negotiation required of them given their relative powerlessness to check Georgia's affront, and one preconditioned by their historical acquiescence to place themselves "under the protection of the United States." The request for recognition thus does capitulate to an agreement to be "bounded" by federal authority, but importantly, the Cherokees imagined limits to those limits. To a certain extent, their bid for recognition as a foreign nation expressly asked for *exclusion* from the U.S. citizenry and from federal authority when they didn't need it, calling for an as-yet-unimagined relationship in which the federal government would protect the self-declared rights of excluded, noncitizen persons.

Though John Ross and former U.S. attorney general William Wirt, the Cherokees' lawyer in the Supreme Court cases, crafted a careful legal argument, the U.S. Constitution's ambiguity on the relationship of Indians to the United States surely suggested that the court's ruling would depend on questions not answered in black letter law. They hoped, for instance, that Chief Justice John Marshall's federalist leanings would incline him to assert federal authority. With little legal precedent, the suit makes its case not least on principles of natural rights, especially ownership of land and establishment of government. The suit, like Boudinot's editorials, also pleads for a humanist sympathy against manifest injustice, particularly insofar as the Cherokees' social progress should leave no doubt that they were capable of managing their own affairs, managing them well, and that injustice committed against them was committed not against a tribe of protohumans but against a duly constituted nation of civilized people. Marshall summarizes the plea:

> They have established a constitution and form of government, the leading features of which they have borrowed from that of the United States. . . . They have established schools for the education of their children, and churches in which the Christian religion is taught; they have abandoned the hunter state, and become agriculturists, mechanics, and herdsmen; and, under provocations long continued and hard to be borne, they have observed, with fidelity, all their engagements by treaty with the United States.
>
> Under the promised "patronage and good neighbourhood" of the United States, a portion of the people of the nation have become civilized Christians and agriculturists; and the bill alleges that in these respects they are willing to submit to a comparison with their white brethren around them.[47]

Once again, Cherokee volition turns the purportedly assimilative civilization program toward the reinforcement of the nation's distinctiveness. As Wald points out, the comparisons the suit makes—on one hand suggesting equality with U.S. polity and on the other insinuating the inferiority of their (and the northern jurists') lower-class "white brethren" on the other—may not have served as well as Wirt and Ross might have hoped, challenging as they were to the United States' ideas of itself as unilaterally sovereign within its declared borders and as inherently superior to its brown brethren.

Wald's reading of the sociopsychological operations of the uncanny in the U.S. response to Cherokee presence is insightful and persuasive. But stopping at a fearful or discomfited reaction to a challenge to the self—and here we must make the leap to a collective and homogeneously imagined self—de-emphasizes other forceful causes of the Cherokees' invasion by Georgia, its rejected claim to nationhood, its abandonment by the U.S. Congress and people, and its loss of land and life. She writes, "*Cherokee Nation* was finally about the incomprehensible hole in the map within the perimeters of Georgia. Marshall's narrative of the Union could make no sense of it, and the Cherokee bid for nationhood American style only further complicated that narrative."[48] It was not simply that the United States *could* not imagine limits to its boundaries and influence in a new relationship based on separate equality, but that it *would* not. Such a relationship stood as a barrier to a national autonarrative not passively characteristic of the zeitgeist but actively produced by and producing a will to accumulate power, appropriate Indian land, and subjugate Indian people. Wald rightly observes, "Ostensibly reading Constitutional law, [Marshall] was in fact writing it," arguing that in his decision he "recast in a distinctly Unionist narrative the often contradictory policies toward indigenous peoples, policies that veered between removal and an assimilation that secured the appropriation of their land and identity."[49] The decisions in the Marshall trilogy—*Cherokee Nation v. Georgia, Worcester v. Georgia,* and *Johnson v. McIntosh*—certainly recast historical precedents, with some glazes more philanthropic than others, but they also add new chapters to the corpus of U.S. colonial law. The contradiction Wald finds in the methods of Indian policy shaped in *Cherokee Nation* are finally only too consistent with their unspoken purpose: the assertion of federal dominance over Indians and their lands, within or without the current national borders. To this overriding pattern all other concerns touching on Indian matters—legal, moral, humanist—could ultimately be molded.

"THE TOLERATION OF DIVERSIFIED VIEWS"

Perhaps Boudinot and Ross came to recognize the doomful consistency of this controlling agenda of U.S. Indian policy, which the weapon of argument—the counter-rhetoric of civilization and Christianity—espoused by them, white allies, anyone, was powerless to stop. Ross revealed the end of the United States' seeming rudderlessness with eloquence approaching epiphany: "The Cherokees . . . are surely the best judges of their own true situation, [and] can properly appreciate . . . the expressed sympathy for their misfortunes, and the avowed benevolence towards the Indian race, all of which amounts simply to this: 'we want, and intend to take your lands, and are sorry you are unwilling for us to do so in our way.' "[50] Boudinot, convinced that the Cherokees would never in the United States be allowed the free exercise of their natural rights or be treated with anything but a pretense of equality; assured of the federal government's indifference to their sufferings in its executive, legislative, and judicial branches; and frightened at the imminent threat of an unofficial genocidal campaign, at some point in 1832 after the *Worcester* decision began to soften his stance against removal. Though he did not specifically argue for it in his editorials, while he was with John Ridge on a fund-raising tour in the northeastern United States, his brother Stand Watie edited the *Phoenix* and perhaps at Boudinot's direction included a notice that the delegation was considering a treaty providing for removal, a possibility the very mention of which Ross would not allow.

Ross and the National Council were unwilling that the *Phoenix* should express anything but a unified front against removal and prohibited Boudinot from writing anything in its pages to the contrary. Whether because he could no longer conscientiously advocate resistance, was dedicated to the freedom of the press, or saw the writing on the wall, he and Ross came to an understanding in August of 1832, and Boudinot resigned as editor. In his letter of resignation printed in the *Phoenix* he explained his irresolvable conflict: "Were I to continue as Editor, I should feel myself in a most peculiar and delicate situation. I do not know whether I could satisfy my own views and the views of the authorities of the nation at the same time. My situation would then be as embarrassing as it would be peculiar and delicate. . . . I love my country and I love my people. . . . I cannot tell them that we will be reinstated in our rights when I have no such hope."[51] The tension between his duties of conscience and of office is exacerbated by his reiterated sense of peculiarity and delicateness, a phrase I'll return to. The words most obviously describe an awkward, or as he has it, potentially "embarrassing" social scene, or might more subtly indicate a recurring sense of oddity and fragility. The quick tendency is to read Boudinot's sense of peculiarity into his personal identity, formed in uncommon social circumstances that were in many ways and places separate from Cherokee people normatively understood, but this reading makes no sense of the vulnerability echoing in the delicacy of his situation. That vulnerability should be read into the comparison he raises not between himself and the people, whom he declares he loves (whether or not they love him back), but between himself and the "authorities of the nation"—that is, between the individual and the state. Whatever misgivings he might have had, he grew increasingly convinced of the necessity of removal in the next years, and in 1835 as a leader of the Ridge/treaty party, acting without authorization, he signed the fraudulent Treaty of New Echota, fully aware that in so doing he gained no security but rather invited his own death. Perhaps even in his earliest misgivings about the compatibility of his thinking with official policy, he became acutely aware that dissent—especially when uncommon or peculiar—entailed vulnerability, and to the very entity possessed of the ultimate coercive power.

Conjecture about the specific cause of his change of course, connected with his signing of the removal treaty, has preoccupied many Boudinot scholars. Most attribute his shift to Jackson's refusal to enforce the *Worcester* decision; McLoughlin, Peyer, and Weaver add the loss of support from political and missionary allies who began to advocate removal. In an influential argument, Perdue predicates Boudinot's intransigency at coming under Georgia's jurisdiction, which might have allowed the Cherokees to stay in the East with subsequent U.S. citizenship, on his experience with the vitriolic antimiscegenation he faced in Cornwall. But according to her line of reasoning, he apparently learned there not only about racism but also how to embrace it. Upon his return from Connecticut, "Boudinot continued to be an ardent advocate of 'civilization,' but so completely did he embrace the tenets of Western culture that he seems to have accepted the dominant white attitudes toward Indians. He began to exhibit racial consciousness. . . . His resistance to the absorption of the Cherokees into white society probably stemmed from a belief that Indians and whites could never be equals. At the very least, Boudinot's encounter with and perhaps subconscious acceptance of white racism reduced to an afterthought the idea of Indian assimilation."[52] In the last sentence, Perdue is referring to assimilation within the citizen-boundaries of the United States, not to the Cherokees' assimilation of the principles of civilization and Christianity. Apparently, not wanting to live among whites, like wanting to live like whites, is also evidence of an internalized colonial consciousness—but such is the adaptable advantage of alleging the shadowy psychology of an assimilationist consciousness. Perdue's wording misses the possibility that Boudinot believed that whites would never *treat* Indians as equals, rather than believing that Indians *were not* whites' equals.

Maureen Konkle, despite her empowering reading of political volition in early American Indian writing, unwittingly reinforces the failure to decode Boudinot's agency in constructing his brand of civilization from a range of traditional dispositions, even as she recovers Cherokee agency in the creation of the nation. She writes, "Apparently rejecting all aspects of Cherokee practices and belief, accepting the EuroAmerican definition of civilization as being essentially 'like' whites, and insisting on natural equality with whites cause problems in the spokesmen's [that is, the treaty party's] discourse . . . Ridge and Boudinot rejected traditional practices outright, characterizing them as the primitive foundation from which the Cherokees were moving ever forward but not something to be retained in any manner whatsoever."[53] This analysis replicates the all-or-nothing dichotomy between assimilation and traditionalism that ignores other practices surviving in the habitus. Not *all* aspects of "Cherokee practices and belief" were rejected out of hand by progressive-minded figures like Ridge and Boudinot—they maintained obvious ties to Cherokee culture, such as in their retention and public use of the language (not small things on their own), insistence on distinct boundaries, strong family ties, deliberate return to Cherokee country, and intellectual advocacy for Cherokee and other Indian groups. I question whether anything short of an early, complete, and permanent removal from Cherokee communities and individuals could effect the type of erasure their critics claim they consciously sought. Additional traditional practices carried on in progressive developments could be found anywhere: in agricultural economics, say, with the common ownership of land and the cultivation of native and newly introduced crops by traditional labor cooperatives like the *gadugi* using technological innovations like plows, or in religion, with dispositions like righteousness and care discussed in the book's first part, or in the principled practices structuring consensus, such as deliberation, debate, and dissent.

The council house—the traditional site where Cherokees congregated and argued for weeks before reaching consensus—gradually emptied as the centralized government assumed control over both internal and external decisions. For a time, the pages of the *Phoenix* promised the nation an alternative place to gather and stay apprised of national goings-on. The potential of that imagined forum was circumscribed, however, by the idea that general dissent and deliberation as impediments to decisive action should yield to the duly delegated if at times obscure authority of the elected government. The general council founded the *Phoenix* with the understanding that it would advocate explicitly nationalist political goals and accordingly provided for only qualified freedom of the press, which Ross explained in his 1828 annual message: "The public press deserves the patronage of the people, and should be cherished as an important vehicle in the diffusion of general information, and as a no less powerful auxiliary in asserting and supporting our political rights. . . . The only legislative provision necessary for conducting the press, in our opinion, is to guard against the admission of scurrilous productions of a personal character, and also against cherishing sectarian principles on religious subjects. The press being the public property of the Nation, it would ill become its character if such infringements upon the feelings of the people should be tolerated. In other respects, the liberty of the press should be as free as the breeze that glides upon the surface."[54] The sole express injunctions against ad hominem attacks and denominational squabbles afford the editor (who may well have been the ghostwriter of the passage) wide latitude, with the proviso that the paper is fundamentally national and that its ends should work toward inculcating a nationalist consciousness. There is little doubt that the nation controls the press, but lost in the shuffle is the matter of who rightfully controls the nation. As "public property," the "public press" suggests a theoretical right of access by the people, access that was in practice sharply curtailed in terms of what material the editor's office expressed and allowed to be expressed by others.

Perhaps anticipating the potential problems in operating a newspaper simultaneously free and bound, the National Council in the Cherokee Constitution made no assurances of freedom of the press. After the conflict with Boudinot, Ross publically clarified the expectations of future editors: "The *views of the public authorities* should continue and ever be in accordance with the *will of the people*; and the *views of the editor of the national paper* be the same. The toleration of *diversified views* to the columns of such a paper would not fail to create fermentation and confusion among our citizens, and in the end prove injurious to the welfare of the nation. The love of our country and people demands *unity of sentiment and action* for the good of *all*."[55] The logic of the passage seems valid and sound enough: the paper depends on the authorities for its views, just as the authorities depend on the people. Perdue goes so far as to argue that Ross in this view "expressed the traditional Cherokee approach to politics in which councils reached a consensus and chiefs had no power to enforce their will."[56] A close reading, however, reveals not a conservative consensual disposition so much as a compulsory display of dramatically concentrated power, couched in the rhetoric of egalitarian tradition.

Ross subtly switches here the legitimating relationship between the polity and the people in a classic reenactment of the government's legally transcendent emergence. The public invests the state with the responsibility to protect the public, a responsibility that extends to protecting the public from itself, effectively elevating the state to a superintendent position outside the rules of its own creation—a state forever in a state of sovereign exception. Its claim to legitimacy endures in tautology: what the state does is best for the people because the people created it to do what is best for them. This unassailable rationale equating the state's operation and the people's best interest excuses the repeated ellipsis of the subject in Ross's injunction. Who might harbor "diversified views"—the editor alone, or the people? Who, exactly, will not tolerate those views and demand "unity of sentiment"? Will it be the people who will police these transgressions of the party line, or will it in fact be the police?[57] The rhetoric of nationalism conveniently sees no conflict of interest. The freedom to express views at odds with the public authorities—that is, elected and sitting officials—would henceforth "be as free as the breeze that glides upon the surface," but would go no deeper.

We might expect a national paper to stick to the party line, but Ross problematically extended his insistence on being able to enforce a nationalist consciousness to the general public. In his annual message of 1833, he spoke at some length on the principles informing his conception of unity:

> It is a self evident truth, that no community can successfully surmount an opposing difficulty and attain the object of desire, unless the members thereof can and do exercise a *controlling* influence of common interest, so as to ensure harmony and perseverance among themselves by unity of sentiment and action, and the force of this truth, is equally applicable to nations. . . . We cannot be too strongly impressed with the necessity of pursuing that course which is best calculated to meet the views, interest and welfare of the people. On all important questions, when a difference of opinion arise in regard to their rights and interest, the sentiments of the majority should prevail, and whatever measure is adopted by that majority for the public good, should be the duty of the minority to yield, and unite in the support of the measure, this is the rule of order, sanctioned by patriotism and virtue; whilst a contrary course would lead to faction, confusion and injury.[40]

Ross takes his turn at adopting the language of the Declaration of Independence, calling acquiescence to the state as the national institution entrusted with "controlling" the common interest a "self evident truth," ironically co-opting the language of a document that articulates the principles of insurrection. His reference to communities smaller than nations gestures toward traditional towns and their anarchistic dispositions of consensus-based decision making, but he trades their traditional practices of persuasion that prevailed in the absence of coercive authority for the practices of "controlling"—a more efficient system, if one less democratic and less traditional. He similarly invokes the traditional principle of harmony but understands it as a condition that may be mandated, again using a dodgy, subjectless language of power and control. Harmony for Ross is a state to be commanded by a "force" that disappears in passive syntax but nevertheless "calculates," "impresses" us to "pursue," and "prevails."

Traditional consensus and deliberation were balancing acts that required recalibration with every movement, agreement, deferral, denial, or compromise. The rule by majority that Ross sanctions by virtue and patriotism, but not by tradition, is less about balancing than about acclimating the people to imbalance. Rule by consensus is the rule of all by all through the only-too-obsolete practices of compromitting—binding together in mutual agreement. Majority rule may be entered into freely, but it also takes advantage of coercive institutions to help those out of balance who might be feeling discomfited adjust to *the* "rule of order." Ross offers majority rule as the only method of order rather than an option among others, subtly turning the "rule of order" into the order of rule: that is, the principle of order sanctions the practice of ruling, of exercising control. He again carefully equivocates subjective agency, dissolving enforcement into the natural order instead of identifying it as a set of coercive practices and institutions under state control. Characteristic in its ellipsis of volitional subjects and objects, the last ambiguous sentence, ostensibly a warning that the body politic may come to harm if dissent prevails, also veils a threat: while "a contrary course would lead to faction . . . and injury," a patriot might well bring injury to a faction.

Ross was committed enough to ideological uniformity that he led or countenanced efforts to unseat from their leadership roles Boudinot and the Ridges, who were impeached by members of the National Council for "maintaining opinions and a policy to terminate the existence of the Cherokee community on the lands of [their] fathers."[59] The treaty party pressed for a trial to defend its members and offer their own account of the obstacles they believed made continued resistance to removal untenable and futile, but Ross declined either to offer them a hearing or to dismiss the charges. These measures he deemed necessary even after he spearheaded the indefinite suspension of elections, a move designed to sustain the government and avoid conflict with Georgia law, which had outlawed any exercise of Cherokee government, but one that engendered resentment among treaty party members who were by degrees removed from policy deliberations.[60] Politically excommunicated, denied access to any venue for public discourse, and effectively silenced, the frustrated treaty party members were convinced both of the necessity of a final, immediate settlement of the Cherokees' deplorable and worsening condition and of their own superior judgment. These and other factors led them to sign the Treaty of New Echota, betraying the trust of the great majority of the Cherokee people and themselves abandoning indigenous anarchism's principled practices of consensus.

In Boudinot's pamphlet *Letters . . . A Reply to John Ross*, written to justify his and the treaty party's actions in signing the New Echota treaty, he describes the conditions that led them to such measures, complaining of the (C)hief source of their discontent:

> We will state what *we* suppose to be the great cause of our present difficulties—our present dissensions. *A want of proper information among the people.* We charge Mr. Ross with having deluded them [the Cherokee people] with expectations incompatible with, and injurious to their interest. He has prevented the discussion of this interesting matter, by systematic measures, at a time when discussion was of the most vital importance. By that means the people have been kept ignorant of their true condition. . . . The original error was in the refusal of the leaders and advisers of this Nation to discuss the question which is now agitated only in the last extremity, and in closing every avenue by which the people might be reached with correct information.[61]

Much of Boudinot's justification for the treaty party's actions hinged on similar claims, that if the people were as aware of the full state of affairs as the leaders, they would consent to relocate the Nation in the West. Many critics have debated the proposition. Most agree that Ross was not entirely forthcoming in his public addresses about the severity of the United States' pressure, its increasing refusal to negotiate on any conditions but total removal, or the concessions for a treaty he had already offered, whether in earnest or as delay tactics.[62] Boudinot's irritation with what he saw of Ross's ambiguity with both the Cherokees and the U.S. government led him to dub Ross "the Delphic Oracle." Despite Boudinot's sarcasm, I am skeptical that reading between the lines of Ross's dealings can reveal a great deal more than we already know about his allegiance to the Cherokees' clear mandate to stay in the East, the Cherokees' commitment to remain in their lands, or the depth of the treaty party's devotion to the Cherokees' distinct survival.

What concerns me more here is Boudinot's expression of the experience of ideological oppression that he articulates on behalf of the treaty party. Though his claim that Ross closed "every avenue" exaggerates the extent to which the treaty party was truly incommunicado (he made this claim in a pamphlet he paid to have printed, after all), it does raise important questions about leader-citizens' responsibility to echo the party and/or public line, their responsibility to act in accordance with their best judgment and conscience, and according to what principles, traditional or progressive, conflicts arising among diverse dispositions should be mediated. Boudinot yearns throughout the documents reprinted in *Letters* for discussion as a "vital," that is, urgent and life-giving practice, once widely enacted but "progressively" constricted. Running counter to his former nationalism, his expressed need for discussion increasingly lines up with indigenist anarchist traditions that didn't just tolerate diversified views but built them in to the very fabric of pluralist, participatory, noncoercive, democratic, consensus-based decision making. His letter of resignation from the *Phoenix* editorship, reprinted in *Letters*, not only confides his reluctance to propagandize against his better judgment but also exhorts "every citizen *to reflect* upon the dangers with which we are surrounded . . . *to talk over* all these matters, and, *if possible*, come to some definite and satisfactory conclusion."[63] His pleas for public deliberation issue perhaps from the embodied, traditional politically anarchistic habitus, disposed as it was to consider matters in due time, concluding only when conclusion was possible, in repeated consultation with various communities, and open to the influence of authorities like clan mothers, elders, and spiritual leaders. He searches for a space of participatory deliberation, a place where dissent belongs: a nation of people conversing with rather than controlling each other. His problem is historically systemic rather than personal, more about the general stricture of spaces, opportunities, and practices of dissent extending from the Cherokees' cession of local authority to central authority than it is about Ross's muzzling of the national newspaper's editor, or even about Boudinot's supposed internalized colonialism.

Though in most of *Letters* Boudinot protests the treaty party's legitimacy too much, he does unwittingly confide some ambivalence in the above passage. His preamble ostensibly promises it will reveal the cause of the treaty party's dissensions, but the syntax is appositive: the "dissensions" unwittingly rename the "cause of the difficulties." Less dissolutive is his general, though belated hesitancy arising from the stupefying complexity of the "interesting matter" of the Cherokees' "difficulties"—problems of such enormity they slip in only as meiosis, as anesthetizing euphemisms staggering in their understatement. As far as the specific case is concerned, Boudinot's defense of the treaty party's actions in *Letters* does not hold up even on its own grounds. At one moment he claims authority for the signers under a written compromise negotiated with Ross but in another disavows the legitimacy of the agreement because of alterations Ross made after the treaty party members signed it. The alterations were in fact approved by John Ridge, the de facto leader of the protreaty contingent, and Boudinot seems to have tacitly approved them as well.[64] Although he rails against what he believed to be disingenuousness on Ross's part, the treaty party had finally forced Ross into a compromise, and treaty advocate leaders John Ridge and Stand Watie were included in a delegation that Ross empowered, "with full powers from the Cherokee people in general council assembled, to make such a Treaty as may appear to us best calculated to ensure the present peace and future posterity of our country."[65]

Ross led this group to Washington to negotiate a "final adjustment of the existing difficulties," as he equivocated to Secretary of War Lewis Cass.[66] While this delegation was in Washington, Boudinot and Major Ridge formed another at New Echota, bent now not on finding some compromise but on exercising control, and the treaty was executed and signed. Following the widespread protest against the New Echota treaty, Boudinot justified it as "the best that can be done for the Cherokees, under present circumstances," and urged Ross to give up his protests and instead convince the Cherokee people of the impossibility of obtaining any better conditions.[67] This Ross should do over and against objections to the treaty party's one-sided negotiations—objections founded on the principle of mutual consent, such as "One party has no right to take away any part of it [a compromise], or to make any additions without the consent of the other. . . . One entire party cannot bind in this manner the other; much less can one individual bind both the contracting parties"—grievances Boudinot himself made against Ross's alteration of the compact with the treaty party but which went unremarked in his own actions.[68]

But proving the treaty party's error and Boudinot's dumbfounding hypocrisy does not require endorsing of all Ross's measures against the signers or even in his rightful defense of Cherokee lands. Too many of his dispositional adjustments tended toward the centralization of power and its alienation—its removal—from the hands of most of the Cherokee people. Perdue justifies Ross's restrictions on the freedom of the press and general freedom of speech with her reading of traditional politics: "In prohibiting dissent, Ross expressed the traditional Cherokee approach to political disputes. Originally, the Cherokees arrived at decisions through consensus, and anyone who could not agree simply withdrew so that the group could present a united front. Since the Cherokees overwhelmingly opposed removal, Boudinot and other pro-removal Cherokees should have withdrawn and maintained silence, according to traditional Cherokee ethics."[69] Though I appreciate the search for enduring dispositions, I believe the interplay between adaptation and perseverance to be more complicated than Perdue here implies. First, as consensus gave way to centralization, the option of withdrawal was dramatically curtailed. Whereas once-existing multiple communities not consenting to decisions could formerly decline to be bound by them without reprisal, withdrawal in the post-constitutional era, at least as far as movement off the land was concerned, entailed disapprobation, disenfranchisement, near-total loss of resources, the possibility of state punishment, and renouncement of the rights of citizenship from the *only* recognized political community, making it an increasingly remote possibility. Indigenous anarchism wasn't what it used to be.

Second, prohibiting dissent in an exercise of political coercion is hardly a traditional disposition. It is true that in a selective departure from tradition, coercive powers were invested in political leaders based on the conservative volition to perpetuate the bulk of the habitus, but even the harmony principle in connection with consensus offers insufficient cause to order or control the people's expression. As discussed in chapter 1, harmony is about developing balance, not enforcing unanimity, and is about participation, not suppression. As Albert Wahrhaftig argues, despite its prominence it was not a superlative principle but one subordinate to the responsibility to lead the people on the right path, even into revolution if necessary. Other adaptations to the habitus, like republican governance itself, to some degree similarly authorize leaders to depart from the wishes of their constituents when they don't align with their better judgment and conscience—"peculiar" as those cases may be.

Most importantly, dissent itself was not—is not—antitraditional. Dissent in fact partly makes up the principled practice of consensus, for only from the toleration of diverse views can consensus be "reached," as Perdue claims it was.[70] I encourage readjusting focus toward the *reaching*, rather than the having, of agreement, for what precedent would be set by agreeing to a version of traditionalism that automatically authorizes state authority over public discourse? Then as now, dissent is vital, in Boudinot's phrase, to push the nation to become as representative of the people as it purports to be, especially on those questions it deems too peculiar, or said to be too momentous to allow the expression of diversified views. Dissent, deliberation, and development belong as much to the Cherokees' habitus as to any group's, and they are crucial to any politics, nationalist or anarchist. No matter the weight of the versions of the public good or tradition narrated by the nation-state, academics, or even the nation-people, we have a responsibility to interrogate their accuracy, utility, and morality.

What might we learn were we to confront head-on the messiness and contradictions in the courses pursued by Ross as well as by Boudinot? Might we see some advocating traditions that required progressive interventions and that superseded even Ross's all-consuming campaign to remain in the eastern homelands? In fact, both regularly argued against removal not only on the grounds that the lands were the homes of their ancestors since time immemorial—and to be sure, they argued this emphatically—but on the right to independent, distinct sovereignty. As Ross stated to Cass in a proposal for land cessions, "It will be impossible for the Indian tribes to be perpetuated as distinct independent communities within the limits of the United States—not because they are destitute of such rights, and do not hold a strong claim on the protection of this Govt.—but because it is evident that . . . the Govt. will not afford that necessary protection which the Indian right demands."[71] Boudinot in *Letters* invokes the same rights of self-governance, reprinting the treaty party's 1834 resolutions that harmonize surprisingly well with Ross's determination that the Cherokees be "perpetuated as [a] distinct independent communit[y]":

> *Resolved,* That it is our decided opinion . . . that our people cannot exist amidst a white population, subject to laws which they have no hand in making . . . that the suppression of the Cherokee Government, which connected this people in a distinct community . . . will completely destroy every thing like civilization among them . . . That, although *we love the land* of our fathers, and should leave the place of our nativity with as much regret as any of our citizens, we consider the lot of the *Exile* immeasurably more to be preferred than a submission to the laws of the States . . . That we are firmly of the opinion, that a large majority of the Cherokee people would prefer to remove if the true state of their condition was properly made known to them.—We believe that if they were told that they had nothing to expect from further efforts to regain their rights as a *distinct community,* and that the only alternative left to them is either to remain amidst a white population, subject to the white man's laws, or to remove to another country, where they *may* enjoy peace and happiness, they would unhesitatingly prefer the latter.[72]

The distinctness so important to both sides of the New Echota treaty debate stands in marked contrast to allegations that advocacy of removal was synonymous with an eradication of all traces of Cherokee culture, for in its mostly unnamed components resided the very distinctness that all sought to preserve. The independence they tried in their respective ways to secure was not exclusively political, although both Boudinot and Ross elevated the political sphere to a superintending role over other cultural principles and practices of nationhood.

Neither supposed that emigration would spell the actual end of Cherokee sovereignty or the nation-people, and once each was finally convinced of removal's inevitability, they turned their attention to reasserting their independence in the western Cherokee Nation. "Peace and happiness" there were hardly as forthcoming as Boudinot had promised, but the dispositions of independence, self-control, and self-sufficiency retained throughout the habitus in practices of governance, dissent, industry, and more perpetuated a distinctly Cherokee identity throughout the period of rebuilding, the violence of the Civil War years, the next round of reunification and rebuilding, and the temporary dissolution of the nation-state in the Dawes era. Most histories of the Cherokees have written their survivance as pointedly political, but the ascendency of the nation-state and its appropriation of traditionalism have obscured alternative and important stories of the nation's people. Independence and distinctness can be claimed by indigenous anarchists as well as nationalists, after all. Perhaps centralization as a means of streamlining the Cherokee government's efficiency was the right answer to U.S. imperialism, and perhaps it was the only answer. But I do not believe it is still the only answer. Since the 1800s, Cherokee Nation governance has continued to centralize, exacerbating tensions with those dissenting from the policies they had no hand in creating, and disempowering or disenfranchising growing numbers according to a reactionary and decidedly untraditional paradigm. Accommodating the rights of Cherokee people today may well require assimilating such alien processes as the toleration of diversified views, slow deliberation, rational dissention, and consensus-based decision making, over and against exclusionary processes that make enemies of allies and ourselves.

ᏕᏢᏉᎩ

CHAPTER 6

Conclusion: Strangers and Kin

After I completed my graduate coursework, my wife and I left upstate New York and returned home to Oklahoma so I could study the Cherokee language and work on my dissertation while immersed in Cherokee country. We moved just south of Tahlequah, the capital of the Cherokee Nation, but a couple hundred miles east of our hometown of Tuttle, a farm and bedroom community in the central part of the state. Growing up in Oklahoma, I had spent some weeks at a time with family in Tahlequah, but they had been long gone by the time my wife and I made it there. There are Cherokees all over Oklahoma, including many like members of my extended family who have migrated far and wide, but the three-hour drive is not all that separates Cherokees who come from Tahlequah and from Tuttle. They do share some similarities—everyone has more or less the same accent and the same sworn allegiance to the University of Oklahoma or Oklahoma State University. Another feature they share ironically separates them: like the residents of many small towns, they are unaccustomed to a great influx of people from far-off places, which results, to my mind, anyway, in communities that for all their friendliness are not always as hospitable to newcomers as outsiders—or perhaps even they—might imagine. They seem in many ways decidedly insular, perhaps more through inexperience than self-conscious standoffishness. I wasn't expecting a throng at the gates when we rolled into Tahlequah, but I was surprised by the cool distances that sometimes echoed the space between the circumstances of my raising among the migrated Cherokees of my extended family and those of people long from Cherokee country. I should not have been, for as I've suggested, my small town was much the same, preferring the familiar and tested to the unknown, which I saw in action against the recently arrived. Just coming off graduate study with an idealistic and simplistic idea of closely affiliating with and working for American Indian communities, I had little sense of the strong familial ties that bind the Cherokee people in northeastern Oklahoma, connections strong and at times rigid by design and habit, and effective at maintaining collective identities.

My wife, Tiffany, who is not Indian, took a job teaching at an elementary school a few miles outside of Tahlequah and so found herself in more regular and much closer contact with Cherokee communities than I did reading about Cherokee culture, holed up in my home office. Though it took her a couple of years of acclimation, by the time she left, according to her, she grew to love the school and the people for the familial regard they mutually developed, more than at any of the other places she had taught in the past. In time, I too found opportunities for connections, but they came about gradually, not by virtue of any single variable like being Cherokee, being present, or even desiring connections. Certain circumstances were more conducive than others when it came to forging connections. Some churches welcomed us readily; others seemed content with their current membership. Some stomp grounds organized themselves strongly around clan and family groups, while others depended more on individual participation. Accustomed to people coming and going, university communities in Tahlequah were generously open to me in my roles both as a Cherokee language student and as an American Indian literature and film instructor. While my wife and I arrived in Cherokee country as outsiders in many respects, in time we became members of *certain* communities, and remained outsiders to others. Bearing in mind how boundaries have been transgressed before, the reasons for communities' caution with strangers makes perfect sense. If some Cherokee groups are insular, it is not because they are inherently separatist, but because they must maintain a measure of social defense, as history has unfailingly demonstrated.

Understanding and respecting people's and communities' boundaries entailed an adjustment to my expectations concerning the degree of intimacy and the amount of time it took to get past superficial associations, in contrast to the urban and university Indian communities more familiar to me. In those, again, strangers appear more regularly, and it seems that they have adapted, allowing them to respond with swifter welcomes. Though they cultivated a patience I did not particularly desire, the more seasoned relationships that by necessity grew out of interactions with people controlling the pace and scope of their development, however, proved as satisfying as I had hoped, though they were not always what I expected. They did not spring fully formed out of my head, but arose in more relaxed and natural relation to circumstance, unfolding at their own pace and in their own directions. By giving up preconceived notions of where and how I would belong in Cherokee country, I found myself belonging more easily and comfortably among people associated in communities variously configured: some established, others temporary; some intimate, others casual. Recognizing their diversity opened several opportunities to contribute to Cherokee communities, opportunities that persist now that I have largely left Cherokee country, though those opportunities come with a fresh set of limitations and participatory parameters imposed by various kinds of distance. The communities in which I now participate are more imaginatively constituted than those possible where larger numbers of Cherokees physically gather, but they are indeed Cherokee communities—intellectual, artistic, familial, religious, and so forth.

In hopes my arguments may stand or fall according to their merits and not in their connection to me personally, I have tried to avoid offering much in terms of analyzing my own subjective position until now. That said, I think this last chapter calls for some commentary on where I come from and where I've been in Indian country. In becoming a member of Cherokee groups new to me, I have reflected on questions surrounding issues of hospitality from the perspectives both of host and stranger, seeing at times people trying to sneak under boundaries to help themselves to the rights of citizenship based on specious or fraudulent claims, at other times, people looking to help others turned away at the gates despite the value of the contributions they might make as cultural allies. Officially, the Cherokee Nation has maintained some boundaries to protect its admittedly finite resources and in other cases has attempted to impose boundaries for less noble purposes, even when there are definite organic, historical connections tying the excluded others to Cherokee people. Discerning when and how to lower our defenses and allow visitors to become members, guests to become family, or aliens to become citizens requires careful weighing of imperatives that may be in competition. I propose that traditional Cherokee dispositions attached to practices of adoption in the private sphere and naturalization in the more broadly political world can help us mediate these demands and refashion contemporary communities in healthy alignment with the ideas of a compassionate, indigenous anarchism, and once more we can find surprisingly innovative principled practices in places we have understood as conservative in too narrow a sense.

Tiffany and I had another personal goal in mind when we moved to Cherokee country, and that was that we hoped we might be able to adopt a Cherokee or Indian child. We signed up with the Nation's child welfare office and enrolled in a foster-adopt program, which is designed to get adoptive parents paired with children who the office believes has a greater than average chance of winding up wards of the court. The Indian Child Welfare (ICW) office tries to find placements as early as possible to minimize children's time in temporary foster care. A year or so after we moved into our home, ICW asked us to take custody of two kids, four and one, whose parent had a protracted history of failing to provide for the children, largely due to a methamphetamine addiction. Furthermore, due to the parent's drug abuse, the youngest child was born with severe medical problems, and what I can only describe as an incomparable sadness in the eyes. The children lived with us for a little more than a year, during which time I made dramatically less progress on my dissertation than I had imagined (going from zero to two kids involved a bit more than I had imagined), but during which the younger child's health steadily improved, with the eyes increasingly taking on the liveliness of the older sibling's. The sadness crept into my wife's and my eyes after we learned that ICW had decided to reunify them with their parent, despite the history of drug abuse, related convictions, and the fact that each of the parent's several children had been taken into the Oklahoma Department of Human Services (DHS) or ICW custody several times over the years.

Like government child welfare offices across the nation, Cherokee ICW follows the mandate that reunification with biological parents is always the best course of action—or at least, it's the course they always follow by default. Only after every attempt has been made to accommodate the parents as they work through their assigned therapeutic and skills programs will parental rights be terminated. As far as bureaucratic dogma goes, this course perhaps sounds reasonable, especially if we consider the points recommending it: its manifest moral imperative to keep families together, the overrepresentation of people from lower socioeconomic brackets in child welfare cases, the social circumstantial burdens that people in poverty face (and Cherokee country does indeed face serious economic problems), the far-reaching ramifications of the criminalization of drug use, the lack of opportunity, the teachable cognitive and personal skills necessary to effective parenting that if absent do not indicate lesser capacity or worth, and the shocking history of the forced-assimilation policy that endorsed outright theft of Indian children from Indian parents and Indian culture prior to the passage of the 1978 Indian Child Welfare Act, which mandated that Indian children in state custody be placed with Indian parents whenever possible.

All these points and more make perfect intellectual and moral sense to me. But the "always" part of the reunification mandate I cannot stand behind. One problem with the current structure, at least of the Cherokee Nation's ICW office, is that a parent's history with Child Welfare essentially resets at the close of a given case: no matter how many times a parent poses a danger to a child, if the case isn't severe enough to warrant swift termination of parental rights, parents can work the program (by, for instance, attending rehab programs and parenting classes, passing drug tests, staying employed) just long enough to get the case closed and bring an end to the monitoring. If they come to Child Welfare's attention again, everything starts from scratch, as if the office were handling a first-time slipup. This was the case with the children who came to us—we came in on the third episode in which the parent's children had been taken into custody, and sadly, I fear it was not the last. Not too long after we lost them, the pain of which I imagine could only compare to having a child die, I saw in a local newspaper's crime report that the parent had been arrested for a methamphetamine-related offense. Privacy laws prevent us from knowing what has become of the children.

Our adoption plan, needless to say, did not work out. But despite the heartbreak that its collapse brought on, I am as convinced as ever that adoption as a social institution represents a powerfully positive force, and not only for the children. W. T. Whitaker, the man who founded a home for the white orphans of Cherokee country and with whose story I led off this book, knew this far better than I. Parents, too, benefit deeply from the opportunity to share their hearts and homes. Friends and family would sometimes compliment my wife and me on accepting a special needs and an older child into our homes as if we were doing something altruistic, but truthfully we were in great measure acting from self-serving motives. I marvel that our course, so blatantly selfish, could yield us benefits so great. I hope, too, that they extended beyond Tiffany and me, and I do believe that the children profited by their time with us, just as I believe that society profits by having its children well taken care of. I think back also on the overwhelming support that we received from the people at the school where Tiffany worked, our neighbors, the families in the Sunday school class we attended, and our extended family, and I am heartened by the compassion they extended in their gifts of toys, time, help, and more.

All told, what I saw from our engagement with adoption was a proliferation of good. Even though I saw also plenty to make me angry—bureaucracy grinding steadily away at good sense and compassion, district court judges who did not require that children and their best interests be represented by counsel separate from the parents', and in whose courtrooms volunteer champions of children, like the Court Appointed Special Advocates (CASA) organization, were not welcome—I only regret that our relationship with the children could not have been longer enduring. Quickly, let me say this again: there are district courts in Oklahoma in which judges have appointed attorneys to children in DHS custody but are allowing them to sit out "nonadversarial" hearings and case reviews on the assumption that the best interests of the parents, as represented by their lawyers, are synonymous with the best interests of the children. For the same reason, these courts believe CASA volunteers are superfluous, and so they cannot offer their advocacy. I can think of several things to call these procedures, but I'll pull up at willfully naïve.

Even though my wife and I did not come to adoption by habituation in a traditionalist Cherokee context, through our experience we learned something of the long-standing practices of adoption not all that different from which an ethical theory of hospitality in the private sphere might be extrapolated. Such a perspective could profitably inform questions involving people in one sense or another outsiders to the public sphere, that is, people moving in transcultural directions. Naturalization as the public extension of adoption, however, has been systematically divested from the Cherokee habitus both through imperialist limitations imposed by U.S. government policy and through a reactionary devaluation of the practice by Cherokees themselves, erasing the institution from collective memory and threatening the compassionate and hospitable values attached to it. In the past several years, the Cherokee Nation has reignited a long-running controversy concerning the place in the nation of the Freedmen, who are the descendants of former Cherokee slaves. In 2007 a controversial special vote was called to consider a constitutional amendment requiring citizens to have an Indian ancestor listed on the admittedly flawed Dawes Rolls, and revoking the citizenship of Freedmen who cannot prove Indian descent. This disenfranchisement has been met by appeals in tribal and federal courts that are still pending, and by a great deal of criticism from many quarters. This chapter, with its dissent from nationalist policies, its advocacy of pluralist equality for organically related communities, and its veneration for (neglected) traditions of adoption, attempts more forcefully an indigenist anarchist discourse that I have earlier mostly been describing. Concerned with the morality of the historical legacy of Cherokee slavery and with the ongoing, dubiously motivated marginalization of people affiliated with the Cherokees, I argue that the nation—its political leaders and its citizens—should reevaluate its exclusionary course with the Freedmen and weigh the benefits of implementing more inclusive political and social ethics. I see these dispositions as part and parcel of a responsible indigenous anarchism that would work against the manifold costs of violating treaties and propagating a specious account of how Cherokees understand what it means to belong among them. Such a narrative offers an attenuated, if not corrupt, version of tradition.

THE UNEXCEPTIONAL PRACTICE OF CHEROKEE SLAVERY

The institution of Cherokee slavery has attracted interest among several recent historians, such as Tiya Miles, Celia Naylor, Fay Yarbrough, Patrick Minges, and other scholars, who have elaborated on and richly detailed Theda Perdue's groundbreaking work in the area. Perdue's 1979 book, *Slavery and the Evolution of Cherokee Society, 1540–1866,* was among the first histories of Cherokee people to unapologetically detail the abuses and colonialist complicities of Cherokee participation in the system. Growing out of traditional practices of slavery, such as those by which captives replaced killed clan members, Cherokee slavery from about the mid-seventeenth century on increasingly issued from economic motivations. At first slaveholders procured slaves from neighboring tribes for trade to English colonies; later they secured mostly African slaves for labor within Cherokee country. Some worked for a handful of the wealthiest families like the Vanns, Rosses, and Ridges on large plantations, while some worked for middle-class families on much smaller farms. According to William McLoughlin and Walter Conser's analysis of census data, in 1835 among Cherokees in the East, in addition to uncounted free black residents, some 1,600 slaves made up a substantial 9 percent of the total population.[1] In some instances, Cherokees married slaves and free black people officially and unofficially, though such marriage was legally prohibited. Clans, too, sometimes found occasion to adopt slaves—black, Indian, and white—into the social order. Relatively few African Cherokees benefited from such inclusion, however, as the laws of the Nation subjected most of them to all the injustices to which the practice of slavery gave rise.

Most scholars, and most Cherokees with whom I have spoken, maintain a belief that Cherokees historically practiced a form of slavery less brutal and more respectful of slaves' lives and dignity than the colonists', often treating slaves like family members. In Celia Naylor's careful study *African Cherokees in Indian Territory: From Chattel to Citizens,* in which she discusses the physical, sexual, emotional, and other abuses of Cherokee slavery and the myriad ways in which African Cherokees resisted it, she takes issue with this inherited rationalization for its tendency to miss the bigger picture. She puts the matter concisely and forcefully: "To believe that Indian cultures made bondage more tenable to African Indians or somehow countered the denigrating process of enslavement is to deny the insidious nature of a system based on the ownership of human beings."[2] Cognizant of Naylor's and others' similar reevaluations, Fay Yarbrough maintains that there were indeed observed differences between Cherokee and Euro-American systems, and that those differences registered in former slaves' own accounts.[3] I admire and am persuaded by her suggestions that those subjectivities need to be respected, a point seconded by Tiya Miles.[4] Yarbrough also makes a compelling case that the alternative ways in which Cherokees organized slavery and in which they constructed racial attitudes could point toward less rigid historical boundaries. I am nevertheless inclined to think that sanitized accounts of Cherokees' compassionate slavery function primarily to assuage well-deserved historical guilt and to deflect criticism that much like the United States was founded upon stolen land, the Cherokee Nation was built in no small part with stolen labor. Whatever the degree to which Cherokee slavery was better than colonial or American slavery, to the extent that it deprived fellow humans of life and liberty, it was surely as bad as anyone would wish it. Acknowledging its legacy and our responsibilities to it remains to us.

New works by Miles, Yarbrough, Naylor and more have made rich use of archival material to offer a detailed picture of slaves lives' among the Cherokee, drawing on and corroborating earlier histories. Unfortunately, these scholars also frequently replicate the dichotomous structure informing them, such as in Perdue's history in *Slavery and the Evolution of Cherokee Society*, where she divides complicated issues too cleanly. Drawing on Albert Memmi's ideas of the effects of colonialism on the colonized's psychology, she writes,

> The reactions which Memmi has described occur at a social as well as an individual level and may drive one segment of a society toward the values and life-style of the colonizer while leading a second group in the rejection of the colonizer's model and the reaffirmation

> of traditional relationships and behavior. The usual result is a deep and unresolvable friction between the two groups.
>
> From initial contact with whites to the American Civil War, the Cherokees gradually developed a severe case of this same social schizophrenia. Confronted with the specter of European exploitation and domination, the Cherokees displayed the *expected* dual reaction and either actively participated in the economic system of Europeans and began to emulate their colonizers or clung to values which sanctioned their aboriginal way of life.[5]

Besides the reductive division of the Cherokees into two forever-irreconcilable camps, there are some problems with this line of thinking, despite the thrust of the critique directed at colonialist policies. Not the least of these issues is the pathologization of the two ostensible responses to colonial intrusion, aspersed on an entire population. This model truncates the open options at complicity or futility, and then defines Cherokees choosing the first as aberrant, even psychologically unhinged, for their victimization. Also troubling is the *expectation* that this template maps a foregone conclusion, structuring the history according to a predetermined and predetermining narrative of how indigenous peoples were divided and conquered. This particular version of the assimilationist/traditionalist binary, again, published in 1979, underwent significant development in both Perdue's own later work and in general scholarship on mixed-bloodedness, as scholars like Louis Owens celebrated the generative, polyglot nature of hybridity, but as I discuss in the introduction, the negatively coded dichotomous tendency that substitutes "elite" or "assimilated" for "mixed-blood" has proved only too resilient. Though they take care to avoid casting the distinction in terms of biology, scholars revisiting thorny and imperative questions of Cherokee racial attitudes by taking recourse to the overworked category of the "Cherokee elite," themselves cling (like traditionalists must ever do to the old ways) to the not-far-removed progressive/conservative binary to grandly narrate the course of several thousand people over several hundred years.

The dichotomy also reifies a "true" body of Cherokees made up of traditionalists and to a lesser extent the dissipating line of progressives, relegating adopted or naturalized society members (among whom numbered blacks, whites, and Indians like the Catawba, categories each enumerated on the 1835 census) to an adjunct status, recapitulating the historical exclusion of slaves and their descendents who would come to be called Freedmen. Some have said that Cherokees brought their slaves with them over the Trail of Tears, but it would be more accurate to say that slaves brought their Cherokee owners over, for it was undoubtedly they who bore the worst part of the disastrous journey, carried the heaviest burdens, first tested dangerous passages, and last sat down to meals. It was also they whose labor helped rebuild the Nation following removal through the Civil War, during which time its laws brought them further under its control even as it further excluded them from official belonging. They remained in this state of exception, to retool Giorgio Agamben's phrase, until the Civil War drew to a close.

Continuing as chief of the reunited nation in Indian Territory, John Ross attempted to maintain Cherokee neutrality in the war, but as surrounding tribal nations joined forces with the Confederacy, he was pressed to follow suit. Many in the nation allied with the Union, as did the revamped religious Keetoowah Society and the so-called "Pin Indians." Here, too, historians have characterized this factional split as caused by antagonism between traditionalists opposed to progressives and their practice of chattel slavery. Surely many were, but I expect that the reasons that thousands of people had for going to war were more diverse and complicated. Perhaps some opposed slavery on moral or religious grounds—was it only coincidence that the adopted white Baptist preacher Evan Jones was so closely affiliated with the Keetoowah Society? Most of the resident missionaries of whatever denominational stripe opposed slavery, and we might well expect that many in their congregations did likewise. With the supposed correlation of Christian conversion and progressivism, is there not a contradiction here as one variety of Cherokee progressivism struggles against another? Others supporting the Union might have looked on the Southern states' promises of respect for Cherokee sovereignty with skepticism approaching incredulousness, given the officially sanctioned abuse those same states doled out only twenty years before. Once more we find aberrations and anomalies adding up and challenging the explanatory capacities of the two basic categories.

Even though many Cherokees fought for the Union and Ross moved the Nation's official alliance to the Union once he was able, when the war was over the United States nevertheless moved to punish the Cherokees by demanding land cessions in the treaty of 1866. The treaty in its ninth article also stipulated that "the Cherokee Nation covenant and agree that slavery shall never hereafter exist in the nation. All freedmen, as well as all free colored persons resident in the nation at the outbreak of the rebellion and now resident therein or who shall return within six months and their descendants, shall have all the rights of native Cherokees. Owners of emancipated slaves shall never receive any compensation therefor [*sic*]."[6] The category of citizen Freedmen was born. While this mandate impinged on the nation's sovereign right to determine its own membership and met with contention, the simple fact of extending citizenship to people not possessed of Cherokee blood was not at issue, for adoption of non-Cherokees continued; rather, the forced acceptance of black people as citizens appears to be the sticking point, as in the current crisis with the Freedmen. Despite the treaty's forthright language calling for the Freedmen's civic equality—is not citizenship a right?—the nation several times tried to deprive them of it, or went so far as to attempt their full disenfranchisement.

THE FREEDMEN CRISIS

The latest attack on Freedmen citizenship began to shape up not long before the 2007 general election, when a petition framed as an assertion of the right of Cherokee citizens to determine citizenship criteria—a petition that basically called for kicking out the Freedmen—garnered enough signatures to bring the question up for a special vote as an amendment to the Constitution. The change in requirements mandating that citizens be able to prove descent from an ancestor listed on the Cherokee-by-blood rolls—effectively unenrolling almost three thousand Freedmen along with nine intermarried whites—passed with 77 percent of the vote (6,702 for and 2,041 against), although only 3.1 percent of the population of about 280,000 voted on the issue (8,743 votes cast), meaning only 2.3 percent voted in favor of it.[7] Meager as that sounds, the turnout was not shockingly low, considering not quite 14,000 voted in the following general election.[8] One of the key objections to the amendment concerns the deeply flawed and subjective process by which the Dawes Rolls were assembled, especially insofar as those doing the enrolling tended to list phenotypically black people on the Freedmen roll regardless of whether they had Cherokee ancestry, resulting in a record of the citizenry not just spotty and arbitrary, but governed by a distinctly racial logic.[9] Like earlier attempts to disenfranchise the Freedmen, the amendment has been appealed in both tribal and federal courts. On August 22, 2011, the Cherokee Supreme Court threw out a district court's earlier voiding of the amendment, claiming the Cherokee Constitution and not the 1866 treaty decided Freedmen citizenship.[10] A federal case is still pending at the time of this writing; another will likely follow long after.

The Descendants of Freedmen of the Five Civilized Tribes Association website offers a thoroughgoing history of the labyrinth of cases, movements, and astounding attempts on the part of Cherokee administrators to stifle debate. The website's mission statement outlines the goals of the organization, and speaks also to the point of the lawsuits they have brought:

> To educate members, supporters and the general public regarding the history, culture and political rights of those particular to the Dawes Freedmen Enrollment. The Association is organized to plan, implement and administer, operate, and evaluate programs to carry out the objectives and purposes of the Association to assist in and promote, restore and preserve the rights of those descendants of the 5 Civilized Tribes . . . particular to the Dawes Freedmen Enrollment. To promote, collect, and preserve Oklahoma Freedmen Genealogy, History and Artifacts and study the unique cultural diversity of Freedmen Descendants for the general benefit and good of the individual and collective Tribes and Representative Communities, in the State and Nation, and to improve the quality of life, to reinvigorate and promote cultural awareness and events relating to our heritage.[11]

The Cherokee Nation may choose not to hear these appeals, but it cannot pretend not to understand them—calls for education, for cultural and political rights, for the support of the nation entrusted with protecting them, for awareness of the importance of kinship, attachment, and the heritage of belonging to an Indian community, all for the sake of self and others, have all issued from Cherokee people in the past. The resemblance is uncanny.

As justified in their claims as I believe the Freedmen are, some of the political saber rattling that has gone on to force the nation into line I find troubling. The controversial disenfranchisement with its patent denial to abide by the provisions of the 1866 treaty provoked members of the Congressional Black Caucus led by then-California representative Diane Watson to introduce legislation in the U.S. House of Representatives that would have terminated the special political relationship between the Cherokee Nation and the United States, as well as legislation that would have cut off federal housing monies to the Nation until it reinstated to the Freedmen the full rights of citizenship. Though Watson has since retired from public office, such disproportionate threats to tribal sovereignty and to the well-being of tribal people remain a possibility in the colonial context of congressional plenary power over Indian affairs. While I believe the Freedmen's exclusion was primarily politically and racially motivated, that does not mean that any conceivable response is justified—would, say, a military intervention be in order, if the Cherokee Nation refuses to admit the Freedmen? Would it be all right to just exterminate the opposition? If they were suddenly deprived by neotermination of reliedon services guaranteed by treaty rights, it would not be an exaggeration to say that many Cherokees would wind up just as dead as from a police action. As could many Freedmen excluded from services, admittedly, but the United States could see that they were taken care of. The history of the disastrous policy of termination, as Vine Deloria termed it in *Custer Died for Your Sins*, may not be as well known to legislators as it is to those more attuned to the various policies by which the United States has pursued the effective erasure of Native peoples. Jumping to the colonialist legislative endgame establishes a dangerous precedent in matters of policy and nation-to-nation relations, as terminating tribes for opposing Congress on potentially any issue could become a commonplace punitive measure, a scenario that would, not coincidentally, conveniently release the United States from the financial and political responsibilities it bears toward tribes. Courting this sort of heavy-handed aid, given as much to erasing the claims of both indigenous and minority peoples as to exerting control over them, will one day seem ruefully naïve when the U.S. nationstate begins finding other groups over whom it can feel morally superior and less beholden to by writing away their identities.

Cherokees themselves should take responsibility for revisiting the question of the Freedmen's inclusion in the body politic. Taking steps in this direction may require other changes first, however, such as opening space for dissent from the official policies of the tribal nation-state and conversing more openly about the moral dimensions involved in the Freedmen's status than we have so far. If we could turn the discourse away from nationalistic rhetoric that collapses the myriad considerations of the legacy of slavery into jingoistic expressions of the people's right to exclude whomsoever they take a notion to, we could discover ways through which a Cherokee social cohesiveness could be bolstered by a willingness to own up to history and by offering others, especially those with whom we have historic and organic connections, the dignity due them.

HOSPITALITY

We have progressive traditional examples to guide us in this. In addition to the celebrated hospitality that clan members extended to one another, by assuring a welcome reception to travelers known or unknown, for instance, the institution of adoption was ingrained in the Cherokee habitus. The reasons for and the particular practices of adoption were myriad but they all tended toward a similar, simple goal: to strengthen people by taking care of selves and others. Just as internal lines demarcating belonging changed over time, so did the lines separating the inside from the outside. These shifted and blurred with circumstances, and led to the development of various ways of receiving strangers, or extending hospitality, if we understand that idea on both local and political levels. Scott Lyons has recently lucidly advocated for a stronger emphasis on citizenship in Native political thinking, arguing that casting belonging as membership, bloodedness, or other depoliticized terms helps relegate Native nations to an almost-but-not-quite national status, effectively reining in their sovereignty. He discusses three major principles recognized in international law by which nations determine citizenship. The first is the right of blood or birth, now broadly construed, he argues, to include language proficiency and other cultural behaviors, but retaining for some nations racial ideas of belonging. The second is the right of soil or place of birth, and the third, which most concerns me here, is naturalization.[12]

Lyons argues that Native nations should take the assertive step of extending citizenship to non-Indians, citing isolated examples of tribes like the Lower Sioux who provide for such adoptions, as positively differentiating between tribes as political entities and as ethnic groups. He further argues that such distinctions could feasibly and productively be built into Native nations' own rules as a hierarchy of citizenship. This intriguing approach suggests some solutions to problems of insularity and cultural needs, but it is not without problems, some of which I will discuss below. Lyons proclaims his bafflement that more governments have not elected to adopt as citizens people connected to the tribe through marriage and other choices, given the availability of the option and its forceful proclamation of control over boundaries. Naturalization, he argues, is basically there for tribal nations to avail themselves of, the U.S. Supreme Court in 1979 having decided in *Santa Clara v. Martinez* that Native nations retain the right of establishing their own membership criteria.[13] While I join him in calling for expanded ideas about citizenship, what naturalization would mean to tribal nations is not a question so easily settled, nor unobstructed in U.S. law.

Lyons takes pointed issue with the language of adoption, urging, "Naturalization as well should go by its proper name; 'adoption' after all, is not a nationalist concept but an ethnological legacy of Lewis Henry Morgan (who was no nationalist)."[14] He here links adoption to Morgan through his ideas of kinship, which Lyons finds alien to indigenous ways of thinking. Given that the U.S. Supreme Court used the language of adopted citizens in 1846 in *United States v. Rogers* and that the Cherokees had passed laws using the specific language of the adoption of intermarried whites as early as 1855, we should be impressed that Morgan's ideas found such purchase before his major works on the subject appeared in print in the late 1870s.[15] Despite this glitch, Lyons's point is well taken—the language of family may not be precise enough in the political world. That claim in turn may be complicated by the sly, effective use nationalism has made of the rhetorical trope of the family (for example, homeland, Great White Father, and so forth) to construct resonant metaphors for the nation. Whatever its difficulties, the language of adoption might yet find a place in our political vocabularies insofar as it concerns ethical relations that our political relations could profit by considering, not in a utilitarian narrative of the nation's naturalness, but with a genuine commitment to the welfare of those outside our national boundaries. It might be idealistic to imagine a place for affective reasoning of this sort, to hope for a nonexploitative way of bringing emotion to bear in the political realm so given over to avoiding the complications of caring, but it is a responsible course.

Jacques Derrida in his discussions of hospitality has broached some of the issues involved in the ethics of welcoming others moving across cultures or nations, offering questions and tentative conclusions that relate to citizenship, politics, and care. He identifies an important paradoxical condition of what he sees as the aporia of hospitality, which is that if it were carried to its ultimate end, it couldn't really exist, because extending hospitality requires the willful opening of gates, or letting down of boundaries, but an absolute hospitality would dissolve boundaries entirely. Drawing boundaries, then, is inevitable, and hospitality is always subject to some conditions, but so too are the boundaries. Strangers appearing at a community's boundaries test them to some degree and call into question the strength of both the limits and the ability to welcome, challenging the hosts' perceptions of themselves. By entering the community, strangers bring themselves under the power of their host. Derrida distinguishes the category of stranger from that of the "absolute other," or an outright enemy, who neither asks nor receives any measure of hospitality. A stranger taken in receives the advantage of certain rights as guest and also takes on some responsibilities, thus entering into a reciprocal relationship with the host. Derrida links this word "host" with its ambivalent meanings of "master of the house" and "enemy" (as in, meeting the host on the field of battle) to other deep-running contradictions between control and welcome, insider and outsider, and more.[16]

In the case at hand, the Freedmen surely need no reminding that the Cherokee Nation has historically been a host of dubious hospitality, to say the least, but many Cherokee people could stand a reminder, for at least two reasons: knowledge of our shared history should first lead us to examine our ideas of ourselves as a hospitable people—if we value this value, we should behave accordingly. Second, it should suggest to us that much like the United States created legal categories to exploit Indian peoples and deny them basic human rights, Cherokees did the same for their slaves. What's to prevent the nation from legislating today's citizens out of the Nation tomorrow?

Here lie two dangers in Lyons's suggestion of a hierarchy of citizenship, which he takes from a model developed in Israel in the 1940s. He proposes distinguishing citizens along three tiers, with full citizens possessing all rights (of voting, land use, resource access, and so on), "nationals" retaining guaranteed treaty rights but removed from policy decisions and divested of the right to vote, and those of lineal descent having bragging rights and the possibility of gaining higher tiers of citizenship. Key to Lyons's suggestion is that nations should require what they want to produce in their people, so that if alarmed by language loss, say, nations requiring proficiency as a condition of citizenship can generate a nation of native language speakers. He also suggests making residency a condition of citizenship. Lyons fails to account for some variables, however. Rules such as these may well bolster targeted traits, but there's little assurance that the groups themselves will be strengthened. According to his logic of requiring what you want to produce, tribal nations should be producing more and more citizens with high blood quantum given commonness of the requirement, but as Lyons himself notes, minimum blood quantum requirements in fact produce "statistical extermination."[17] If tribes today instituted a Native language proficiency requirement, is it more likely we'd see a tribe of ten thousand members dip to nine thousand speakers and rising, or a drop to one thousand speakers and falling? The economies of bureaucratic requirements have all sorts of hidden costs and inverse effects that we would do well to think through.

More importantly, distinguishing among citizens can easily become discriminating against citizens, or making of them the almost-citizens that have raised such a stink in the past. Derrida reminds us of France's Algerian nationals, and we might remember the protests of American Indians denied citizenship and representation prior to 1924. Creating layers of exception and classes of excepted does less to strengthen a nation than it does to perpetuate the logic of excepting, which will proceed, I fear, to find other ways by which some are accounted deficient. Maybe they speak a corrupt dialect of the Native tongue, attend the wrong church or stomp grounds, don't attend at all, grew up away from the homelands, make too much or too little money, don't have dark enough skin, or have skin too dark. How much value should be placed on a "national"? Maybe some compromise would give these almost-citizens three-fifths of a vote. I don't intend to be flip about either histories of racist policies or Lyons's carefully considered suggestions, but I do want to point out that having classes of officially differentiated, reduced-rights citizens lacking means of redress can create conditions very like those the Freedmen now face.

With these caveats borne in mind, we should remember, however, that boundary drawing—that is, exclusion—is inevitable and was surely a Cherokee disposition as old as any we could hope to find. Externally, Cherokee people distinguished themselves from other tribes and fiercely maintained control over land boundaries, and internally they distinguished all sorts of rights for citizens according to age, gender, ability, and so on, in addition to the traditional slave status, whose members fell outside the protection of the clans. All this is to say that a society inevitably distinguishes internally among its members, by withholding rights from certain groups, such as children, criminals, incapacitated people, and others. These matters then become subject to questions of morality and functionality. To help settle them, Derrida offers up the idea of "intermediate schemas," which calls to my ears favorable echoes of pragmatism and cognizance of the at-times indissociable relationship between the host and guest.[18] Thinking historically of the Freedmen's position, this indissociability is incontrovertible, and so we must examine the reciprocity of that relationship. In the current context of impending disenrollment, the Freedmen stand to the Cherokee much like strangers to hosts. The Freedmen are not absolute others, enemies looking to usurp the host's position. They are asking for the right to participate in Cherokee political society, a society built upon their labor. Neither are they parasites, another class of outsider-come-in that Derrida distinguishes, which is to say they are not exploiters. No, it could hardly be responsibly said that the Freedmen exploited the Cherokee—just the opposite. Living in America, Cherokee people know that even after many years, it's hard to find recompense for an injustice—but it may be harder still to offer it for one we have committed. It is no less imperative for that. We might accomplish it by the reproduction of a more compassionate and just adoptive disposition that works toward a politics of inclusion for those with whom we have organic, reciprocal relations, not a model in which we do unto others simply as we have been done unto.

ADOPTION AND NATURALIZATION

The importance of these organic bonds gave rise to dispositions of inclusion that, as historian John Phillip Reid argues, Cherokees traditionally enacted in two modes, the local and the national, which despite their operational differences shared the objective of formally recognizing and solidifying out of the ordinary relationships.[19] At the local level, though all the clans could and did adopt others to replace members who had passed on, the practice of adoption was so ingrained in the Cherokee culture that one particular clan, the Long Hair, was designated to handle it by default. The clan was even known alternatively by the term "Strangers," establishing socially and linguistically the ongoing presence of strangers among us. Several early examples of adoption of people connected to Cherokees, especially in war and marriage, survive in the written historical record, including those of French soldier Antoine Bonnefoy, American teenager Joseph Brown, the children of the Cherokee man Shoe Boots by his slave Doll, the slave Molley, and a Shawnee slave of the Cherokee warrior Black Dog.[20] Many of these have been well interpreted by historians as evidence of social thinking not as preoccupied with race as would be seen in the elaborations of slavery laws that came to dictate suitable marriage partners. Before the legislature took it upon itself to regulate such matters, individuals were left to take their solitary ways when it came to choosing partners, and clan agents could decide for themselves whether to extend full protections, rights, and responsibilities to outsiders. Taken together, however, the various instances of adoption we know about suggest that adoption practices extended beyond the loci of family and clan to strengthen still larger communities, conceived along tribal, national, religious, and other lines.

The social disposition of adoption translated to the civic practice of naturalization, the extension of citizenship to non-Cherokees, following the ratification of the national Constitution, though those naturalized were still referred to as "adopted" citizens. This process most often concerned the adoption of white men, by the government rather than by the clans, who had married Cherokee women and wanted to gain access to the rights of citizenship. The most important of these was access to land, which could mean significant economic advantage, for Cherokee citizens had usufruct access to as much of the communally held land as they could improve. On occasion the nation adopted other allies, like the Baptist missionary and staunch Cherokee advocate Evan Jones, who lived fifty some-odd years with Cherokee people, spoke Cherokee, and led a contingent during removal. In 1843, a few years after the main body of the nation arrived in Indian Territory, the government looked to bring an end to conflict with tribes already present there and entered into a peace agreement with the Creeks and Osages. A remarkable provision of this compact provided that "any citizen of one Nation may be admitted to citizenship in any other Nation, party thereto, by consent of the proper authorities of such Nation."[21] Such adoptions were not only honorific displays designed to aid in transnational diplomacy, but also served to strengthen transcultural relationships between Cherokees and their strongest affiliates and to prioritize their allegiance to the Cherokee communities.

By 1843 intermarrying white men who desired citizenship, for instance, were required to take an oath of allegiance to the Cherokee Nation and to renounce their U.S. citizenship.[22] They also had to pony up a ten dollar fee and secure the signatures of ten Cherokee citizens who could vouch for them. The "Intermarriage of White Men and Foreigners" law in section 67 of Article XV of the *Compiled Laws of the Cherokee Nation* under the heading "Miscellaneous Acts," elaborates that a white or foreign prospective groom would "be required to present to the said clerk a certificate of good moral character, signed by at least ten (10) respectable citizens of the Cherokee Nation who are Cherokees, Delawares, or Shawnees by blood, and who shall have been acquainted with him at least six months immediately preceding."[23] The act also described various scenarios by which intermarried citizens could lose their rights of citizenship, as in divorce, abandonment, or the death of the Cherokee spouse. As Yarbrough notes, these and other regulations governing inheritance helped prevent property, both private and communal in real estate, from passing out of Cherokee hands in the face of widespread exogamous marriage, thereby providing for communal continuity to keep pace with the changing habits of intermarriage.

It is important to remember that intermarriage hardly began and ended with Cherokees marrying white people, as is revealed by Article XVI, "Intermarriage of Cherokees with Other Indians," which averred, "Whereas, quite a number of our own citizens have intermarried with Indians, members of other tribes of this Territory, and it has always been the custom of the Cherokee people to recognize such marriages as lawful . . . therefore, any Indian, a member of any of the tribes of this Territory who has married, or shall hereafter marry a Cherokee, a citizen of this Nation at the time of such marriage, in accordance with the law regulating marriage between native citizens thereof, shall be, and . . . is hereby deemed a Cherokee to all intents and purposes, and entitled to the rights of other Cherokees (Dec. 22, 1880)."[24] With a later provision in Article XX that reads, "No particular form of marriage shall be required . . . *provided,* that citizens of the United States, or those of other than Indian nationalities, intermarrying among the Cherokees, shall first comply with the law governing such cases," it does not appear that non-Cherokee Indians were required to renounce their former citizenship, take an oath of allegiance, or procure the signatures of character witnesses.[25] While we might understand this difference as an early example of a racialized Indian preference, I suspect it had more to do with Cherokee legislators' general social and historical senses that Indian partnerships were far less prone to schemes on Cherokee land.

Residency in the nation constituted a key dimension the government considered in extending citizenship. The residency clause is found in the fifth section of the amendment to Article III of the Constitution, which with its provision for Freedmen citizenship is worth quoting: "All native born Cherokees, all Indians, and whites legally members of the nation by adoption, and all freedmen who have been liberated by voluntary act of their former owners or by law, as well as free colored persons who were in the country at the commencement of the rebellion, and are now residents therein, or who may return within six months from the 19th day of July, 1866, and their descendants, who reside within the limits of the Cherokee Nation, shall be taken, and deemed to be, citizens of the Cherokee Nation."[26] The lawful provision offering easy and apparently automatic Cherokee citizenship to members of other Indian tribes who married citizens and moved to Cherokee country, without a great deal of bureaucratic hoop-jumping, testifies to the former political hospitality that Cherokee people through their government extended to people with whom they had strong, natural connections.

Requiring that adoptees produce several references and reside in the nation helped ascertain the veracity and strength of those connections, and while certainly some looking to marry an acreage gamed the system—in some cases securing signatures and licenses before sweethearts, according to Yarbrough—the signatures also likely intended to embed intermarrying whites and others in local communities. Yarbrough also notes that the readiest candidates for referees were probably the wives' family members, who could thus exert some influence over the partnerships entered into.[27] The requirement could well have worked, too, to impart a sense of responsibility for the intermarried adoptees on the part of the signers. Having publicly endorsed an outsider, community members had some vested interest in the good conduct of those they sponsored. More broadly, the signature requirement implicitly communicated to citizens that the health of their Cherokee communities facing changing patterns of intermarriage and outsider influx required their careful attention. It also affirmed the priority that Cherokee leaders placed on organic connections to community, and while legislative rules are hardly best suited to creating such natural ties in this instance the rules do seem to have focused more on core community cohesion than on consolidating bureaucracy. Even when the Cherokees effected larger-scale adoptions of other tribal peoples—and these did muddy the national motives in their more dramatic plays for power and resources—they were still at least partially prompted by the motivations to strengthen and to care for both Us and Them, and they again channeled change through existing traditions.

Other tribal peoples were formally adopted en masse by the Cherokees several times throughout the nation's history, further rendering celebrations of historical Cherokee-only citizenship, such as those sometimes heard against Freedmen inclusion, untenable. Some earlier examples of national naturalization include the Natchez in the seventeenth century; the Catawbas, who were enumerated in the 1835 census; and the Taskigis, who Reid claims were "nearly extinct as an identifiable group by 1819."[28] The practice, in which neighboring tribes came under the protection of the Nation, entered into full citizenship, and also maintained separate identities to varying degrees, continued throughout the nineteenth century.

Two cases in point, involving the Delawares in 1867 and the Shawnees in 1869, even naturalized former enemies. In these arrangements (more transnational than transcultural, given the bureaucratic contention involved), the Nation entered into agreements with the tribes and the United States that involved the transfer of a great deal of land and money, after which with the Delawares, "all the members of the tribe . . . shall become members of the Cherokee Nation, with the same rights and immunities, and the same participation (and no other,) in the national funds, as native Cherokees . . . And the children hereafter born of such Delawares so incorporated into the Cherokee Nation, shall in all respects be regarded as native Cherokees."[29] The language of the Shawnee agreement is even more accommodating: "And it is further agreed by the parties hereto that in consideration of the said payments and acts agreed upon . . . that the said Shawnees shall be incorporated into and ever after remain a part of the Cherokee Nation, on equal terms in every respect, and with all the privileges and immunities of native citizens of said Cherokee Nation; *provided,* that all of said Shawnees who shall elect to avail themselves of the provisions of this agreement, shall register their names, and permanently locate in the Cherokee country."[30] As had happened who knows how many times in the past, hundreds of people took advantage of these hospitable arrangements. According to a census count, over 20 percent of the nation were adopted citizens by 1880[31]—citizens, not just residents—and the categories of adoptees (white, black, Delawares, Shawnees, Creeks, and miscellaneous) likely do not account for the adoptions of earlier eras, such as the Natchez, Catawbas, and Taskigis.

Saying "Cherokee," then, can mean no clear-cut thing, without the willful forgetting, in Benedict Anderson's sense, of a long history of admixture both political and social. To be clear, I am not arguing that we can never mean more than hopelessly indeterminate mixedness by the word, the concept, the name of our people and nation, but I am saying that to be Cherokee is to be to some extent part of a corporate body made heterogeneous by several historical forces, many of which we ourselves deployed through traditional, diversifying dispositions. When we recognize these specific histories and also reject blanket statements of synchronic impurity, pointing to definable Cherokee communities on one hand and admitting to interrelatedness or hybridity on the other are not mutually exclusive. With the basic tool of a measure of *degree*, rectifying these critical positions of national/social distinctness and cosmopolitanism is aided by precise narratives of cohesive plurality—again, not so paradoxical a thing if done in detail. It's not unlike other constructions that binarism has conditioned us to think of as mutually exclusive—constructions like full-blood/mixed-blood, progressive/traditional, Christian/Indian, Cherokee/Freedmen, and so on. By measure of degree, I mean that through assessing the scale of change and continuity in cultural dispositions, measured against a broad consideration of the habitus's continuation in historical moments, we can tell more precise stories of the arc of Indian peoples' histories and can shape more empowering strategies for our futures.

Adoption or naturalization in the past was not, however, everywhere seamless or benevolent. The Delawares who joined the Cherokees, for instance, found occasion to complain that the Nation meant to exclude them from proceeds from lands leased in the Cherokee Outlet on the grounds that the lands belonged exclusively to Cherokee citizens and not to the recently adopted Delawares. In 1890 the Delawares brought suit against the Nation and prevailed in the 1894 *Cherokee Nation v. Journeycake* decision.[32] In the 1904 suit *Delaware Indians v. Cherokee Nation* in which the Delawares hoped for the right to sell off lands as individual owners, John G. Pratt, a U.S. government agent to the Delawares, testified that back in 1867, they were not wholly satisfied with the articles under which they were incorporated with the Cherokees, particularly that they would not hold title to their own lands, but "they signed because it was the best they could do."[33] Though they officially held all the rights of Cherokee citizens and were incorporated into the nation, many Delawares long maintained their distinct identity and desired to leave off and constitute their own government, perhaps in part because of discriminatory policies on the part of the Cherokees. The Cherokee Nation, however, until very recently stridently opposed Delaware attempts to secede, winning a 2004 U.S. Court of Appeals decision in *Cherokee Nation v. Norton* that blocked federal recognition for the tribe *at the same time* it was insisting that only Cherokees by blood should be allowed citizenship vis-à-vis the Freedmen.[34] Occasionally someone would mutter something about adopted Delawares and Shawnees being allowed to remain, but without explaining the reasons for the exception—perhaps because race is the only logic that could explain it.

Adopted Shawnees, though not as visible in court records as the Delawares, also looked for opportunities to separate from the Cherokee Nation. After some wrangling, the tribes came to terms in 2000, and the Shawnee Tribe (sometimes called the Loyal Shawnee) left under provisions of a law passed by Congress—with careful input from the Cherokee Nation—that prohibits them in Cherokee jurisdictional boundaries from taking land into trust or operating federal programs.[35] The Delawares, who in seeking independent federal recognition already had the backing of the Department of the Interior, finally negotiated an end to Cherokee opposition to their independence in 2009, under conditions similar to the arrangement with the Shawnees that require that any land taken into trust be outside of Cherokee jurisdiction—no *imperium in imperio* again—and that the Cherokee Nation would retain the administration of several programs for which the Delawares are eligible, to the tune of about $9 million in 2004.[36] The Delawares, then, were something like wards in a state of pupilage. The Cherokee Nation, it appears, flexed a great deal of political muscle to preclude competition over federal monies for which it has contracted and over casino profits. Very recently, the U.S. Department of the Interior notified the Cherokee Nation that it was not authorized to administer other tribes' affairs, and the Cherokee Tribal Council voted to move out of the way of the Delawares' funding. With any luck, the Shawnees, too, will soon be managing their own affairs.[37] This pattern of obstruction, however, is not the best lesson transculturalism could learn from transnational history.

Unstated in the Nation's rhetorical posturing over the right to determine its own membership, held up as a sacrosanct and fundamental precept of sovereignty, is the fact that the United States in its judicial development of colonialist law has already circumscribed that right, despite Scott Lyons's claim that the Supreme Court issued its "first and final word regarding the absolute right of Indian nations to determine their own citizenship criteria."[38] In the landmark 1845 Supreme Court case *United States v. Rogers*, Chief Justice Roger Taney (he of the *Dred Scott* decision), took a dramatic step toward legally defining what it means to be Indian along racial lines. The case involving the murder of one white man by another white man—both of them Cherokee citizens—challenged the jurisdiction of U.S. courts over white citizens of Indian nations and by extension the right of Indian nations to establish their communities' boundaries. William Rogers, the alleged murderer, and Jacob Nicholson, the victim, had both married Cherokee wives and resided in the Cherokee Nation. Claiming he had renounced his U.S. citizenship, Rogers wanted to be tried in a Cherokee court. Whether the men in this case renounced their U.S. citizenship, garnered any required signatures, or took an oath of allegiance to the Cherokee Nation I do not know, but these facts as far as the Taney court was concerned were immaterial. Writing for the unanimous court, Taney reviewed Rogers's claim in light of an exception to the 1834 Indian Nonintercourse Act that took Indian-on-Indian crimes out of federal hands. Taney found,

> And we think it very clear, that a white man who at mature age is adopted in an Indian tribe does not thereby become an Indian, and was not intended to be embraced in the exception above mentioned. He may by such adoption become entitled to certain privileges in the tribe, and make himself amenable to their laws and usages. Yet he is not an Indian; and the exception is confined to those who by the usages and customs of the Indians are regarded as belonging to their race. It does not speak of members of a tribe, but of the race generally,—of the family of Indians; and it intended to leave them both, as regarded their own tribe, and other tribes also, to be governed by Indian usages and customs. . . . Whatever obligations the prisoner may have taken upon himself by becoming a Cherokee by adoption, his responsibility to the laws of the United States remained unchanged and undiminished. He was still a white man, of the white race, and therefore not within the exception in the act of Congress.[39]

To say "Cherokee" for Taney, and for the many progeny of the *Rogers* case, is to say "Indian," which is and can only ever be a race of man, defined by an ineffable but all determining essence. Though the Cherokee Nation continued to make citizens of adopted white men, it would not so far as the United States was concerned be able to make Indians of them. Indian nations can define their membership however they please, apparently, so long as it doesn't concern the federal government—but more than a little of life in Indian country concerns the federal government. As long as the federal government has the final say over who is eligible for the programs it funds and over jurisdictional matters, Indian tribes' naturalization of non-Indians will be in many ways gestural only, though pressing the court to explain inconsistencies such as the inclusion of the Freedmen might open other avenues of more thoroughgoing inclusion.

Even as *United States v. Rogers* ensconced race in federal Indian law, it blurred as much as it brought to light—an adult white male might be precluded from going Native, but what about women and children? Might they somehow pull off the switch? Scholars of the case have rightfully critiqued it for its extension of power over Indian identity based on racialized ideology, but it also makes sense to see the ruling as protecting the boundaries of white male power from the instability of race conceived as social, political, or cultural construct.[40] If whites could lay claim to the rights of Indians, perhaps too little prevented Indians from laying claim to those of whites. Positioning whites at the top of a racial hierarchy may be one of the few consistencies maintained in federal Indian law, for contradictions and confusion elsewhere abound. Who can be an Indian? Adult white men—no. Black people without Indian blood? Sometimes yes. Mixed-blood Indians? Sometimes no. Full-blood Indians? Yes, but not if their tribe lacks treaty history with the United States. These irregularities, exceptions, and anomalies tend not toward diversifying and strengthening communities, but toward undermining and weakening attempts at coherence. When the Cherokee Nation fights against allowing the Freedmen to remain citizens, when it fights against allowing the Shawnees and Delawares to withdraw, is it not replicating the vagaries of Taney's race-based thinking, disguised as expressions of legitimate political authority? When it declares it is only exercising its sovereignty in line with the will of the people, is it not disingenuous to remain silent about the colonialist superintendence that delimits the scope of that sovereignty?

CONCLUSION

No phrase has so clearly pointed up the irrationality of federal Indian law than Marshall's "domestic dependent nations," a paradox that has given birth to innumerable intrusions on Indian nations' sovereignty, but locking into a binaristic mode of thinking threatens us with an even deeper irrationality. In terms of sovereignty, binaristic thinking predisposes us to think of it as functioning outside of degree, as something exercised absolutely or not at all. However it may be defined or theorized, sovereignty as actually held by governments is never absolute, certainly not for any length of time. No empire has ever controlled the planet. Like hospitality, sovereignty is always conditional and negotiated, by nations in relation to other nations and by governments with the people who ultimately govern them. This goes for tribal nations as well as for the U.S. government, for no matter its historically benevolent posturing, Native military power, legal maneuvering, the court of public opinion, international law, and more have held its expansionist impulses in check to some degree.

If we understand sovereignty as the unfettered discretionary exertion of power, we run the risks of forgetting the history of successful resistance and of relinquishing our sovereign rights of the citizenry, synchronically styling the U.S. government as always having been in control of the country as its natural inheritors, just as the American nationalist myth would have it. Similarly, if we support the Cherokee Nation's efforts to expand its sovereignty in this direction, that is, toward putting ever-greater powers at the government's disposal with less need for democratic input and fewer opportunities for review, we also risk falling for a dangerously nationalist version of traditionalism and of progressivism and of accepting, even supporting, a sovereignty that allows a government to pursue any course couched as the people's prerogative. Perhaps the Cherokee Nation has started to think that an action taken by a sovereign government is beyond reproach, rather than a particular course taken to address a problem that may require revisiting and renegotiation as circumstances dictate. When we affirm that the actions of sovereigns are subject to review and response—by the people governed, by other peoples and governments, by all sorts of interested parties—we come not just to a more practical but also to a more respectful approach to politics.

Crying foul against critiques of such actions as the disenfranchisement of the Freedmen on the grounds that they threaten Indian sovereignty dodges a crucial issue: because a nation can do something does not necessarily mean it should. Neither is it the case that because a majority of voters decides on something that it's necessarily the right thing to do. Majorities of American and Cherokee lawmakers once decided that slavery was a justified, even humanitarian, idea. Scholars in American Indian studies have zeroed in on the legacy bequeathed us by colonialism and demonstrated that much of the limited opportunity, the poverty, the losses of parts of our cultures, and more troubles that we face can be traced to policies of oppression, exploitation, and discrimination, but our governments are loath to confess their, and our, own culpability in our similar treatment of others. There's no time like the present to end this hypocrisy.

Cherokee people need to have better conversations about Freedmen than we have so far, conversations that acquaint us with histories and dispositions ignored and forgotten. These ought to include practices concerned with the welfare not just of those we style ourselves, but also those we consider strangers. If adoption taught me one thing, it is how crucial it is that we care for those who have been pushed outside of the boundaries marking off what we think of as natural or normal, because sure as the river runs, someone before long will try to move them closer in. We need to be able to explain how very much we might lose and how very much harm we might inflict in doing that, and for certain, those in opposition to the disenfranchisement need to speak against it more loudly and publicly than we have. In addition to being in conversation with elected officials, being involved in public life, and working toward making the government redundant, Cherokee people need also to cultivate better spaces for public discourse. Ironically enough, with a little tweaking the nationalist goals of Elias Boudinot's 1826 fund-raising tour could also work toward these anarchistic goals of fostering consensual communities. A Cherokee institution of higher education and a press, both as independent as possible of the government in funding and oversight, could offer forums that promote scrutiny of the state and improvement of the lives of local collectives and, by extension, larger society, from the exercise of democratic agency. Finally, so long as the government is with us, we should cultivate leaders committed to consensus building and also to *leading*, such as when doing the right thing cuts against the grain of popular opinion. Building consensus will take an uncommon vision and an enormous amount of work given the diversity of opinion in our worlds today.

But as I hope I have shown, the traditional world was in fact no less complex than ours. We have always been many, in communities of infinite constellations that in their diversity strengthened the whole, yet leaders in the past were able to achieve common ground, not strictly because of their powers of persuasion nor even the power of their arguments, but also because the people themselves venerated consensus, respect for individuals' sovereignty, and Cherokee ways of doing things. These traditions they carried into uncertain futures, persuaded of their utility as the nation progressed. Over time, circumstances necessitated many changes to these principled practices, but they are not lost to us. Even should the way forward today take us a long ways back, we will no doubt find that the past and present belong in conversation with each other, and if we listen in, we may hear of ways of being Cherokee that we might never have dreamed of. For centuries, the Cherokees have stood as an example of progress, tradition, and perseverance—we should embrace the best of our inherited dispositions and through them offer the world a more compassionate modern society built upon the participatory consensus of the people.

Notes

Preface

Epigraph: "Orphan Child," *Cherokee Hymn Book* (Tahlequah, Okla.: Cherokee Nation, 2005) 112–13. I have slightly reworked and condensed the translation.

1. W. T. Whitaker, "Support of Certain Destitute Orphan Children. Letter from the Acting Secretary of the Interior, Transmitting Letters from W. T. Whitaker and Others . . ." Committee on Indian Affairs, Senate, 57th Cong., 1st Sess., Doc. 337, May 3, 1902, LexisNexis, Serial-Set-ID 4241 S.doc.337.

2. Alvin Rucker, "Oklahoma 'Clicks' as Daddy to Orphans," *Daily Oklahoman*, July 15, 1928, D1+, microfilm.

3. Jace Weaver, *That the People Might Live* (New York: Oxford UP, 1996) 1–36; Daniel Heath Justice, " 'Go Away, Water!' Kinship Criticism and the Decolonization Imperative," *Reasoning Together: The Native Critics Collective,* ed. Craig S. Womack, Justice, and Christopher B. Teuton (Norman: U of Oklahoma P, 2008) 147–68; Daniel Heath Justice, *Our Fire Survives the Storm: A Cherokee Literary History* (Minneapolis: U of Minnesota P, 2006) 7–10; Craig S. Womack, "The Integrity of American Indian Claims (Or, How I Learned to Stop Worrying and Love My Hybridity)," *American Indian Literary Nationalism,* by Jace Weaver, Womack, and Robert Warrior (Albuquerque: U of New Mexico P, 2006) 91–177; Craig S. Womack, *Red on Red: Native American Literary Separatism* (Minneapolis: U of Minnesota P, 1999) 1–20; Craig S. Womack, "Theorizing American Indian Experience," *Reasoning Together,* 353–410.

4. To be clear, I am using "progressive" to refer to attitudes held, or thought to be held, among Native people who are concerned more with modernizing and adapting to present and future circumstances than with maintaining traditions. I am not using it in connection with the social-activist Progressive era or movement in the

United States around the turn of the twentieth century, though many progressive Indians were also Progressive.

5. Pierre Bourdieu, *The Logic of Practice*, trans. Richard Nice (1980; Paris: Minuit; Stanford: Stanford UP, 1990) 53.

6. Justice, *Our Fire* 19–42; Mary Churchill, *Walking the White Path: Toward a Cherokee-Centric Hermeneutic for Interpreting Cherokee Literature*, diss., U of Calif. at Santa Barbara, 1997 (Ann Arbor: UMI, 1997) 137–87; Weaver, *That the People* vii–xiv, 26–45; Eva Marie Garroutte, *Real Indians: Identity and the Survival of Native America* (Berkeley: U of California P, 2003) 99–152.

Introduction

1. Sean Kicummah Teuton, *Red Land, Red Power: Grounding Knowledge in the American Indian Novel* (Durham: Duke UP, 2008) 16–17. For more postpositivist realists on experience, also see William Wilkerson, "Is There Something You Need to Tell Me? Coming Out and the Ambiguity of Experience," *Reclaiming Identity: Realist Theory and the Predicament of Postmodernism*, ed. Paula Hoya and Michael Hames-García (Berkeley: U of California P, 2000) 251–78; and John Zammito, "Reading 'Experience': The Debate in Intellectual History among Scott, Toews, and LaCapra," *Reclaiming Identity*, 279–311. For an earlier consonant pragmatist take, see W. V. O. Quine, "Two Dogmas of Empiricism," *Quintessence: Basic Readings from the Philosophy of W. V. Quine*, ed. Roger Gibson (Cambridge: Belknap-Harvard UP, 2004) 31–53.

2. Sean Kicummah Teuton 141, 168.

3. Robert Warrior, *Tribal Secrets: Recovering American Indian Intellectual Traditions* (Minneapolis: U of Minnesota P, 1995) 106; Womack, *Red on Red* 271–303.

4. Womack, *Red on Red* 60.

5. Justice, *Our Fire* 24.

6. Jace Weaver, "Splitting the Earth: First Utterances and Pluralist Separatism," *American Indian Literary Nationalism* 15.

7. Warrior, *Tribal Secrets* 87–98; Elizabeth Cook-Lynn, "Literary and Political Questions of Transformation: American Indian Fiction Writers," *Anti-Indianism in Modern America: A Voice from Tatekeya's Earth* (Urbana: U of Illinois P, 2001) 41–42; Womack, *Red on Red* 59.

8. Benedict Anderson, *Imagined Communities: Reflections on the Origin and Spread of Nationalism*, rev. ed. (New York: Verso, 1983) 5–7.

9. Jace Weaver, "More Light Than Heat: The Current State of Native American Studies," *American Indian Quarterly* 31.2 (2007): 239; Robert Warrior, "Native Critics in the World," *American Indian Literary Nationalism* 214; Craig S. Womack, *Art as Performance, Story as Criticism: Reflections on Native Literary Aesthetics* (Norman: U of Oklahoma P, 2009) 95–114.

10. Jace Weaver, *Turtle Goes to War: Of Military Commissions, the Constitution and American Indian Memory* (New Haven: Trylon and Perisphere, 2002).

11. Weaver, "Splitting the Earth" 46.

12. Elvira Pulitano, *Toward a Native American Critical Theory* (Lincoln: U of Nebraska P, 2003) 61–62, 70, 87–88, 97–100; Eric Cheyfitz, *The Columbia Guide to American Indian Literatures of the United States since 1945*, ed. Cheyfitz (New York: Columbia

UP, 2004) 104–106; Arnold Krupat, *Red Matters: Native American Studies* (Philadelphia: U of Pennsylvania P, 2002) 26–28.

13. Womack, *Red on Red* 3.

14. Womack, "Integrity" 101; Warrior, *Tribal Secrets* xvi–xxi.

15. Weaver, "Splitting the Earth" 39–40; Womack, "Integrity" 100.

16. Krupat, *Red Matters* 13, 17.

17. Krupat, *Red Matters* 10.

18. Krupat, *Red Matters* 10.

19. Krupat, *Red Matters* 5, citing Jonathan Ree's "Cosmopolitanism and the Experience of Nationality" in *Cosmopolitics: Thinking and Feeling beyond the Nation*, ed. Pheng Cheah and Bruce Robbins (Minneapolis: U of Minnesota P, 1998) 87.

20. Krupat, *Red Matters* 18.

21. Frantz Fanon, *The Wretched of the Earth,* trans. Constance Farrington, 1961 (New York: Grove, 1963) 246; Krupat, *Red Matters* 7, 22.

22. Fanon 227.

23. Fanon 203–204.

24. Bruce Robbins, "Introduction Part I: Actually Existing Cosmopolitanism," *Cosmopolitics: Thinking and Feeling beyond the Nation*, ed. Pheng Cheah and Robbins (Minneapolis: U of Minnesota P, 1998) 9, but also see Pheng Cheah, "Introduction Part II: The Cosmopolitical—Today," *Cosmopolitics*, 22.

25. Kwame Anthony Appiah, *The Ethics of Identity* (Princeton: Princeton UP, 2005) ix–x.

26. Appiah, *Ethics* 245.

27. Kwame Anthony Appiah, *Cosmopolitanism: Ethics in a World of Strangers* (New York: Norton, 2006) 163, emphasis added.

28. Arnold Krupat, *The Turn to the Native: Studies in Criticism and Culture* (Lincoln: U of Nebraska P, 1996) 105, 112.

29. Krupat, *Red Matters* 18.

30. Krupat, *Red Matters* 5.

31. Krupat *Red Matters* 3.

32. Justice, "'Go Away, Water!'" 151.

33. Ernest Gellner, *Nations and Nationalism* (Ithaca: Cornell UP, 1983) 3–5.

34. "Cherokee Nation Industries Employees Tour Bell Helicopter Assembly Center," News and Events, Cherokee Nation Industries website, Nov. 14, 2008, Sept. 21, 2009, <http://www.cherokee.org/News/Stories/23806.aspx>; Mark Thompson, "V-22 Osprey: A Flying Shame," *Time* Sept. 26, 2007, Sept. 21, 2009, <http://www.time.com/time/nation/article/ 0,8599,1665835-1,00.html>.

35. Scott Lyons, *X-Marks: Native Signatures of Assent* (Minneapolis: U of Minnesota P, 2010) 12.

36. Lyons 139, citing his "Rhetorical Sovereignty: What Do Indians Want from Writing?" *College Composition and Communication* 51.3 (Feb. 2000): 447–68.

37. Lyons 160, 163, 11, respectively.

38. Fanon 246.

39. Cheah 24.

40. Edward Said, *Culture and Imperialism* (New York: Vintage, 1994) 228–29.

41. Krupat, *Red Matters* 119–20.

42. For examples of cosmopolitanist worries about nativism and insistence on particularity, see Krupat, *Turn to the Native* 54–55, 68–69, 106–107; Pulitano 86–89.

43. Jacques Derrida, *Of Grammatology*, trans. Gayatri Chakravorty Spivak (1967; Paris: Minuit; Baltimore: Johns Hopkins UP, 1976) 141–64.

44. Renato Rosaldo, "Imperialist Nostalgia," *Representations* 26 (Spring 1989): 107–22.

45. Louis Owens, *Mixedblood Messages: Literature, Film, Family, Place* (Norman: U of Oklahoma P, 1998) 25–41.

46. Owens 11–12, 17–18.

47. Bourdieu, *Logic of Practice* 53.

48. Bourdieu, *Logic of Practice* 52.

49. Bourdieu, *Logic of Practice* 60–61.

50. Bourdieu, *Logic of Practice* 55.

51. Lyons 186, emphasis in original.

52. Lyons 186.

53. Lyons 181.

54. Elizabeth Cook-Lynn, "The American Indian Fiction Writers: Cosmopolitanism, Nationalism, the Third World, and First Nation Sovereignty," *Why I Can't Read Wallace Stegner and Other Essays: A Tribal Voice* (Madison: U of Wisconsin P, 1996) 78–96; Cook-Lynn, "Literary and Political Questions," 34–44; Warrior, *Tribal Secrets* 1–44.

55. Noam Chomsky, "Goals and Visions," *Chomsky on Anarchism* (Oakland: AK, 2005) 190–211.

56. Colin Ward, *Anarchism: A Very Short Introduction* (New York: Oxford UP, 2004) 31.

57. Chomsky 195.

58. Unfortunately, not many anarchist writers have explored this connection or even seem particularly conscious of it. Crispin Sartwell is a notable exception. See his *Against the State: An Introduction to Anarchist Political Theory* (Albany: State U of New York P, 2008) 5.

59. Taiaiake Alfred, *Wasáse: Indigenous Pathways of Action and Freedom* (Peterborough, Ont.: Broadview, 2005) 45.

60. Jacqueline Lasky, "Indigenism, Anarchism, Feminism: An Emerging Framework for Exploring Post-Imperial Futures," *Affinities* 5.1 (2011): 16, June 18, 2012, <http://www.affinitiesjournal.org/index.php/affinities/article/view/72/0>.

61. Lasky 21.

62. Jane Lawrence, "The Indian Health Service and the Sterilization of Native American Women," *American Indian Quarterly* 24.3 (2000): 400–19; Will Chavez, "CBC Wants to Deny Tribe Housing Funds," *Cherokee Phoenix* May 2008: A1–2.

63. Steve Russell, *Sequoyah Rising* (Durham: Carolina Academic, 2010) 85–86.

64. Raymond Fogelson, "Who Were the Aní-Kutánî? An Excursion into Cherokee Historical Thought," *Ethnohistory* 31.4 (1984): 255–63.

65. Russell 71–72.

66. Cherokee Nation Registrar v. Nash, SC-2011-02, Supreme Ct. of the Cherokee Nation, 2011; Lenzy Krehbiel-Burton, "Frustrations Grow as Cherokee Election Drags On," *Tulsa World*, July 19, 2011, Feb. 16, 2012, http://www.tulsaworld.com/site/printerfriendlystory.aspx?articleid=20110719_11_A1_CUTLIN889989.

67. Will Chavez, "Freedmen Descendants Have Citizenship Restored," *Cherokee Phoenix* Oct. 2011: 1+; Lenzy Krehbiel-Burton, "Bill John Baker Named Official Winner in Cherokee Chief Election," *Tulsa World*, Oct. 13, 2011, Feb. 16, 2012, <http://www.tulsaworld.com/news/article.aspx?subjectid=520&articleid=20111013_16_A1_CUTLIN132201>.

68. "4 Ex-Employees Sue Chief for Wrongful Termination," Associated Press, *Cherokee Phoenix*, Feb. 8, 2012, Feb. 16, 2012, <http://www.cherokeephoenix.org/Article/Index/5947>.

69. Chadwick Allen, *Trans-Indigenous: Methodologies for Global Native Literary Studies* (Minneapolis: U of Minnesota P, 2012) xiv.

70. Shari Huhndorf, *Mapping the Americas: The Transnational Politics of Contemporary Native Culture* (Ithaca: Cornell UP, 2009) 4.

71. James Cox, *The Red Land to the South: American Indian Writers and Indigenous Mexico* (Minneapolis: U of Minnesota P, 2012) 20, citing Rachel Adams, *Continental Divides: Remapping the Cultures of North America* (Chicago: U of Chicago P, 2009) 35.

Chapter 1. Paths of Righteousness

1. I offer still less about other stomp-dance-religion societies like the Four Mothers or the Seven Clans societies, which are less conspicuous in the historical record, for reasons that might include greater reticence, factional disputes, lower membership numbers, or others.

2. Robert Thomas, "Cherokee Values and World View," unpublished ms., U of North Carolina, 1958.

3. Fred Gearing, "Priests and Warriors: Social Structures for Cherokee Politics in the 18th Century," Memoir 93 in *American Anthropologist* 64.5, pt. 2 (Oct. 1962): 31.

4. As it turns out, Chief John Ross regularly invoked harmony in his rhetoric, and to multiple audiences, during the factional disputes over removal. John Ross, *The Papers of Chief John Ross*, ed. Gary Moulton, vol. 1 (Norman: U of Oklahoma P, 1985) 265, 271, 303, 337.

5. Churchill, *Walking the White Path* 137–87; Justice, *Our Fire* 27–34.

6. Robert Thomas, *The Origin and Development of the Redbird Smith Movement*, master's thesis, U of Arizona, 1953, 150.

7. Albert Wahrhaftig, "We Who Act Right: The Persistent Identity of Cherokee Indians," *Currents in Anthropology: Essays in Honor of Sol Tax*, ed. Robert Henshaw (New York: Mouton, 1979) 263.

8. Crosslin Smith, "The Good Mind," lecture, 14th Annual Symposium of the American Indian, Northeastern State U, Tahlequah, Okla., Apr. 1986, videocassette.

9. Churchill 183, citing Janet Etheridge Jordan, "Politics and Religion in a Western Cherokee Community: A Century of Struggle in a White Man's World," diss., U of Connecticut, 1975 (Ann Arbor: Xerox U Microfilms, 1975) 127.

10. Garroutte 118.

11. Garroutte 118–27.

12. Garroutte 128.

13. Garroutte 129.

14. Garroutte 136.

15. Garroutte 137, emphasis and editorial comments in original.

16. Jace Weaver, *That the People* 32.
17. Weaver, *That the People* 37.
18. Weaver, *That the People* 28.
19. Weaver, *That the People* 31.
20. Weaver, *That the People* 43.
21. Weaver, *That the People* 45.
22. Weaver *That the People* 39, emphasis added.
23. Garroutte 132.

24. Garroutte admittedly avoids these critiques through her additional requirements that belonging to a community also requires a state of "being," that is, of having "a connection to ancestry rooted in the individual's fundamental nature" (120) and that that connection be recognized by others in the community. The incorporation of community acceptance does not fully extract us from the repetitious logic that seeks to know by whose criteria a community's claims to Indianness, like an individual's, are established. It seems to me that by including personal assertions, communal affirmations, and the opinions of outsiders to the community as variables in the assessment of identity claims, theorists have made sufficient allowances and must at some point make a pragmatic—that is, telically and realistically oriented—decision, a jumping into the circle, that need not control under all past, present, and future conditions.

25. The practice of "moving the fire" is one example of a method providing for the transplantation and sanctification of a new stomp grounds. See Thomas, *Origin* 153, 161–64; Benny Smith, "The Keetoowah Society of the Cherokee Indians," master's thesis, Northwestern State College, Alva, Okla., 1967, 27–28; Janey Hendrix, "Redbird Smith and the Nighthawk Keetoowahs," *Journal of Cherokee Studies* 8.1 (1983): 36.

26. George Tinker, *Spirit and Resistance: Political Theology and American Indian Liberation* (Minneapolis: Fortress, 2004) 12–27, 95–98, 112.

27. Wyman Kirk, my Cherokee language instructor at Northeastern State University and one of the most erudite people I know on Cherokee matters, introduced me to this practice, for which I am indebted to him. Any errors in its description owe to my failures as a listener and interpreter, not to his careful and considered explanations.

28. Hendrix 8.1: 26–27.

29. See Thomas, *Origin* 180; Howard Meredith and Virginia Milan, eds., *A Cherokee Vision of Eloh'*, trans. Wesley Proctor (Muskogee, Okla.: Indian UP, 1981) 21; Janey Hendrix, "Redbird Smith and the Nighthawk Keetoowahs," *Journal of Cherokee Studies* 8.2 (1983): 84.

30. Benny Smith 20.

31. While they might work together, gaining knowledge and community vetting are not necessarily linked in traditionalist thinking; I have yoked them so conspicuously and regularly by my own devices.

32. Rennard Strickland, *Fire and the Spirits: Cherokee Law from Clan to Court* (Norman: U of Oklahoma P, 1975) 45.

33. Howard Tyner, "The Keetoowah Society in Cherokee History," master's thesis, Tulsa U, 1949, 28.

34. Raymond Fogelson, "Who Were the Aní-Kutánî?" 255–63. Cherokee author Robert Conley's first several novels in the Real People series (*The Way of the Priests,*

The Dark Way, and *The White Path*) fictionalize the story, with a troublesome villainizing of the antagonist priests as homosexual.

35. James Adair, *Adair's History of the American Indians*, ed. Samuel Williams, new edition (1775; London: Edward and Charles Dilly; Johnson City, Tenn.: Watauga, under auspices of Natl. Soc. of Colonial Dames of America, 1930; New York: Promontory, [1974?]) 245.

36. Rennard Strickland 45.

37. Thomas, *Origin* 47.

38. William McLoughlin, *Cherokees and Missionaries, 1789–1839* (New Haven: Yale UP, 1984; Norman: U of Oklahoma P, 1994) 8–9.

39. McLoughlin, *Cherokees and Missionaries* 8.

40. James Mooney, "Myths of the Cherokee," Smithsonian Inst., Bureau of Amer. Ethnology, 19th Annual Rept., Pt. 1, 1897–98 (Washington: GPO, 1900): 396–97. While I consulted the original ethnographic reports Mooney authored, they have been reprinted by several presses as facsimiles, thus generally retaining the original pagination. *Myths of the Cherokee and Sacred Formulas of the Cherokees* (Nashville: Charles and Randy Elder; Cherokee, N.C.: Cherokee Heritage, 1982) is a faithful and readily available version, as are many electronic copies.

41. McLoughlin, *Cherokees and Missionaries* 33–34.

42. The historical power dynamic was still dicey, as revealed by a 1787 report to the Continental Congress regarding the need for Georgia and North Carolina to cede land to the federal government to use as treating currency. Though it dates somewhat earlier than the major period of missionary entry, it reveals the trepidation with which the young America regarded the still-dangerous southeastern tribes:

> The committee conceive that several other considerations cannot escape the observation of the two states, which may be urged in favor of the cessions. . . . The committee believe that the two states . . . will be disposed to follow the liberal examples of the other states in a similar situation . . . that by making the proposed cessions, those difficulties they now experience will be removed, that is, the controversies respecting Indian affairs, and those dispersed settlements which tend to render the governments weak and feeble, and to produce expensive and calamitous wars with the Indians.

("Committee Report," *Journals of the Continental Congress, Documents from the Continental Congress and the Constitutional Convention, 1774–1789, American Memory*, Library of Congress, June 8, 2009, <http://memory.loc.gov/cgi-bin/query/r?ammem/bdsbib:@field(M010+90898156)):>).

43. See in general McLoughlin, *Cherokees and Missionaries* 35–212.

44. McLoughlin, *Cherokees and Missionaries* 51–53.

45. William McLoughlin, *Cherokees and Christianity, 1794–1870: Essays on Acculturation and Cultural Persistence*, ed. Walter Conser (Athens: U of Georgia P, 1984) 36.

46. Rennard Strickland 10–39.

47. Theda Perdue, *Cherokee Women: Gender and Culture Change, 1700–1835* (Lincoln: U of Nebraska P, 1998) 10.

48. Perdue, *Cherokee Women* 25–27. Also see Paula Gunn Allen, *The Sacred Hoop: Recovering the Feminine in American Indian Traditions* (Boston: Beacon, 1986) 1–42.

49. While historians might cast Cherokee women as everywhere alike in their traditionalism, we should be aware of the falsely homogenizing influence of such tendencies, as Chandra Mohanty has argued in "Under Western Eyes: Feminist Scholarship and Colonial Discourses." Such leveling enables the dichotomization of women as traditional or progressive, ignorant or educated, authentic or corrupt. Spurred by Mohanty's astute perception of the mainstream theoretical construction of third world female subjectivity, and with focus on the contradictions posed by Christian Cherokee women, it's worth disrupting the "already constituted, coherent group with identical interests and desires, regardless of class, ethnic or racial location or contradictions" that reinscribes the prevailing cultural versions and indices of value. See Chandra Talpade Mohanty, "Under Western Eyes: Feminist Scholarship and Colonial Discourses," *Boundary 2* 12.3 (1984): 336–37.

50. Partha Chatterjee, *The Nation and Its Fragments: Colonial and Postcolonial Histories*, Princeton: Princeton UP, 1993, rpt. in *The Partha Chatterjee Omnibus* (New Delhi: Oxford UP, 1999) 6.

51. Chatterjee, *Nation and Its Fragments* 117.

52. Judith Lowder Newton, "Power and the Ideology of 'Woman's Sphere,'" *Feminisms: An Anthology of Literary Theory and Criticism*, ed. Robyn Warhol and Diane Price Herndl, rev. ed. (New Brunswick: Rutgers UP, 1997) 880–95.

53. Chatterjee, *Nation and Its Fragments* 3–6.

54. McLoughlin, *Cherokees and Missionaries* 27, 147; McLoughlin, *Cherokees and Christianity* 84, 209–10, 331.

55. Carolyn Ross Johnston, *Cherokee Women in Crisis: Trail of Tears, Civil War, and Allotment, 1838–1907* (Tuscaloosa: U of Alabama P, 2003) 133; Thomas, *Origin* 180–81, 196; Tyner 79; Benny Smith 12, 14.

56. Churchill 24–25.

57. Churchill 35–61.

58. Churchill 72, 77.

59. Churchill 24–26, 62, 77–82.

60. In his reply to Churchill, Hudson regrets using "abominable" and "anomalous" synonymously and explains he intended no pejorative connotations and thus no facile good versus bad opposition between categories. He further objects to the ostensible poststructuralism in her critique. Charles Hudson, "Reply to Mary Churchill," *American Indian Quarterly* 24.3 (2000): 495–96.

61. Churchill 72–73.

62. Churchill 67.

63. Churchill 178.

64. Churchill 67.

65. Claude Lévi-Strauss, *Structural Anthropology*, 1958, trans. Claire Jacobson and Brooke Grundfest Schoepf (New York: Basic, 1963) 229.

66. Churchill 72n178.

67. Churchill 183, emphasis added.

68. Benny Smith 15, 16.

69. Churchill 183.

70. Churchill 83.

71. Churchill 186, emphasis added. Churchill here refers to the work of Jack and Anna Kilpatrick in *Run to the Nightland: Magic of the Oklahoma Cherokees* (Dallas:

Southern Methodist UP, 1967) and *Walk in Your Soul: Love Incantations of the Oklahoma Cherokees* (Dallas: Southern Methodist UP, 1965).

72. Catherine Belsey, *Poststructuralism: A Very Short Introduction* (New York: Oxford UP, 2002) 43.

73. Justice, *Our Fire* 28.

74. Justice, *Our Fire* 24.

75. Justice, *Our Fire* 20.

76. Justice, *Our Fire* 30.

77. Justice, *Our Fire* 30.

78. Justice, *Our Fire* 19–20.

79. Justice, *Our Fire* 27.

80. Justice, *Our Fire* 216.

81. Justice, *Our Fire* 23.

82. Wayne Booth, *Critical Understanding: The Powers and Limits of Pluralism* (Chicago: U of Chicago P, 1979) 3.

83. This line of structuralism's critique I borrow from Pierre Bourdieu, *In Other Words: Essays Towards a Reflexive Sociology*, trans. Matthew Adamson (Stanford: Stanford UP, 1990) 9–10.

Chapter 2. Gaining Knowledge and Religious Improvisation in Catharine Brown's Memoir

1. Much of the material on Catharine Brown in this chapter is reprinted from my article "Integrated Circuitry: Catharine Brown across Race, Gender, and Religion," *American Indian Culture and Research Journal* 30.1 (2006): 17–31, by permission of the American Indian Studies Center, University of California, Los Angeles, for which I am grateful.

2. Catharine Brown, *Memoir of Catharine Brown: A Christian Indian of the Cherokee Nation*, ed. Rufus Anderson, 2nd ed. (N.p.: Armstrong, 1824; Boston: Crocker and Brewster, 1825; Signal Mountain, Tenn.: Mountain, [1998?]) 19; Arnold Krupat, *Native American Autobiography: An Anthology* (Madison: U of Wisconsin P, 1994) 114; Theda Perdue, "Catharine Brown: Cherokee Convert to Christianity," *Sifters: Native American Women's Lives*, ed. Perdue (New York: Oxford UP, 2001) 88; Clara Sue Kidwell, Homer Noley, and George Tinker, *A Native American Theology* (Maryknoll, N.Y.: Orbis, 2001) 44–45. For a historical summary of people, places, and events see Mary Higginbotham, "The Creek Path Mission," *Journal of Cherokee Studies* 1.2 (1976): 72–85. Many primary sources survive in the Papers of the American Board of Commissioners for Foreign Missions in the Houghton Library's archives at Harvard University, and several references to Brown may be found in Joyce Phillips and Paul Phillips, eds., *The Brainerd Journal: A Mission to the Cherokees, 1817–1823* (Lincoln: U of Nebraska P, 1998). Brown's (misnamed) memoir was published in 1824 in a now-difficult-to-find first edition by Samuel Armstrong; in a second edition the following year by John Haven publishers in New York and by Crocker and Brewster in Boston; and in at least a third edition by the American Sunday School Union in Philadelphia in 1832. Mountain Press's 1998 reprinting of the second edition, which I have used, ameliorates the scarcity of those prior. (This date is taken from the publisher's website, <http://www.mountainpress.com/books/na/details

/gn-0153w.html>, accessed May 1, 2004, and is not found in the edition itself.) There are differences among the editions in the way of deleted passages that bear closer scrutiny. For the sake of clarity, each subsequent reference to this volume will attempt to identify either Brown or Anderson as the primary speaker—would that conclusive differentiation could be definitive.

3. Joel Martin, *The Land Looks after Us: A History of Native American Religion* (New York: Oxford UP, 2001) 28.

4. James Treat, "Introduction: Native Christian Narrative Discourse," *Native and Christian: Indigenous Voices on Religious Identity in the United States and Canada*, ed. Treat (New York: Routledge, 1996); James West, "Indian Spirituality: Another Vision," *Native and Christian: Indigenous Voices on Religious Identity in the United States and Canada*, ed. Treat (New York: Routledge, 1996) 6–13, 34–36.

5. Laura Donaldson, *American Samson: Haunting the Native-Christian Encounter* (Chapel Hill: U of North Carolina P, forthcoming); Perdue, *Cherokee Women* 3–11; Brown 25; Phillips and Phillips 91.

6. McLoughlin, *Cherokees and Missionaries* 35–45, 110.

7. James Mooney, "Myths of the Cherokee" 83.

8. Wendy Doniger, Foreword, *Myth and Meaning: Cracking the Code of Culture*, Claude Lévi-Strauss, rev. ed. (New York: Schocken, 1995) viii–ix.

9. Claude Lévi-Strauss, *Myth and Meaning: Cracking the Code of Culture*, rev. ed. (New York: Schocken, 1995) 23.

10. Fredric Jameson, *The Prison-House of Language: A Critical Account of Structuralism and Russian Formalism* (Princeton: Princeton UP, 1972): 5–22.

11. Anne McClintock, *Imperial Leather: Race, Gender, and Sexuality in the Colonial Contest* (New York: Routledge, 1995) 5.

12. Jameson 96–98.

13. Perdue, *Cherokee Women* 170–71.

14. Ruth Bradley Holmes and Betty Sharp Smith, *Beginning Cherokee*, 5th ed. (Norman: U of Oklahoma P, 1976) 22, 248–49; Durbin Feeling, *Cherokee-English Dictionary*, ed. William Pulte (Tahlequah, Okla.: Heritage, 1975) 141, 177. Holmes and Smith offer a rich genealogy of the verb *kanesdi* (ᎧᏁᏍᏗ), which means to speak or address, and is found in variations in words like gospel, song, psalm, history, story, poem, treaty, testimony, and tradition, all of which connote announcing or heralding.

15. William Pulte and Durbin Feeling, "Outline of Cherokee Grammar," *Cherokee-English Dictionary*, by Durbin Feeling, ed. William Pulte (Tahlequah, Okla.: Heritage, 1975) 241–305.

16. Perdue, *Cherokee Women* 159–84; Johnston 40–54; Elias Boudinot, *Cherokee Editor: The Writings of Elias Boudinot*, ed. Theda Perdue (Knoxville: U of Tennessee P, 1983; Athens: U of Georgia P, 1996) 8–12.

17. Mark Custalow, "Native American Church Planting," North American Mission Board, Southern Baptist Convention, Apr. 19, 2004, <http://www.namb.net/lightupthenation/body_cpt_12_nativeamerican.asp>; also see Mark Custalow, "Biblical Guidelines for Contextualizing Native American Church Ministry," Church Planting Village website, North American Mission Board, Southern Baptist Convention, n.d., 12 pp., June 22, 2009, <http://www.churchplantingvillage.net/atf/cf/%7B0938A074-4176-42D7-8428-77A665D9544E%7D/Bible%20Guidelines%20for%20 Contextualization.pdf>.

18. Bill Sherman, "Oklahoma Baptists Elect First Native American President," *Tulsa World*, Nov. 11, 2008, June 15, 2009, <http://www.tulsaworld.com/news/article.aspx?articleID=20081111_1__Onewe02724>; "Southern Baptists Choose Johnny Hunt New President," Associated Press, *Fort Worth Star Telegram*, June 10, 2008, June 15, 2009, <http://www.star-telegram.com/804/story/692978.html>.

19. Martin 71.

20. Mooney, "Myths of the Cherokee" 333.

21. Mooney, "Myths of the Cherokee" 331–36; Martin 71–72; Richard Bushyhead, "The Little People and the Nunnehi," Kathi Smith Littlejohn, "The Cherokee Little People" and "Nunnehi, the Gentle People," and Barbara Duncan, "Edna Chekelelee," all in *Living Stories of the Cherokee*, comp. and ed. Barbara Duncan (Chapel Hill: U of North Carolina P, 1998) 183–87, 68–74, 125–26, respectively; also see Jeannie Reed, ed., *Stories of the Yûñwï Tsunsdi': The Cherokee Little People* (Cullowhee, N.C.: Western Carolina U, 1991).

22. Albert Wahrhaftig, "We Who Act Right" 264; Thomas, *Origin* 40, 92, 124, 190, and especially 213–14, 217; Raymond Fogelson, "Cherokee Notions of Power," *The Anthropology of Power: Ethnographic Studies from Asia, Oceania, and the New World*, ed. Fogelson and Richard Adams (New York: Academic, 1977) 189; Mary Ellen Meredith and Howard Meredith, *Reflection on Cherokee Literary Expression* (Lewiston, N.Y.: Mellen, 2003) 40; Martin 71–73.

23. Brown 59, 66.

24. In case anyone wants to track them down, see Brown 41, 15, 54, 59, 74, 81, 82, 83, 90, 94, 100; Anderson, in Brown 19, 54, 58, 122.

25. Perdue, "Catharine Brown" 80–81.

26. Garroutte, *Real Indians* 129; Weaver, *That the People* 32; Crosslin Smith, "The Good Mind."

27. Barbara Welter, "The Cult of True Womanhood: 1820–1860," *American Quarterly* 18.2 (1966): 152.

28. Theda Perdue, "Southern Indians and the Cult of True Womanhood," *Half Sisters of History: Southern Women and the American Past*, ed. Catherine Clinton (Durham: Duke UP, 1994) 43.

29. Perdue, "Southern Indians" 51.

30. Wilma Dunaway, "Rethinking Cherokee Acculturation: Agrarian Capitalism and Women's Resistance to the Cult of Domesticity, 1800–1838," *American Indian Culture and Research Journal* 21.1 (1997): 171.

31. Shirley Samuels, introduction, *The Culture of Sentiment: Race, Gender, and Sentimentality in Nineteenth-Century America*, ed. Samuels (New York: Oxford UP, 1992) 4.

32. A handful of quotes from Hopkins's *Historical Memoirs: Relating to the Housatunnuk Indians* may illustrate: "Tho' the *Indians* are sunk below the Dignity of human Nature, and their Lust after Drink exposes them to be cheated out of what little they have; yet this gives us no Right to deal unjustly by them. They have a natural Right to Justice, and many, with great Propriety, challenge it at our Hand, feeling we profess to be subject to the Law of Christ, which teach us to do *that which is altogether just*" (169); "We should also exercise that Kindness and Generosity towards them, that shall convince them that it is for their Interest to be in Friendship with us." He anticipates an objection that Indians' ungratefulness ought to

preclude such kindness: "We have good Authority for being *kind to the Unthankful and to the Evil.* And if that good Being who recommends it to us, had not given an Example of it, in his Dealings with us, how deplorable had our State been?" (174). See also Joseph Conforti, "Samuel Hopkins and the New Divinity: Theology, Ethics, and Social Reform in Eighteenth-Century New England," *William and Mary Quarterly* 34.4 (1977): 584.

33. Conforti, "Samuel Hopkins" 574.

34. Martin 75.

35. Leonard Sweet, "The Female Seminary Movement and Woman's Mission in Antebellum America," *Church History* 54.1 (1985): 52.

36. Sweet 44.

37. Genevieve McCoy, "The Women of the ABCFM Oregon Mission and the Conflicted Language of Calvinism," *Church History* 64.1 (1995): 69; Joseph Conforti, "Mary Lyon, the Founding of Mount Holyoke College, and the Cultural Revival of Jonathan Edwards," *Religion and American Culture* 3.1 (1993): 83.

38. Brown 66.

39. R. Palmer Howard, "Cherokee History to 1840: A Medical View," *Oklahoma State Medical Assn. Jour.* 63 (1970): 73, qtd. in Russell Thornton, *The Cherokees: A Population History* (Lincoln: U of Nebraska P, 1990) 49; Phillips and Phillips 513; William McLoughlin, *Cherokee Renascence in the New Republic* (Princeton: Princeton UP, 1986) 385.

40. McLoughlin, *Cherokee Renascence* 206–59, 411–27.

41. Perdue, "Catharine Brown" 81.

42. Anderson, in Brown 40.

43. Brown 93.

44. Perdue, "Catharine Brown" 89.

45. See for instance, Mooney, "Myths of the Cherokee" 229, 392; James Mooney, "The Sacred Formulas of the Cherokees," Smithsonian Inst., Bureau of Amer. Ethnology, 7th Annual Rept., 1885–88 (Washington: GPO, 1891) 318–19. Much of the research literature on Cherokee religion relies heavily on James Mooney's ethnological work in the Qualla Boundary in North Carolina near the beginning of the twentieth century. Most of his research relies on the male informant named Swimmer. The vast and geographically diverse territory once inhabited by the Cherokees, the degree of town autonomy, the privacies of clans, the separation of social gender roles, and the dynamism of culture and religion generally should lead us to question the nearly sacrosanct status afforded Mooney's early work, itself shaped by the protoanthropological, social evolutionary theories of the likes of John Powell, Daniel Brinton, Frederic Putnam, Lewis Morgan, and others, preceding Francis Boas's cultural relativism. For a concise introduction to the theoretical history of the Bureau of American Ethnology and the broader fields of ethnography, ethnology, and anthropology, see Lee Baker, *From Savage to Negro: Anthropology and the Construction of Race, 1896–1954* (Berkeley: U of California P, 1998) 26–53; for a critical biography of Mooney's early years and his time working with the Cherokee see L. G. Moses, *The Indian Man: A Biography of James Mooney*, rev. ed. (Urbana: U of Illinois P, 1984; Lincoln: U of Nebraska P, 2002) 1–51. Craig Womack's chapter "In the Storyway" in *Red on Red*, 75–101, offers an insightful deconstruction of the narrative wiggle room in ethnological retellings of oral traditions.

46. Brown 61.
47. Brown 66.
48. Brown 46.
49. Brown 50.
50. Isaac Watts, "LVI [Hymn 56]. The Song of Moses and the Lamb: Or, Babylon Falling, Rev. xv, 3, and xvi, 19, and xvii, 6," *Hymns and Spiritual Songs*, 7th ed., [Boston?]: [Bristol?], [1720?], Early American Imprints, Series I: Evans, 1639–1800; An Archive of Americana Collection, no. 29733, rec. no. w038649, <http://docs.newsbank.com.proxy.library.cornell.edu/openurl?ctx_ver=z39.88-2004&rft_id=info:sid/iw.newsbank.com:EVAN&rft_val_format=info:ofi/fmt:kev:mtx:ctx&rft_dat=0F2F820D6CD2D2B0&svc_dat=Evans:eaidoc&req_dat=0D0CB4F0E6B93180>, 66–67.
51. Andrea Smith, *Native Americans and the Christian Right: The Gendered Politics of Unlikely Alliances* (Durham: Duke UP, 2008) ix–xxxv, 200–75.
52. Anderson, in Brown 41.
53. Anderson, in Brown 120–21. Anderson's allusion is to Song of Solomon 2:11, in a piquant reference to the most erotic book of the Bible. He perhaps suggests that marriage of Indian women to white men numbers among the ordinances they should fully enjoy.
54. McLoughlin, *Cherokees and Christianity* 71.
55. Anderson, in Brown 25.
56. "Resolution by Missionaries," *Cherokee Phoenix* Jan. 1, 1831, rpt. in Samuel Worcester, *New Echota Letters: Contributions of Samuel A. Worcester to the "Cherokee Phoenix,"* ed. Jack Frederick Kilpatrick and Anna Gritts Kilpatrick (Dallas: Southern Methodist UP, 1968) 83–84.
57. Althea Bass, *Cherokee Messenger*, 1936 (Norman: U of Oklahoma P, 1996) 138–60; McLoughlin, *Cherokees and Christianity* 55.
58. McLoughlin, *Cherokees and Christianity* 73, 93, 115.
59. McLoughlin, *Cherokees and Christianity* 102.
60. McLoughlin, *Cherokees and Christianity* 117–26.
61. Bethany Schneider, *From Place to Populace: Indian Removal and State-Formation in Antebellum American Literature*, diss., Cornell U, 2003 (Ann Arbor: UMI, 2003) 162.
62. Worcester 43–53, McLoughlin, *Cherokees and Missionaries* 136–37, McLoughlin, *Cherokees and Christianity* 194–97, 199, 211, 205, 200–201; Mooney, "Sacred Formulas" 336.
63. McLoughlin, *Cherokees and Christianity* 205, 207.
64. McLoughlin, *Cherokees and Christianity* 66.
65. Worcester 5–9, 14–33, 41–42, 59–69; Anderson, in Brown 46. Worcester also made some perfunctory attempts at Cherokee ethnology; see Worcester 43–47, 53.
66. Anna Gambold, "Diary Year 1807," July 16, 1807, *The Moravian Springplace Mission to the Cherokees*, ed. Rowena McClinton, Indians of the Southeast, vol. 1: 1805–1813 (Lincoln: U of Nebraska P, 2007) 199–200.
67. Anderson, in Brown 39–40, 42; Phillips and Phillips 114–15.
68. In the first case, Anderson, in Brown 40, and also see Phillips and Phillips 158; Anderson, in Brown 42, quoting a letter from David Brown dated Sept. 24, 1824.
69. Phillips and Phillips 176.
70. McLoughlin, *Cherokees and Christianity* 116–17.

71. William McLoughlin, *After the Trail of Tears: The Cherokees' Struggle for Sovereignty, 1839–1880* (Chapel Hill: U of North Carolina P, 1993) 189.
72. Anderson, in Brown 58–59, 78, 127–28.
73. Anderson, in Brown 42–43.
74. Anderson, in Brown 115–16.
75. Benny Smith 8.
76. Martin 70–71.
77. Perdue, "Catharine Brown" 86.
78. Johnston 43.
79. Krupat, *Native American Autobiography* 115.
80. Womack, *Red on Red* 183.
81. Anderson, in Brown 38.
82. McLoughlin, *Cherokees and Missionaries* 335–52; McLoughlin, *Cherokees and Christianity* 152–218.
83. Mooney, "Myths of the Cherokee" 242–49; Perdue, *Cherokee Women* 13–15; Johnston 24–27.
84. Perdue, *Cherokee Women* 17–40.

Chapter 3. Gathering Strength in Sequoyah Guess's **Kholvn**

1. Sequoyah Guess, *Kholvn* (Kansas, Okla.: Kholvn, 1992), inside back cover.
2. Chris Teuton, "Scary Stories: An Interview with Traditional Keetoowah/Cherokee Storyteller, Novelist, and Filmmaker Mr. Sequoyah Guess," *Mississippi Quarterly* 60.1 (2006–2007) 151.
3. James Mooney, "Myths of the Cherokee" 225.
4. Thomas, *Origin* 119.
5. Thomas, *Origin* 145–46.
6. Thomas, *Origin* 112–13.
7. Howard Meredith and Virginia Milan, eds., *A Cherokee Vision of Eloh'*, trans. Wesley Proctor (Muskogee, Okla.: Indian UP, 1981); Floyd Lounsbury, "Iroquois-Cherokee Linguistic Relations," *Symposium on Cherokee and Iroquois Culture*, ed. William Fenton and John Gulick, Bull. 180, Smithsonian Inst., Bureau of Amer. Ethnology, Washington: GPO, 1961, 9–18; William McGoun, "Adoption of Whites by 18th Century Cherokees," *Journal of Cherokee Studies* 9.1 (1984): 37–41.
8. "Keetoowah Constitution and Bylaws," n.d., Appendix B, in Howard Tyner, "The Keetoowah Society in Cherokee History," master's thesis, Tulsa U, 1949, 123, 124. The date of the exclusion is uncertain. Tyner indicates that the original document is in Cherokee and that John Smith, Redbird Smith's son, authored this draft in English. The preamble of sorts refers to the Keetoowah Society's constitution of 1859, the English version of which does not include such a prohibition, and also says the constitution was amended in 1889, but what the amendments included or even if the two constitutions are at all related is ambiguous (100, 121).
9. "Keetoowah Constitution" 131–32. Tyner reprints the constitution and of it writes, "Appendix B is the constitution of the Nighthawk Keetoowahs and was written by John Smith, son of Redbird Smith who was the first chief of the Nighthawks. The original copy is at the Oklahoma Historical Society, Oklahoma City, Oklahoma" (100).

10. Charles Hudson, *Elements of Southeastern Indian Religion* (Leiden, Neth.: Brill Academic, 1984) 13.

11. Mooney, "Sacred Formulas" 340–41.

12. Thomas, *Origin* 122.

13. Benny Smith 27. Smith also describes the Keetoowah practice of sacrifice, which some surely thought incompatible with Christianity (15). The amendment, however, references a biblical counterpart.

14. Guess 109–10.

15. Chris Teuton 155.

16. Chris Teuton 172.

17. Guess 93.

18. Chris Teuton 176.

19. Guess 216.

20. Guess 100.

21. Crosslin Smith, "The Good Mind."

22. Mooney, "Myths of the Cherokee" 431.

23. Chris Teuton 175.

24. Guess 207–208.

25. Mooney, in "Myths of the Cherokee" 240, 421, comments on Cherokee cedar symbolism, and Matthew 6:28, Song of Solomon 2:1, and the hymn "Lily of the Valley" link Christ to the lily.

26. Guess 208.

27. Guess, n.p. This quote is found in the unnumbered section titled "A Word from the Author" found at the beginning of *Kholvn*.

28. Chris Teuton 162.

29. Guess 169.

30. Chris Teuton 162.

31. Chris Teuton 162.

32. Guess 144.

33. Thomas, *Origin* 217.

34. Guess 3.

35. Guess 222. The punctuation is as it appears in the original.

36. Chad Smith, "Letter to Cherokee Citizens from Chad Smith," *Cherokee Phoenix* Aug. 2005: 30, July 16, 2009, <http://www.cherokeephoenix.org/1512/Article.aspx>.

37. Teddye Snell, "Trust Land Status OK'd for UKB Casino," *Tahlequah Daily Press* July 31, 2012: 1A–2A.

38. "Keetoowah History Essay," United Keetoowah Band of Cherokee Indians website, n.d., July 7, 2009, <http://www.keetoowahcherokee.org/documents/history/historyessay.pdf>; "UKB Chief Responds to CNO's Public Statement," United Keetoowah Band of Cherokee Indians website, Jan. 18, 2008, July 7, 2009, <http://www.keetoowahcherokee.org/1182008.html>.

39. Guess 221.

40. Guess iii. "Complete people" is an alternative rendering of the Cherokees' name for themselves, *aniyvwiya*, usually translated "real people."

Chapter 4. Deliberation in Town and Country

1. Betty Anderson Smith, "Distribution of Eighteenth-Century Cherokee Settlements," *The Cherokee Indian Nation: A Troubled History*, ed. Duane King (Knoxville: U of Tennessee P, 1979) 46–57; Thornton, *Cherokees* 32; McLoughlin, *Cherokee Renascence* 8.

2. Raymond Fogelson and Paul Kutsche, "Cherokee Economic Cooperatives: The Gadugi," *Symposium on Cherokee and Iroquois Culture*, ed. William Fenton and John Gulick, Bulletin 180, Smithsonian Inst., Bureau of Amer. Ethnology (Washington: GPO, 1961) 88. Durbin Feeling has "town" as *gaduhvi* in his *Cherokee-English Dictionary*, ed. William Pulte, Cherokee Nation (Tahlequah: Heritage, 1975) 93.

3. Betty Anderson Smith 47, 57.

4. Raymond Fogelson, in "Who Were the Aní-Kutánî?" 255–63, assembles the most complete account of the priests' fall.

5. Gearing, "Priests and Warriors" 23–27; Fogelson and Kutsche 91–92; Duane Champagne, "Symbolic Structure and Political Change in Cherokee Society," *Journal of Cherokee Studies* 8 (1983): 87; Duane Champagne, "Institutional and Cultural Order in Early Cherokee Society: A Sociological Interpretation," *Journal of Cherokee Studies* 15 (1990): 12–19; V. Richard Persico, "Early Nineteenth-Century Cherokee Political Organization," *The Cherokee Indian Nation: A Troubled History*, 93–95.

6. Perdue, *Cherokee Women* 41–59, 111–45, 228; Rennard Strickland, *Fire and the Spirits* 22–26; Laura Donaldson, "But We Are Your Mothers, You Are Our Sons: Gender, Sovereignty and the Nation in Early Cherokee Women's Writing," *Indigenous Women and Feminism: Politics, Activism, Culture*, ed. Cheryl Suzack, et al. (Vancouver: U of British Columbia P, 2010) 43–55; also see Raymond Fogelson, "Cherokee Notions of Power," *The Anthropology of Power: Ethnographic Studies from Asia, Oceania, and the New World*, ed. Fogelson and Richard Adams (New York: Academic, 1977) 192–93.

7. Champagne, "Institutional and Cultural Order" 21, 15–16.

8. Rennard Strickland 27.

9. Rennard Strickland 25–26; Persico 95; Perdue, *Cherokee Women* 46; Champagne, "Institutional Order" 11–12; Fogelson and Kutsche 90–91; McLoughlin, *Cherokee Renascence* 11.

10. Gearing 4–5; also see Rennard Strickland 56; Fogelson and Kutsche 93.

11. Rennard Strickland 10–12, 22; McLoughlin, *Cherokee Renascence* 15–16; Mooney, "Sacred Formulas" 318; Raymond Fogelson, "The Conjuror in Eastern Cherokee Society," *Journal of Cherokee Studies* 5.2 (1980): 61; Benny Smith 6.

12. Champagne, "Institutional and Cultural Order" 12–14.

13. Gearing 30–36; John Loftin, "The 'Harmony Ethic' of the Conservative Eastern Cherokees: A Religious Interpretation," *Journal of Cherokee Studies* 8.1 (1983): 40–45; Wahrhaftig, "We Who Act Right" 262–64; Champagne, "Institutional and Cultural Order" 10.

14. Champagne, "Institutional and Cultural Order" 17, 19; McLoughlin, *Cherokee Renascence* 8–11; Fogelson and Kutsche 97; Persico 93–95.

15. Champagne, "Institutional and Cultural Order" 15.

16. Gearing 39.

17. Fogelson, "Cherokee Notions of Power" 189; Benny Smith 20.

18. Fogelson and Kutsche 97–98; Gearing 31, 37–41; Persico 93–94, 100; McLoughlin, *Cherokee Renascence* 11; Champagne, "Institutional and Cultural Order" 15–16, but also see Loftin 41.

19. Gearing 39; William Strickland, "Cherokee Rhetoric: A Forceful Weapon," *Journal of Cherokee Studies* 2.3 (1977): 377; Loftin 42.

20. Gearing 37–42.

21. Champagne, "Institutional and Cultural Order" 16. For more on the traditional consensus-based model of governance, see McLoughlin, *Cherokee Renascence* 10–12; Champagne, "Institutional and Cultural Order" 10–19; Persico 94.

22. Benny Smith 1, 12–16; Gearing 41–42.

23. William Strickland 375–84; Gearing 40–45; Champagne, "Institutional and Cultural Order" 14–15; Fogelson, "Cherokee Notions of Power" 190–92.

24. Wahrhafting 266.

25. McLoughlin, *Cherokee Renascence*, 44–45, 139–42, 156–67, 284–89; Rennard Strickland 51–52; Persico 95–108; Champagne, "Symbolic Structure" 91–92. Gearing (85–112) and Champagne ("Symbolic Structure" 87–96) locate the shift somewhat earlier, in the mid-1700s.

26. Persico 99–108; McLoughlin, *Cherokee Renascence* 407.

27. Champagne, "Symbolic Structure" 91–92; McLoughlin, *Cherokee Renascence* 224–27; Rennard Strickland 40–52; Perdue, *Cherokee Women* 138–58.

28. Perdue, *Cherokee Women* 136–41; Rennard Strickland 41, 44–50; McLoughlin, *Cherokee Renascence* 140.

29. William McLoughlin and Walter Conser, "The Cherokees in Transition: A Statistical Analysis of the Federal Cherokee Census of 1835," *Journal of American History* 64 (1977): 679–703; Thornton 47–54.

30. McLoughlin and Conser 693. Scholars reiterate the minority position of the mixed-blood group—but one-quarter is no small minority.

31. Circe Sturm, *Blood Politics: Race, Culture, and Identity in the Cherokee Nation of Oklahoma* (Berkeley: U of California P, 2002) 56.

32. Mark Rifkin, *Manifesting America: The Imperial Construction of U.S. National Space* (New York: Oxford UP, 2009) 6.

33. Rifkin, 19–20, is interrogating a quote from Womack's *Red on Red* here.

34. Rifkin 54.

35. Partha Chatterjee asks similar questions of Benedict Anderson's assumption that nationalism in the third world only ever copied the model established by the first. Like Chatterjee, I am interested both in culturally specific innovations to the postcolonial nation and in exploring its limitations, or as he more eloquently puts it, "the twists and turns, the suppressed possibilities, the contradictions still unresolved" (22). See his *Nationalist Thought and the Colonial World: A Derivative Discourse?* London: Zed for United Nations U of Tokyo, 1986, rpt. in *The Partha Chatterjee Omnibus* (New Delhi: Oxford UP, 1999) 19–22.

36. Rifkin 7.

37. McLoughlin and Conser 700.

38. Signers are listed in "Treaty with the Cherokees, 1835," *The Cherokee Removal: A Brief History with Documents*, ed. Theda Perdue and Michael Green (Boston: Bedford, 1995) 144. Census entries for some can be found in *1835 Cherokee Census*, Monograph 2 (Park Hill, Okla.: Trail of Tears Assn., 2002), 2, 3, 9, 12, 13, 14, 16, 17, 46, 51, 53, 55, 57, 62.

39. Rifkin 54.

40. Rifkin 55.

41. Cherokee Nation v. the State of Georgia, 30 US 1, Supreme Ct. of the U.S., 1831, 25.

42. Priscilla Wald, *Constituting Americans: Cultural Anxiety and Narrative Form* (Durham: Duke UP, 1995) 25.

43. Partha Chatterjee, *The Nation and Its Fragments: Colonial and Postcolonial Histories*, Princeton: Princeton UP, 1993, rpt. in *The Partha Chatterjee Omnibus* (New Delhi: Oxford UP, 1999) 3–13; Womack, *Red on Red* 35–41.

44. I know most anarchists would reject this suggestion that valuing wealth and maintaining private property could be part of anarchistic reform, but in given economic realities, it is not only pragmatic and necessary to insist that Indians individually and collectively have the right to accumulate resources and to control land independent of an external state, but it is also radically imperative as part of anticolonial action. Furthermore, I believe that a careful study of traditional dispositions regarding economics and ownership would demonstrate that Indian communities' concepts and practices of control of material and place were consistent with indigenous religious, spiritual, and social beliefs that hold land as sacred and intimately connected with communities, with fundamental anarchistic principles of equality and liberty, and to a greater extent than we have yet dared to think, with capitalist principles of growth, creativity, profit, independence, competition, and more.

45. Gary Moulton, *John Ross: Cherokee Chief* (Athens: U of Georgia P, 1978) 5–13; McLoughlin, *Cherokees and Missionaries* 51–57.

46. Moulton 12–13, 80, 100–101; Maureen Konkle, *Writing Indian Nations: Native Intellectuals and the Politics of Historiography, 1827–1863* (Chapel Hill: U of North Carolina P, 2004) 48. I have found no corroboration of Konkle's suggestion that Quatie spoke no English.

47. Moulton 15; Boudinot ("Letters and Other Papers Relating to Cherokee Affairs: Being in Reply to Sundry Publications Authorized by John Ross," Athens: Southern Banner, 1837, *Sabin Americana, 1500–1926*, Gale, Cengage Learning; also rpt. in Sen. Doc. 121, 25th Cong., 2nd sess.) 186; Boudinot 229.

48. Moulton 139–43, 182, 193–96.

49. Moulton 15–37; Stanley Hoig, *The Cherokees and Their Chiefs: In the Wake of Empire* (Fayetteville: U of Arkansas P, 1998) 124–32.

50. Bernd Peyer, *The Tutor'd Mind: Indian Missionary-Writers in Antebellum America* (Amherst: U of Massachusetts P, 1997) 214.

51. Peyer 169.

52. Thurman Wilkins's history has the brothers Major Ridge and David Watie's mother as one-half Cherokee, but Starr claims both men were full-bloods. Such ambiguity proliferates, indicating a much more relaxed and possibly metaphorical attitude toward blood quantum in early years. See Wilkins, *Cherokee Tragedy: The Story of the Ridge Family and the Decimation of a People* (New York: Macmillan, 1970) 4, and Emmet Starr, *History of the Cherokee Indians and Their Legends and Folklore* ([Warden?]: Oklahoma City, 1921, rpt., Baltimore: Genealogical, 2003) 473.

53. Boudinot 3–9; Ralph Gabriel, *Elias Boudinot, Cherokee, and His America* (Norman: U of Oklahoma P, 1941) 22–34; Peyer 177–81. For discussion of Ross's religious

attitudes, see McLoughlin, *Cherokees and Missionaries* 349; Moulton 7. See McLoughlin, *Cherokees and Missionaries* 2–3, 35–81 and in general for the linkage between the educational programs of the federal civilization policy and missionary work.

54. Homi Bhabha, *The Location of Culture* (New York: Routledge, 1994) 86, 89.

55. Boudinot 8–11; Gabriel 57–92; Theresa Strouth Gaul, *To Marry an Indian: The Marriage of Harriet Gold and Elias Boudinot in Letters, 1823–1839* (Chapel Hill: U of North Carolina P, 2005) 1–52.

56. Boudinot 15–25, 87–89; Bethany Schneider, "Boudinot's Change: Boudinot, Emerson, and Ross on Cherokee Removal," *English Literary History* 75.1 (2008): 151–77; Robert Martin, "The *Cherokee Phoenix*: Pioneer of Indian Journalism," *Chronicles of Oklahoma* 25.2 (1947): 102–18; Peyer 182–89; Gabriel 106–27.

57. On this period in particular, see Roy Harvey Pearce, *Savagism and Civilization: A Study of the Indian and the American Mind*, rpt. and rev. ed. of *The Savages of America* (Baltimore: Johns Hopkins, 1953; Berkeley: U of California P, 1988) 53–75.

58. Grant Foreman, *Indian Removal*, 1989 ed. (Norman: U of Oklahoma P, 1932) 229–30; Kenneth Penn Davis, "Chaos in the Indian Country: The Cherokee Nation, 1828–35," *The Cherokee Indian Nation: A Troubled History* 129–47.

59. McLoughlin, *Cherokee Renascence* 428–38; Thurman Wilkins (202–207) recounts the story of Chewoyee who was beaten to death after he accompanied Major Ridge on an expedition to drive out intruding settlers; Foreman 236; Kenneth Penn Davis, 142, 144, mentions the attempted rapes and the killing of a Cherokee man named Bread Baker by John Fields, another Cherokee who was working for the government as an enrollment agent. For an account of the Bread Baker story, see the *Cherokee Phoenix* Feb. 8, 1834: 3, col. 4. Elijah Hicks was the editor of the *Phoenix* during this time.

60. Robert Davis, "*State v. George Tassel*: States' Rights and the Cherokee Court Cases, 1827–1830," *Journal of Southern Legal History* 12 (2004): 51–53, 67. Davis relies on an 1830 summary of the trial for this little-known event he uncovered in the *Georgia Journal*, but notes that other sources at greater remove from the events also name Andrew Falon and a man named Saunders as Tassel's victim.

61. Lindsay Robertson, *Conquest by Law: How the Discovery of America Dispossessed Indigenous Peoples of their Lands* (New York: Oxford UP, 2005) 129–30.

62. Foreman 233–35; Thurman Wilkins 207–29; McLoughlin, *Cherokee Renascence* 438–47.

63. Thurman Wilkins, 229–78, has a thorough account of the events leading up to the treaty signing; also see Kenneth Penn Davis 139–44; Foreman 244–50, 264–69; Moulton 50–86; Grace Steele Woodward, *The Cherokees* (Norman: U of Oklahoma P, 1963) 171–90.

64. Thurman Wilkins 36–38; Rennard Strickland 77–78.

65. For closer treatment of events following the signing through removal and the assassinations in Indian Territory, see Foreman 269–312; Thurman Wilkins 279–326; Moulton 87–126; Woodward 192–218.

Chapter 5. The Removal Rhetoric of Elias Boudinot and John Ross

1. Boudinot ("An Address to the Whites Delivered in the First Presbyterian Church, on the 26th of May, 1826, by Elias Boudinott, a Cherokee Indian," Philadelphia: William Geddes, 1826) 72.

2. Boudinot 69–70.

3. Boudinot 13; Edward Said, *Orientalism* (New York: Vintage, 1978) 21; also see Pearce 56–58, 63–75.

4. Boudinot ("Indian Clans," *Cherokee Phoenix* Feb. 18, 1829: 2, col. 5) 108. While many issues of the *Cherokee Phoenix* are publicly available online through websites like the Digital Library of Georgia (http://neptune3.galib.uga.edu/ssp/cgi-bin/tei-news-idx.pl?sessionid=7f000001&type=years&id=CHRKPHNX) and nearly all are available through university libraries' database subscriptions, I have confined my references to Boudinot's writing to that found in Theda Perdue's helpful and representative sampling in *Cherokee Editor,* although I have included reference information for the original sources. In just a very few cases, I quietly corrected punctuation and spelling to accord with the original.

5. Boudinot 32–33.

6. Boudinot 3.

7. Ellen Cushman, *The Sequoyah Syllabary: Writing the People's Perseverance* (Norman: U of Oklahoma P, 2011) 118, 127.

8. Maureen Konkle, *Writing Indian Nations: Native Intellectuals and the Politics of Historiography, 1827–1863* (Chapel Hill: U of North Carolina P, 2004) 48.

9. Ross ("To James Monroe," Jan. 19, 1824) 59. Ross's name appears at the head of others who signed the letter.

10. Ross ("To John Q. Adams," Mar. 12, 1825) 105. Ross's signature appears above those of G[eorge] Lowrey and Elijah Hicks.

11. Boudinot 33.

12. Ross ("Letter from John Ross . . . in Answer to Inquiries from a Friend Regarding the Cherokee Affairs with the United States," [Washington?]: n.p., July 1836) 455.

13. Boudinot 13.

14. Boudinot ("Address") 72–74.

15. Boudinot (editorial, *Cherokee Phoenix* Apr. 21, 1830: 2, col. 5) 116, emphasis in original.

16. Boudinot ("Address") 74. Boudinot refers to Sequoyah's English name, which has also been spelled (George) Guess and Gist.

17. Ross ("To George Gist," Jan. 12, 1832) 234–35.

18. Boudinot (editorial, *Cherokee Phoenix* May 14, 1828: 3, col. 2) 100.

19. McLoughlin, in *Cherokee Renascence* 76, points to Presbyterian Gideon Blackburn's ban on Cherokee.

20. Boudinot (editorial, *Cherokee Phoenix* Jan. 28, 1829: 2, col. 5) 105.

21. McLoughlin, *Cherokee Renascence* 355; McLoughlin, *Cherokees and Missionaries* 49–53; Anderson, in Brown 38–43.

22. McLoughlin, *Cherokee Renascence* 254.

23. McLoughlin, *Cherokee Renascence* 253–59, 355. It appears unlikely the sale was ever accomplished as the United States was holding out for the sale of *all* lands. There are scattered references to other educational funds, like the U.S. education fund established by the Civilization Fund Act in 1819, but they appear to be unassociated. The Cherokees did benefit from these funds channeled through missionaries like the ABCFM to establish schools.

24. Ross ("To Lewis Cass," Jan. 28, 1833) 258.

25. Boudinot ("Address") 77.

26. Boudinot ("National Academy," *Cherokee Phoenix* Feb. 18, 1829: 2, col. 4–5) 106–107.

27. McLoughlin, *Cherokee Renascence* 400, 407.

28. McLoughlin, *Cherokees and Missionaries* 232. For more on the importance Cherokees saw in education, see McLoughlin, *Cherokee Renascence* 72–73, 254, 354–55, 400.

29. See for instance Ross ("Memorial to the Senate and House of Representatives," May 17, 1834) 290; Ross ("To the Senate and House of Representatives," June 21, 1836) 427; Ross ("Letter") 491; Cherokee Nation v. State of Georgia, 30 U.S. 1, Supreme Ct. of the U.S., 1831, 2–12.

30. I am indebted to Angela Pulley Hudson for sharing her article on Boudinot's constitutional language for this reading. See her " 'Forked Justice': Elias Boudinot, the US Constitution, and Cherokee Removal," *American Indian Rhetorics of Survivance: Word Medicine, Word Magic*, ed. Ernest Stromberg (Pittsburgh: U of Pittsburgh P, 2006) 50–65. My earlier suggestion that his language also recalls the Declaration of Independence owes to her.

31. Boudinot (editorial, *Cherokee Phoenix* Jan. 28, 1829: 2, col. 5) 105–106.

32. Boudinot ("High Movement," *Cherokee Phoenix* Jan. 8, 1831: 2, col. 2) 121.

33. Boudinot (editorial, *Cherokee Phoenix* May 15, 1830: 2, col. 5) 118.

34. Boudinot (editorial, *Cherokee Phoenix* June 19, 1830: 3, col. 1) 119.

35. Respectively, Boudinot (editorial, *Cherokee Phoenix* May 15, 1830: 2, col. 5) 118; Boudinot (editorial, *Cherokee Phoenix* Nov. 12, 1831: 2, col. 2) 142.

36. Boudinot (editorial, *Cherokee Phoenix* Dec. 24, 1831: 3, col. 3) 144–45. Perdue dates the smudged issue December 21; the Sequoyah Research Center's online archives believe it to be December 24, which by the calendar accords with the indicated Saturday day of publication. Regarding Boudinot's ironic use of Marshall's language of guardianship, see again Hudson, 56–57, for an insightful reading.

37. Ross ("To the Senate and House of Representatives," Apr. 15, 1824) 77–78.

38. Ross ("Letter . . . to a Gentleman of Philadelphia") 502–503.

39. Boudinot (editorial, *Cherokee Phoenix* Sept. 9, 1829: 3, col. 3) 111.

40. Boudinot (editorial, *Cherokee Phoenix* June 17, 1829: 2, col. 4) 109.

41. Jace Weaver, *That the People* 55. For more on Apess's Christian reflections, see Robert Warrior, *The People and the Word: Reading Native Nonfiction* (Minneapolis: U of Minnesota P, 2005) 28–32.

42. Weaver, *That the People* 75.

43. Boudinot (editorial, *Cherokee Phoenix* Dec. 24, 1831: 3, col. 3) 144.

44. Wald 27.

45. Wald 28, citing Homi Bhabha, "Of Mimicry and Man: The Ambivalence of Colonial Discourse" *October* 28 (Spring 1984): 126.

46. Wald 36.

47. Cherokee Nation v. State of Georgia, 30 U.S. 1, Supreme Ct. of the U.S., 1831, 6.

48. Wald 26.

49. Wald 24–25.

50. Ross ("To the Senate and House of Representatives," June 21, 1836) 436–37.

51. Boudinot ("To the Readers of the *Cherokee Phoenix*," *Cherokee Phoenix* Aug. 11, 1832: 2, col. 3–4) 163–64.
52. Boudinot 10–11.
53. Konkle 47.
54. Ross ("Annual Message," Oct. 13, 1828) 141.
55. Ross ("To the General Council," Aug. 4, 1832) 250.
56. Boudinot 165, 227n14.
57. I find it telling that one of the most outspoken opponents of the treaty party, Thomas Foreman, was a sheriff.
58. Ross ("Annual Message," Oct. 15, 1833) 271, emphasis added.
59. Thurman Wilkins 253, 356n68, 64, citing "Currey to Lewis Cass, Sept. 15, 1834, in National Archives RG 75, Letters received by Office of Indian Affairs: Cherokee Agency (East) 1834–36 (M-234, Roll 76, frames 0315-45)."
60. Boudinot ("Letters") 211–12; Thurman Wilkins 252–55, 235–36.
61. Boudinot ("Letters") 161–62.
62. Moulton 57, 61–71; Boudinot 158; see for instance Boudinot 178, 191, 200.
63. Boudinot ("Letters") 163, all emphasis added.
64. Boudinot ("Letters") 195, 185, 183, 181.
65. Ross ("To John F. Schermerhorn," Oct. 30, 1835) 372.
66. Ross ("To Lewis Cass," Jan. 2, 1836) 378.
67. Boudinot ("Letters") 216.
68. Boudinot ("Letters") 183.
69. Boudinot 26.
70. Boudinot 165, 227n14.
71. Ross ("To Lewis Cass," Feb. 14, 1835) 321.
72. Boudinot ("Letters") 176–77.

Chapter 6. Conclusion: Strangers and Kin

1. McLoughlin and Conser 686, 681.
2. Celia Naylor, *African Cherokees in Indian Territory: From Chattel to Citizens* (Chapel Hill: U of North Carolina P, 2008) 205.
3. Fay Yarbrough, *Race and the Cherokee Nation* (Philadelphia: U of Pennsylvania P, 2008) 122–23.
4. Tiya Miles, *The Ties that Bind: The Story of an Afro-Cherokee Family in Slavery and Freedom* (Berkeley: U of California P, 2005) 40–43.
5. Theda Perdue, *Slavery and the Evolution of Cherokee Society, 1540–1866* (Knoxville: U of Tennessee P, 1979), xiii, emphasis added.
6. Charles Royce, *The Cherokee Nation of Indians*, Bureau of American Ethnology 5th Annual Rept, 1887 rpt. (Chicago: Aldine; Smithsonian Institution P, 1975) 214.
7. Naylor 212.
8. Will Chavez, "Smith Wins Another Term," *Cherokee Phoenix*, July 11, 2007, June 22, 2011, <http://www.cherokeephoenix.org/Article/Index/1932>.
9. Naylor 181.
10. Cherokee Nation Registrar v. Nash, SC-2011-02, Supreme Ct. of the Cherokee Nation, 2011, 8.

11. "Mission: Purposes and Mission Statement of the Descendants of Freedmen Association," Descendants of Freedmen of the Five Civilized Tribes website, Feb. 5, 2012, <http://freedmen5tribes.com/Mission.htm>.

12. Lyons 174–75.

13. Lyons 178–89.

14. Lyons 181–82.

15. "Intermarriage of White Men and Foreigners," sec. 72, art. 15, *Compiled Laws of the Cherokee Nation* (Tahlequah, Indian Territory, 1881): Cherokee Nat. Council, Natl. Advocate Print, 277, facsim., *Google Books*, June 6, 2011, <http://books.google.com/books?id=dvg9AAAAIAAJ&printsec=frontcover&dq=compiled+laws+of+the+cherokee+nation&hl=en&ei=KDhdTs_OKoKPsQLAvpk7&sa=X&oi=book_result&ct=result&resnum=1&ved=0CDUQ6AEwAA#v=onepage&q&f=false>. Morgan's *League of the Iroquois* was published in 1851, and his studies focused on kinship, *Systems of Consanguinity and Affinity of the Human Family* and *Ancient Society*, came out in 1871 and 1877, respectively.

16. Jacques Derrida, *Of Hospitality* (Stanford: Stanford UP, 2000) 3–73.

17. Lyons 181.

18. Derrida, *Of Hospitality* 147.

19. John Phillip Reid, *A Law of Blood: The Primitive Law of the Cherokee Nation* (New York: New York UP, 1970; rpt., DeKalb: Northern Illinois UP, 2006) 196–200.

20. Duane King, "Lessons in Cherokee Ethnology from the Captivity of Joseph Brown: 1788–1789," *Journal of Cherokee Studies* 2.2 (Spring 1977): 219–29, discusses Bonnefoy and Brown; Tiya Miles's *The Ties that Bind* chronicles Shoe Boots's family in depth; see Yarbrough 25–38 on Molley; and Reid 192–93 on Black Dog.

21. "Compact between the Several Tribes of Indians," art. 1, chap. 17, "Compacts with Tribes of Indians," *Compiled Laws* 338.

22. Yarbrough 53.

23. "Intermarriage of White Men and Foreigners," sec. 67, art. 15, *Compiled Laws* 275.

24. "Intermarriage of Cherokees with Other Indians," sec. 76, art. 16, *Compiled Laws* 278.

25. "Marriage and Divorce," sec. 96, art. 20, *Compiled Laws* 286, emphasis in original.

26. *Compiled Laws* 31.

27. Yarbrough 62.

28. Reid 198.

29. "Articles of Agreement with the Delawares," art. 2, chap. 17, "Compacts with Tribes of Indians," *Compiled Laws* 344.

30. "Agreement between Shawnees and Cherokees, Concluded June 7th, 1869, Approved by the President June 9th, 1869," art. 3, chap. 17, "Compacts with Tribes of Indians," *Compiled Laws* 347–48.

31. Of a total population of 19,735, there were 15,307 Cherokees by blood; 1,032 whites; 1,976 blacks; 672 Delawares; 503 Shawnees; 232 Creeks; and 13 listed under miscellaneous; see Yarbrough 87.

32. Cherokee Nation v. Journeycake, 155 U.S. 196, 15 Supreme Ct. of the U.S 55, 1894.

33. Delaware Indians v. Cherokee Nation, 193 U.S. 127, 24 Supreme Ct. of the U.S. 342, 1904, 16.

34. Cherokee Nation v. Norton, 389 F.3d 1074 U.S. Court of Appeals, 10th Circuit, 2004.

35. "Congress Grants Loyal Shawnees Federal Recognition," Cherokee Nation News Release, Dec. 15, 2000, July 17, 2011, <http://cherokee.org/PressRoom/22874/Press_Article.aspx>.

36. Jami Custer, "Delaware Tribe Eligible for Federal Funds," *Cherokee Phoenix* Nov. 2009: 4; Travis Snell, "Delawares' Sovereignty Rehearing Denied," *Cherokee Phoenix* Feb. 2005: 5. Also see Robert Sher, "Notes: Cherokee Nation of Oklahoma v. Norton, 389 F.3d (10th Cir. 2004)," *American Indian Law Review* 30.2 (2005/2006): 443–60, for a history prior to the 2009 negotiated separation.

37. Tesina Jackson, "Delaware Tribe to Receive Federal Funds Directly from Feds," *Cherokee Phoenix* Sept. 2013: 7.

38. Lyons 181.

39. United States v. Rogers, 45 U.S. 567, 4. How., 1847, 572–73.

40. David Wilkins, *American Indian Sovereignty and the U.S. Supreme Court* (Austin: U of Texas P, 1997) 38–51, Garroutte, *Real Indians* 69; Yarbrough 67–69.

Works Cited

Primary Sources

Adair, James. *Adair's History of the American Indians.* London: Edward and Charles Dilly, 1775. Ed. Samuel Cole Williams. Johnson City, Tenn.: Watauga, under auspices of Natl. Soc. of Colonial Dames of America, 1930. New York: Promontory, [1974?].

"Agreement between Shawnees and Cherokees, Concluded June 7th, 1869, Approved by the President June 9th, 1869." Art. 3, ch. 17. "Compacts with Tribes of Indians." *Compiled Laws* 345–48.

"Articles of Agreement with the Delawares." Art. 2, ch. 17. "Compacts with Tribes of Indians." *Compiled Laws* 340–45.

Boudinot, Elias. *Cherokee Editor: The Writings of Elias Boudinot.* Ed. Theda Perdue. Knoxville: U of Tennessee P, 1983. Athens: U of Georgia P, 1996.

Brown, Catharine. *Memoir of Catharine Brown: A Christian Indian of the Cherokee Nation.* N.p.: Armstrong, 1824. Ed. Rufus Anderson. 2nd ed. Boston: Crocker and Brewster, 1825. Signal Mountain, Tenn.: Mountain, [1998?].

Cherokee Nation Registrar v. Nash. SC-2011-02. Supreme Ct. of the Cherokee Nation. 2011.

Cherokee Nation v. Journeycake. 155 U.S. 196. 15 Supreme Ct. of the U.S. 1894.

Cherokee Nation v. Norton. 389 F.3d 1074. U.S. Ct. of Appeals. 10th Circuit. 2004.

Cherokee Nation v. State of Georgia. 30 U.S. 1. Supreme Ct. of the U.S. 1831.

"Committee Report." *Journals of the Continental Congress. Documents from the Continental Congress and the Constitutional Convention, 1774–1789. American Memory,* Lib. of Cong. <http://memory.loc.gov/cgi-bin/query/r?ammem/bdsbib:@field (M010+90898156)):>.

"Compact between the Several Tribes of Indians." Art. 1, ch. 17 "Compacts with Tribes of Indians." *Compiled Laws* 336–39.

Compiled Laws of the Cherokee Nation. Tahlequah, Indian Territory, 1881: Natl. Advocate Print, pub. by authority of Cherokee Natl. Council. Facsim. *Google Books.* June 6, 2011. <http://books.google.com/books?id=dvg9AAAAIAAJ&printsec=frontcover&dq=compiled+laws+of+the+cherokee+nation&hl=en&ei=KDhdTs_OKoKP-sQLAvpk7&sa=X&oi=book_result&ct=result&resnum=1&ved=0CDUQ6AEwAA#v=onepage&q&f=false>.

"Congress Grants Loyal Shawnees Federal Recognition." Cherokee Nation news release. Dec. 15, 2000. July 17, 2011. <http://cherokee.org/PressRoom/22874/Press_Article.aspx>.

Constitution of the Cherokee Nation. Sec. 5, Amendments to Art. 3. *Compiled Laws* 31.

Delaware Indians v. Cherokee Nation. 193 U.S. 127. 24 Supreme Ct. of the U.S. 342. 1904.

1835 Cherokee Census. Monograph 2. Park Hill, Okla.: Trail of Tears Assn., 2002.

Gambold, Anna. "Diary Year 1807." July 16, 1807. *The Moravian Springplace Mission to the Cherokees.* Ed. Rowena McClinton. Indians of the Southeast. Vol. 1: 1805–1813. Lincoln: U of Nebraska P, 2007. 199–200.

Guess, Sequoyah. *Kholvn.* Kansas, Okla.: Kholvn, 199[illegible]

[Hicks, Elijah?]. [Account of Bread Baker's murder by John Fields.] *Cherokee Phoenix* Feb. 8, 1834: 3, col. 4

Hopkins, Samuel. *Historical Memoirs, Relating to the Housatunnuk Indians.* Boston: S. Kneeland, 1753. *Google Books.* June 6, 2009. <http://books.google.com/books?id=Hr0OAAAAQAAJ&printsec=frontcover&dq=hopkins+historical+memoirs+relating+indians>.

"Intermarriage of Cherokees with Other Indians." Sec. 76, art. 16. *Compiled Laws* 278.

"Intermarriage of White Men and Foreigners." Sec. 72, art. 15. *Compiled Laws* 274–78.

"Keetoowah Constitution and Bylaws." Tyner 121–33.

"Marriage and Divorce." Sec. 96, art. 20. *Compiled Laws* 286.

"Mission: Purposes and Mission Statement of the Descendants of Freedmen Association." Descendants of Freedmen of the Five Civilized Tribes website. N.d. Feb. 5, 2012. <http://freedmen5tribes.com/Mission.htm>.

"Resolution by Missionaries." *Cherokee Phoenix* Jan. 1, 1831. Rpt. In Worcester 83–84.

Ross, John. *The Papers of Chief John Ross.* Ed. Gary Moulton. Vol. 1. Norman: U of Oklahoma P, 1985.

Royce, Charles. *The Cherokee Nation of Indians.* Bureau of Amer. Ethnology 5th Annual Rept. 1887. Chicago: Aldine; Smithsonian Inst. P, 1975.

Rucker, Alvin. "Oklahoma 'Clicks' as Daddy to Orphans." *Daily Oklahoman* July 15, 1928: D1+, microfilm.

Smith, Benny. "The Keetoowah Society of the Cherokee Indians." Master's thesis. Northwestern State College, Alva, Okla. 1967.

Smith, Crosslin. "The Good Mind." Lecture. 14th Annual Symposium of the Amer. Indian. Northeastern State U, Tahlequah, Okla. Apr. 1986. Videocassette.

———. "The Way of the Sacred Eagle." Lecture. 16th Annual Symposium of the Amer. Indian. Northeastern State U, Tahlequah, Okla. Apr. 1988. Videocassette.

"Treaty with the Cherokees, 1835." *The Cherokee Removal: A Brief History with Documents*. Ed. Theda Perdue and Michael Green. Boston: Bedford, 1995.

United States v. Rogers. 45 U.S. 567, Supreme Ct. of the U.S. 4. How. 1847.

Watts, Isaac. "LVI [Hymn 56]. The Song of Moses and the Lamb: Or, Babylon Falling. Rev. xv, 3, and xvi, 19, and xvii, 6." *Hymns and Spiritual Songs*, 7th ed. [Boston?]: [Bristol?], [1720?]. Early American Imprints, Series I: Evans, 1639–1800; An Archive of Americana Collection. No. 29733, rec. no. w038649, 66–67. <http://docs.newsbank.com.proxy.library.cornell.edu/openurl?ctx_ver=z39.88-2004&rft_id=info:sid/iw.newsbank.com:EVAN&rft_val_format=info:ofi/fmt:kev:mtx:ctx&rft_dat=0F2F820D6CD2D2B0&svc_dat=Evans:eaidoc&req_dat=0D0CB4F0E6B93180>.

Whitaker, W. T. "Support of Certain Destitute Orphan Children. Letter from the Acting Secretary of the Interior, Transmitting Letters from W. T. Whitaker and Others . . ." Committee on Indian Affairs. Senate. 57th Cong., 1st Sess. Doc. 337. May 3, 1902. LexisNexis. Serial-Set-ID 4241 S.doc.337.

Worcester, Samuel. *New Echota Letters: Contributions of Samuel A. Worcester to the "Cherokee Phoenix."* Ed. Jack Frederick Kilpatrick and Anna Gritts Kilpatrick. Dallas: Southern Methodist UP, 1968.

Secondary Sources

Alfred, Taiaiake. *Wasáse: Indigenous Pathways of Action and Freedom*. Peterborough, Ont.: Broadview, 2005.

Allen, Chadwick. *Trans-Indigenous: Methodologies for Global Native Literary Studies*. Minneapolis: U of Minnesota P, 2012.

Allen, Paula Gunn. *The Sacred Hoop: Recovering the Feminine in American Indian Traditions*. Boston: Beacon, 1986.

Anderson, Benedict. *Imagined Communities: Reflections on the Origin and Spread of Nationalism*. Rev. ed. New York: Verso, 1983.

Appiah, Kwame Anthony. *Cosmopolitanism: Ethics in a World of Strangers*. New York: Norton, 2006.

———. *The Ethics of Identity*. Princeton: Princeton UP, 2005.

Baker, Lee. *From Savage to Negro: Anthropology and the Construction of Race, 1896–1954*. Berkeley: U of California P, 1998. 26–53.

Bass, Althea. *Cherokee Messenger*. 1936. Norman: U of Oklahoma P, 1996.

Belsey, Catherine. *Poststructuralism: A Very Short Introduction*. New York: Oxford UP, 2002.

Bhabha, Homi. *The Location of Culture*. New York: Routledge, 1994.

Booth, Wayne. *Critical Understanding: The Powers and Limits of Pluralism*. Chicago: U of Chicago P, 1979.

Bourdieu, Pierre. *In Other Words: Essays Towards a Reflexive Sociology*. Trans. Matthew Adamson. Stanford: Stanford UP, 1990.

———. *The Logic of Practice*. Trans. Richard Nice. Paris: Minuit, 1980. Stanford: Stanford UP, 1990.

Brooks, Lisa. "At the Gathering Place." Weaver, Womack, and Warrior 225–46.

Bushyhead, Richard. "The Little People and the Nunnehi." Duncan, *Living Stories* 183–87.

Champagne, Duane. "Institutional and Cultural Order in Early Cherokee Society: A Sociological Interpretation." *Journal of Cherokee Studies* 15 (1990): 3–26.

———. "Symbolic Structure and Political Change in Cherokee Society." *Journal of Cherokee Studies* 8 (1983): 87–96.

Chatterjee, Partha. *The Nation and Its Fragments: Colonial and Postcolonial Histories.* Princeton Studies in Culture/Power/History. Princeton: Princeton UP, 1993. Rpt. in *The Partha Chatterjee Omnibus*. New Delhi: Oxford UP, 1999.

———. *Nationalist Thought and the Colonial World: A Derivative Discourse?* London: Zed for United Nations U of Tokyo, 1986. Rpt. in *The Partha Chatterjee Omnibus.* New Delhi: Oxford UP, 1999.

Chavez, Will. "CBC Wants to Deny Tribe Housing Funds." *Cherokee Phoenix* May 2008: A1–2.

———. "Freedmen Descendants Have Citizenship Restored." *Cherokee Phoenix* Oct. 2011: 1+.

———. "Smith Wins Another Term." *Cherokee Phoenix* July 11, 2007. June 22, 2011. <http://www.cherokeephoenix.org/Article/Index/1932>.

Cheah, Pheng. "Introduction Part II: The Cosmopolitical—Today." Cheah and Robbins. 20–41.

Cheah, Pheng, and Bruce Robbins, eds. *Cosmopolitics: Thinking and Feeling beyond the Nation*. Minneapolis: U of Minnesota P, 1998.

"Cherokee Nation Industries Employees Tour Bell Helicopter Assembly Center." News and Events, Cherokee Nation Industries website. Nov. 13, 2008. Sept. 21, 2009. <http://www.cherokee.org/News/Stories/23806.aspx>.

Cheyfitz, Eric. *The Columbia Guide to American Indian Literatures of the United States since 1945.* Ed. Cheyfitz. New York: Columbia UP, 2004.

Chomsky, Noam. "Goals and Visions." *Chomsky on Anarchism*. Oakland: AK, 2005. 190–211.

Churchill, Mary. *Walking the White Path: Toward a Cherokee-Centric Hermeneutic for Interpreting Cherokee Literature.* Diss. U of California at Santa Barbara, 1997. Ann Arbor: UMI, 1997.

Conforti, Joseph. "Mary Lyon, the Founding of Mount Holyoke College, and the Cultural Revival of Jonathan Edwards." *Religion and American Culture* 3.1 (1993): 69–89.

———. "Samuel Hopkins and the New Divinity: Theology, Ethics, and Social Reform in Eighteenth-Century New England." *William and Mary Quarterly* 34.4 (1977): 572–89.

Cook-Lynn, Elizabeth. "The American Indian Fiction Writers: Cosmopolitanism, Nationalism, the Third World, and First Nation Sovereignty." *Why I Can't Read Wallace Stegner and Other Essays: A Tribal Voice.* Madison: U of Wisconsin P, 1996. 78–96.

———. "Literary and Political Questions of Transformation: American Indian Fiction Writers." *Anti-Indianism in Modern America: A Voice from Tatekeya's Earth.* Urbana: U of Illinois P, 2001. 34–44.

Cox, James. *The Red Land to the South: American Indian Writers and Indigenous Mexico.* Minneapolis: U of Minnesota P, 2012.

Cushman, Ellen. *The Sequoyah Syllabary: Writing the People's Perseverance*. Norman: U of Oklahoma P, 2011.

Custalow, Mark. "Biblical Guidelines for Contextualizing Native American Church Ministry." Church Planting Village website. North American Mission Board, Southern Baptist Convention. N.d.: 12 pp. June 22, 2009. <http://www.churchplantingvillage.net/atf/cf/%7B0938A074-4176-42D7-8428-77A665D9544E%7D/Bible%20Guidelines%20for%20 Contextualization.pdf>.

———. "Native American Church Planting." North American Mission Board, Southern Baptist Convention. N.d. Apr. 19, 2004. <http://www.namb.net/ lightupthenation/body_cpt_12_nativeamerican.asp>.

Custer, Jami. "Delaware Tribe Eligible for Federal Funds." *Cherokee Phoenix* Nov. 2009: 4.

Davis, Kenneth Penn. "Chaos in the Indian Country: The Cherokee Nation, 1828–35." King, *Cherokee Indian Nation* 129–47.

Davis, Robert. "*State v. George Tassel*: States' Rights and the Cherokee Court Cases, 1827–1830." *Journal of Southern Legal History* 12 (2004): 41–71.

Derrida, Jacques. *Of Grammatology*. Trans. Gayatri Chakravorty Spivak. Paris: Minuit, 1967. Baltimore: Johns Hopkins UP, 1976.

———. *Of Hospitality*. Stanford: Stanford UP, 2000.

Donaldson, Laura. *American Samson: Haunting the Native-Christian Encounter*. Chapel Hill: U of North Carolina P, forthcoming.

———. "But We Are Your Mothers, You Are Our Sons: Gender, Sovereignty and the Nation in Early Cherokee Women's Writing." *Indigenous Women and Feminism: Politics, Activism, Culture*. Ed. Cheryl Suzack, et al. Vancouver: U of British Columbia P, 2010. 43–55.

Doniger, Wendy. Foreword. *Myth and Meaning: Cracking the Code of Culture*. By Claude Lévi-Strauss. Rev. ed. New York: Schocken, 1995. vii–xv.

Dunaway, Wilma. "Rethinking Cherokee Acculturation: Agrarian Capitalism and Women's Resistance to the Cult of Domesticity, 1800–1838." *American Indian Culture and Research Journal* 21.1 (1997): 155–92.

Duncan, Barbara. "Edna Chekelelee." Duncan, *Living Stories* 125–26.

———, comp. and ed. *Living Stories of the Cherokee*. Chapel Hill: U of North Carolina P, 1998.

Fanon, Frantz. *The Wretched of the Earth*. 1961. Trans. Constance Farrington. New York: Grove, 1963.

Feeling, Durbin. *Cherokee-English Dictionary*. Ed. William Pulte. Tahlequah, Okla.: Heritage, 1975.

Fogelson, Raymond. "Cherokee Notions of Power." *The Anthropology of Power: Ethnographic Studies from Asia, Oceania, and the New World*. Ed. Fogelson and Richard Adams. New York: Academic, 1977. 185–94.

———. "The Conjuror in Eastern Cherokee Society." *Journal of Cherokee Studies* 5.2 (1980): 60–87.

———. "Who Were the Aní-Kutánî? An Excursion into Cherokee Historical Thought." *Ethnohistory* 31.4 (1984): 255–63.

Fogelson, Raymond, and Paul Kutsche. "Cherokee Economic Cooperatives: The Gadugi." *Symposium on Cherokee and Iroquois Culture*. Ed. William Fenton and

John Gulick. Smithsonian Inst., Bureau of Amer. Ethnology. Bull. 180. Washington: GPO, 1961. 83–123.

Foreman, Grant. *Indian Removal: The Emigration of the Five Civilized Tribes of Indians*. 1932. Norman: U of Oklahoma P, 1989.

"4 Ex-Employees Sue Chief for Wrongful Termination." *Cherokee Phoenix*. Feb. 8, 2012. Feb. 16, 2012. <http://www.cherokeephoenix.org/Article/Index/5947>.

Gabriel, Ralph Henry. *Elias Boudinot, Cherokee, and His America*. Norman: U of Oklahoma P, 1941.

Garroutte, Eva Marie. *Real Indians: Identity and the Survival of Native America*. Berkeley: U of California P, 2003.

Gaul, Theresa Strouth. *To Marry an Indian: The Marriage of Harriet Gold and Elias Boudinot in Letters, 1823–1839*. Chapel Hill: U of North Carolina P, 2005.

Gearing, Fred. "Priests and Warriors: Social Structures for Cherokee Politics in the 18th Century." Memoir 93 in *American Anthropologist* 64.5, pt. 2 (Oct. 1962).

Gellner, Ernest. *Nations and Nationalism*. Ithaca: Cornell UP, 1983.

Hendrix, Janey. "Redbird Smith and the Nighthawk Keetoowahs." *Journal of Cherokee Studies* 8.1, 8.2 (1983): 22–40, 73–85.

Higginbotham, Mary. "The Creek Path Mission." *Journal of Cherokee Studies* 1.2 (1976): 72–85.

Hoig, Stanley. *The Cherokees and Their Chiefs: In the Wake of Empire*. Fayetteville: U of Arkansas P, 1998.

Holmes, Ruth Bradley, and Betty Sharp Smith. *Beginning Cherokee*. 5th ed. Norman: U of Oklahoma P, 1976.

Hoya, Paula M. L., and Michael Hames-García, eds. *Reclaiming Identity: Realist Theory and the Predicament of Postmodernism*. Berkeley: U of California P, 2000.

Hudson, Angela Pulley. "'Forked Justice': Elias Boudinot, the US Constitution, and Cherokee Removal." *American Indian Rhetorics of Survivance: Word Medicine, Word Magic*. Ed. Ernest Stromberg. Pittsburgh: U of Pittsburgh P, 2006. 50–65.

Hudson, Charles. *Elements of Southeastern Indian Religion*. Leiden: Brill, 1984.

———. "Reply to Mary Churchill." *American Indian Quarterly* 24.3 (2000): 495–96.

Huhndorf, Shari. *Mapping the Americas: The Transnational Politics of Contemporary Native Culture*. Ithaca: Cornell UP, 2009.

Jackson, Tesina. "Delaware Tribe to Receive Federal Funds Directly from Feds." *Cherokee Phoenix* Sept. 2013: 7.

Jameson, Fredric. *The Prison-House of Language: A Critical Account of Structuralism and Russian Formalism*. Princeton: Princeton UP, 1972.

Johnston, Carolyn Ross. *Cherokee Women in Crisis: Trail of Tears, Civil War, and Allotment, 1838–1907*. Tuscaloosa: U of Alabama P, 2003.

Justice, Daniel Heath. "'Go Away, Water!' Kinship Criticism and the Decolonization Imperative." Womack, Justice, and Teuton 147–68.

———. *Our Fire Survives the Storm: A Cherokee Literary History*. Minneapolis: U of Minnesota P, 2006.

"Keetoowah History Essay." United Keetoowah Band of Cherokee Indians website. N.d. July 7, 2009. <http://www.keetoowahcherokee.org/documents/history/historyessay.pdf>.

Kidwell, Clara Sue, Homer Noley, and George Tinker. *A Native American Theology.* Maryknoll, N.Y.: Orbis, 2001.

King, Duane, ed. *The Cherokee Indian Nation: A Troubled History.* Knoxville: U of Tennessee P, 1979.

———. "Lessons in Cherokee Ethnology from the Captivity of Joseph Brown, 1788–1789." *Journal of Cherokee Studies* 2.2 (1977): 219–29.

Konkle, Maureen. *Writing Indian Nations: Native Intellectuals and the Politics of Historiography, 1827–1863.* Chapel Hill: U of North Carolina P, 2004.

Krehbiel-Burton, Lenzy. "Bill John Baker Named Official Winner in Cherokee Chief Election." *Tulsa World* Oct. 13, 2011. Feb. 16, 2012. <http://www.tulsaworld.com/news/article.aspx?subjectid=520&articleid=20111013_16_A1_CUTLIN132201>.

———. "Frustrations Grow as Cherokee Election Drags On." *Tulsa World* July 19, 2011. Feb. 16, 2012. <http://www.tulsaworld.com/site/printerfriendlystory.aspx?articleid=20110719_11_A1_CUTLIN889989>.

Krupat, Arnold. *Native American Autobiography: An Anthology.* Madison: U of Wisconsin P, 1994.

———. *Red Matters: Native American Studies.* Philadelphia: U of Pennsylvania P, 2002.

———. *The Turn to the Native: Studies in Criticism and Culture.* Lincoln: U of Nebraska P, 1996.

Lasky, Jacqueline. "Indigenism, Anarchism, Feminism: An Emerging Framework for Exploring Post-Imperial Futures." *Affinities* 5.1 (2011): 3–36. June 18, 2012. <http://www.affinitiesjournal.org/index.php/affinities/article/view/72/0>.

Lawrence, Jane. "The Indian Health Service and the Sterilization of Native American Women." *American Indian Quarterly* 24.3 (2000): 400–19.

Lévi-Strauss, Claude. *Myth and Meaning: Cracking the Code of Culture.* Rev. ed. New York: Schocken, 1995.

———. *Structural Anthropology.* 1958. Trans. Claire Jacobson and Brooke Grundfest Schoepf. New York: Basic, 1963.

Littlejohn, Kathi Smith. "The Cherokee Little People" and "Nunnehi, the Gentle People." Duncan, *Living Stories* 68–74.

Loftin, John. "The 'Harmony Ethic' of the Conservative Eastern Cherokees: A Religious Interpretation." *Journal of Cherokee Studies* 8.1 (1983): 40–45.

Lounsbury, Floyd. "Iroquois-Cherokee Linguistic Relations." *Symposium on Cherokee and Iroquois Culture.* Ed. William Fenton and John Gulick. Smithsonian Inst., Bureau of Amer. Ethnology. Bull. 180. Washington: GPO, 1961. 9–18.

Lyons, Scott. *X-Marks: Native Signatures of Assent.* Minneapolis: U of Minnesota P, 2010.

Martin, Joel. *The Land Looks after Us: A History of Native American Religion.* New York: Oxford UP, 2001.

Martin, Robert. "The Cherokee Phoenix: Pioneer of Indian Journalism." *Chronicles of Oklahoma* 25.2 (1947): 102–18.

McClintock, Anne. *Imperial Leather: Race, Gender, and Sexuality in the Colonial Contest.* New York: Routledge, 1995.

McCoy, Genevieve. "The Women of the ABCFM Oregon Mission and the Conflicted Language of Calvinism." *Church History* 64.1 (1995): 62–82.

McGoun, William. "Adoption of Whites by 18th Century Cherokees." *Journal of Cherokee Studies* 9.1 (1984): 37–41.

McLoughlin, William. *After the Trail of Tears: The Cherokees' Struggle for Sovereignty, 1839–1880*. Chapel Hill: U of North Carolina P, 1993.

———. *Cherokee Renascence in the New Republic*. Princeton: Princeton UP, 1986.

———. *Cherokees and Christianity, 1794–1870: Essays on Acculturation and Cultural Persistence*. Ed. Walter Conser. Athens: U of Georgia P, 1984.

———. *Cherokees and Missionaries, 1789–1839*. New Haven: Yale UP, 1984. Norman: U of Oklahoma P, 1994.

McLoughlin, William, and Walter Conser. "The Cherokees in Transition: A Statistical Analysis of the Federal Cherokee Census of 1835." *Journal of American History* 64 (1977): 678–703.

Meredith, Howard L., and Virginia E. Milan, eds. *A Cherokee Vision of Eloh'*. Trans. Wesley Proctor. Muskogee, Okla.: Indian UP, 1981.

Meredith, Mary Ellen, and Howard L. Meredith. *Reflection on Cherokee Literary Expression*. Lewiston, N.Y.: Mellen, 2003.

Miles, Tiya. *The Ties that Bind: The Story of an Afro-Cherokee Family in Slavery and Freedom*. Berkeley: U of California P, 2005.

Mohanty, Chandra Talpade. "Under Western Eyes: Feminist Scholarship and Colonial Discourses." *Boundary 2* 12–13 (1984): 333–58.

Mooney, James. "Myths of the Cherokee." Smithsonian Inst., Bureau of Amer. Ethnology. 19th Annual Rept., Pt. 1, 1897–98. Washington: GPO, 1900.

———. "The Sacred Formulas of the Cherokees." Smithsonian Inst., Bureau of Amer. Ethnology. 7th Annual Rept., 1885–88. Washington: GPO, 1891.

Moses, L. G. *The Indian Man: A Biography of James Mooney*. Rev. ed. Urbana: U of Illinois P, 1984. Lincoln: U of Nebraska P, 2002.

Moulton, Gary. *John Ross: Cherokee Chief*. Athens: U of Georgia P, 1978.

Naylor, Celia. *African Cherokees in Indian Territory: From Chattel to Citizens*. Chapel Hill: U of North Carolina P, 2008.

Newton, Judith Lowder. "Power and the Ideology of 'Woman's Sphere.'" *Feminisms: An Anthology of Literary Theory and Criticism*. Ed. Robyn Warhol and Diane Price Herndl. Rev. ed. New Brunswick: Rutgers UP, 1997. 880–95.

Owens, Louis. *Mixedblood Messages: Literature, Film, Family, Place*. Norman: U of Oklahoma P, 1998.

Pearce, Roy Harvey. *Savagism and Civilization: A Study of the Indian and the American Mind*. Berkeley: U of California P, 1988. Rpt. and rev. ed. of *The Savages of America*, Baltimore: Johns Hopkins, 1953.

Perdue, Theda. "Catharine Brown: Cherokee Convert to Christianity." *Sifters: Native American Women's Lives*. Ed. Perdue. New York: Oxford UP, 2001.

———. *Cherokee Women: Gender and Culture Change, 1700–1835*. Lincoln: U of Nebraska P, 1998.

———. *Slavery and the Evolution of Cherokee Society, 1540–1866*. Knoxville: U of Tennessee P, 1979.

———. "Southern Indians and the Cult of True Womanhood." *Half Sisters of History: Southern Women and the American Past*. Ed. Catherine Clinton. Durham: Duke UP, 1994. 36–55.

Persico, V. Richard. "Early Nineteenth-Century Cherokee Political Organization." King, *Cherokee Indian Nation* 92–109.

Peyer, Bernd. *The Tutor'd Mind: Indian Missionary-Writers in Antebellum America*. Amherst: U of Massachusetts P, 1997.

Phillips, Joyce, and Paul Phillips, eds. *The Brainerd Journal: A Mission to the Cherokees, 1817–1823*. Lincoln: U of Nebraska P, 1998.

Pulitano, Elvira. *Toward a Native American Critical Theory*. Lincoln: U of Nebraska P, 2003.

Pulte, William, and Durbin Feeling. "Outline of Cherokee Grammar." *Cherokee-English Dictionary*. By Durbin Feeling. Ed. Pulte. Tahlequah, Okla.: Heritage, 1975.

Quine, W. V. O. "Two Dogmas of Empiricism." *Quintessence: Basic Readings from the Philosophy of W. V. Quine*. Ed. Roger Gibson. Cambridge: Belknap-Harvard UP, 2004. 31–53.

Reed, Jeannie, ed. *Stories of the Yûñwï Tsunsdi': The Cherokee Little People*. Cullowhee, N.C.: Western Carolina U, 1991.

Reid, John Phillip. *A Law of Blood: The Primitive Law of the Cherokee Nation*. New York: New York UP, 1970. DeKalb: Northern Illinois UP, 2006.

Rifkin, Mark. *Manifesting America: The Imperial Construction of U.S. National Space*. New York: Oxford UP, 2009.

Robbins, Bruce. "Introduction Part I: Actually Existing Cosmopolitanism." Cheah and Robbins. 1–19.

Robertson, Lindsay. *Conquest by Law: How the Discovery of America Dispossessed Indigenous Peoples of Their Lands*. New York: Oxford UP, 2005.

Rosaldo, Renato. "Imperialist Nostalgia." *Representations* 26 (Spring 1989): 107–22.

Russell, Steve. *Sequoyah Rising*. Durham: Carolina Academic, 2010.

Said, Edward. *Culture and Imperialism*. New York: Vintage, 1994.

———. *Orientalism*. New York: Vintage, 1978.

Samuels, Shirley, ed. Introduction. *The Culture of Sentiment: Race, Gender, and Sentimentality in Nineteenth-Century America*. New York: Oxford UP, 1992. 3–8.

Sartwell, Crispin. *Against the State: An Introduction to Anarchist Political Theory*. Albany: State U of New York P, 2008.

Schneider, Bethany. "Boudinot's Change: Boudinot, Emerson, and Ross on Cherokee Removal." *English Literary History* 75.1 (2008): 151–77.

———. *From Place to Populace: Indian Removal and State-Formation in Antebellum American Literature*. Diss. Cornell U, 2003. Ann Arbor: UMI, 2003.

Sher, Robert. "Notes: Cherokee Nation of Oklahoma v. Norton, 389 F.3d (10th Cir. 2004)." *American Indian Law Review* 30.2 (2005–2006): 443–60.

Sherman, Bill. "Oklahoma Baptists Elect First Native American President." *Tulsa World* Nov. 11, 2008. June 15, 2009. <http://www.tulsaworld. com/news/article.aspx?articleID=20081111_1__Onewe02724>.

Smith, Andrea. *Native Americans and the Christian Right: The Gendered Politics of Unlikely Alliances*. Durham: Duke UP, 2008.

Smith, Betty Anderson. "Distribution of Eighteenth-Century Cherokee Settlements." King, *Cherokee Indian Nation* 46–60.

Smith, Chad. "Letter to Cherokee Citizens from Chad Smith." *Cherokee Phoenix* Aug. 2005: 30. July 16, 2009. <http://www.cherokeephoenix.org /1542/Article.aspx>.

Snell, Travis. "Delawares' Sovereignty Rehearing Denied." *Cherokee Phoenix* Feb. 2005: 5.

———. "Trust Land Status OK'd for UKB Casino." *Tahlequah Daily Press* July 31, 2012: 1A–2A.

"Southern Baptists Choose Johnny Hunt New President." Associated Press. *Fort Worth Star Telegram* June 10, 2008. June 15, 2009. <http://www.star-telegram.com/804/story/692978.html>.

Starr, Emmet. *History of the Cherokee Indians and Their Legends and Folklore.* [Warden?]: Oklahoma City: 1921. Baltimore: Genealogical, 2003.

Strickland, Rennard. *Fire and the Spirits: Cherokee Law from Clan to Court.* Norman: U of Oklahoma P, 1975.

Strickland, William. "Cherokee Rhetoric: A Forceful Weapon." *Journal of Cherokee Studies* 2.3 (1977): 375–84.

Sturm, Circe. *Blood Politics: Race, Culture, and Identity in the Cherokee Nation of Oklahoma.* Berkeley: U of California P, 2002.

Sweet, Leonard. "The Female Seminary Movement and Woman's Mission in Antebellum America." *Church History* 54.1 (1985): 41–55.

Teuton, Chris. "Scary Stories: An Interview with Traditional Keetoowah/Cherokee Storyteller, Novelist, and Filmmaker Mr. Sequoyah Guess." *Mississippi Quarterly* 60.1 (2006–2007): 151–77.

Teuton, Sean Kicummah. *Red Land, Red Power: Grounding Knowledge in the American Indian Novel.* Durham: Duke UP, 2008.

Thomas, Robert. "Cherokee Values and World View." Unpublished ms. U of North Carolina, 1958.

———. *The Origin and Development of the Redbird Smith Movement.* Master's thesis. U of Arizona, 1953.

Thompson, Mark. "V-22 Osprey: A Flying Shame." *Time* Sept. 26, 2007. Sept. 21, 2009. <http://www.time.com/time/nation/article/ 0,8599,1665835-1,00.html>.

Thornton, Russell. *The Cherokees: A Population History.* Lincoln: U of Nebraska P, 1990.

Tinker, George. *Spirit and Resistance: Political Theology and American Indian Liberation.* Minneapolis: Fortress, 2004.

Treat, James. "Introduction: Native Christian Narrative Discourse." *Native and Christian: Indigenous Voices on Religious Identity in the United States and Canada.* Ed. Treat. New York: Routledge, 1996. 1–26.

Tyner, Howard. "The Keetoowah Society in Cherokee History." Master's thesis. Tulsa U. 1949.

"UKB Chief Responds to CNO's Public Statement." United Keetoowah Band of Cherokee Indians website. Jan. 18, 2008. July 7, 2009. <http://www.keetoowahcherokee.org/1182008.html>.

Wahrhaftig, Albert. "We Who Act Right: The Persistent Identity of Cherokee Indians." *Currents in Anthropology: Essays in Honor of Sol Tax.* Ed. Robert Henshaw. New York: Mouton, 1979. 255–69.

Wald, Priscilla. *Constituting Americans: Cultural Anxiety and Narrative Form.* Durham: Duke UP, 1995.

Ward, Colin. *Anarchism: A Very Short Introduction.* New York: Oxford UP, 2004.

Warrior, Robert. "Native Critics in the World." Weaver, Womack, and Warrior 179–223.

———. *The People and the Word: Reading Native Nonfiction*. Minneapolis: U of Minnesota P, 2005.

———. *Tribal Secrets: Recovering American Indian Intellectual Traditions*. Minneapolis: U of Minnesota P, 1995.

Weaver, Jace. "Splitting the Earth: First Utterances and Pluralist Separatism." Weaver, Womack, and Warrior 1–89.

———. *That the People Might Live*. New York: Oxford UP, 1996.

———. *Turtle Goes to War: Of Military Commissions, the Constitution and American Indian Memory*. New Haven: Trylon and Perisphere, 2002.

Weaver, Jace, Craig S. Womack, and Robert Warrior. *American Indian Literary Nationalism*. Albuquerque: U of N. Mex. P, 2006.

Welter, Barbara. "The Cult of True Womanhood: 1820–1860." *American Quarterly* 18.2 (1966): 151–74.

West, James. "Indian Spirituality: Another Vision." *Native and Christian: Indigenous Voices on Religious Identity in the United States and Canada*. Ed. James Treat. New York: Routledge, 1996. 29–37.

Wilkerson, William. "Is There Something You Need to Tell Me? Coming Out and the Ambiguity of Experience." Hoya and Hames-García 251–78.

Wilkins, David. *American Indian Sovereignty and the U.S. Supreme Court*. Austin: U of Texas P, 1997.

Wilkins, Thurman. *Cherokee Tragedy: The Story of the Ridge Family and the Decimation of a People*. New York: Macmillan, 1970.

Womack, Craig S. *Art as Performance, Story as Criticism: Reflections on Native Literary Aesthetics*. Norman: U of Oklahoma P, 2009.

———. "The Integrity of American Indian Claims (Or, How I Learned to Stop Worrying and Love My Hybridity)." Weaver, Womack, and Warrior 91–177.

———. *Red on Red: Native American Literary Separatism*. Minneapolis: U of Minnesota P, 1999.

———. "Theorizing American Indian Experience." Womack, Justice, and Teuton 353–410.

Womack, Craig S., Daniel Heath Justice, and Christopher B. Teuton, eds. *Reasoning Together: The Native Critics Collective*. Norman: U of Oklahoma P, 2008.

Woodward, Grace Steele. *The Cherokees*. Norman: U of Oklahoma P, 1963.

Yarbrough, Fay. *Race and the Cherokee Nation*. Philadelphia. U of Pennsylvania P, 2008.

Zammito, John. "Reading 'Experience': The Debate in Intellectual History among Scott, Toews, and LaCapra." Hoya and Hames-García 279–311.

Index